The Loss of the USS *Thresher*

Loss of the USS *Thresher*

Hearings
before the
Joint Committee
on Atomic Energy Congress
of the
United States
Eighty- Eighth Congress
First and Second Sessions on
The Loss of the USS *Thresher*

June 26, 27, July 23, 1963, and July 1, 1964

GOVERNMENT REPRINTS PRESS.
Washington, D.C.

Printed in The United States of America
Ross & Perry, Inc. Publishers
717 Second St., N.E., Suite 200
Washington, D.C. 20002
Telephone (202) 675-8300
Facsimile (202) 675-8400
info@RossPerry.com

SAN 253-8555

Government Reprints Press Edition 2001

Government Reprints Press is an Imprint of Ross & Perry, Inc.

Library of Congress Control Number: 2001094514
http://www.GPOreprints.com

ISBN 1-931641-93-5

♾ The paper used in this publication meets the requirements for permanence established by the American National Standard for Information Sciences "Permanence of Paper for Printed Library Materials" (ANSI Z39.48-1984).

In Memoriam

Men Who Perished With the Loss of *Thresher*—April 10, 1963

Harvey, John W., LCDR, USN.
Garner, Pat M., LCDR, USN.
Di Nola, Michael J., LCDR, USN.
Lyman, John S., Jr., LCDR, USN.
Smarz, John (n), Jr., LT, USN.
Parsons, Guy C., Jr., LTJG, USN.
Henry, James J., Jr., LTJG, USN.
Babcock, Ronald C., LTJG, USN.
Wiley, John J., LTJG, USN.
Malinski, Frank J., LTJG, USN.
Collier, Merrill F., LT, USN.
Grafton, John G., LTJG, USN.
Arsenault, Tilmon J., ENCA(SS)–P2, USN.
Bain, Ronald E., EN2(SS)–P2, USN.
Bell, John E., MM1–P2, USN.
Bobbitt, Edgar S., EM2(SS)–P2, USN.
Boster, Gerald C., EM3(SS)–P1, USN.
Bracey, George (n), SD3(SS), USN.
Brann, Richard P., EN2(SS)–P2, USN.
Carkoski, Richard J., EN2(SS), USN.
Cayey, Steven G., TM2(SS), USN.
Christiansen, Edward (n), SN(SS), USN.
Claussen, Larry W., EM2(SS)–P2, USN.
Clements, Thomas E., ETR3(SS), USN.
Cummings, Francis M., SOS2(SS), USN.
Carmody, Patrick W., SK2, USN.
Dabruzzi, Samuel J., ETN2(SS), USN.
Day, Donald C., EN3(SS), USN.
Denny, Roy O., Jr., EM1(SS)–P2, USN.
DiBella, Peter J., SN, USN.
Dundas, Don R., ETN2(SS), USN.
Dyer, Troy E., ET1(SS)–P1, USN.
Davison, Clyde E., III, ETR3–P1, USN.
Forni, Ellwood H., SOCA(SS)–P1, USN.
Foti, Raymond P., ET1(SS), USN.
Freeman, Larry W., FTM2(SS), USN.
Fusco, Gregory J., EM2(SS)–P2, USN.
Gallant, Andrew J., Jr., HMC(SS), USN.
Garcia, Napoleon T., SD1(SS), USN.
Garner, John E., YNSN(SS), USN.
Gaynor, Robert W., EN2(SS), USN.
Gosnell, Robert H., SA (SS), USNR.
Graham, William E., SOC(SS)–P1, USN.
Gunter, Aaron J., QM1(SS), USN.
Hall, Richard C., ETR2(SS)–P2, USN.
Hayes, Norman T., EM1–P2, USN.
Heiser, Laird G., MM1–P2, USN.

SHIP'S COMPANY—continued

Helsius, Marvin T., MM2, USN.
Hewitt, Leonard H., EMCA(SS), USN.
Hoague, Joseph H., TM2(SS), USN.
Hodge, James P., EM2, USN.
Hudson, John F., EN2(SS), USN.
Inglis, John P., FN, USNR.
Johnson, Brawner G., FTG1(SS)–P2, USN.
Johnson Edward A., ENCA(SS), USN.
Johnson, Richard L., RMSA, USN.
Johnson, Robert E., TMC(SS)–P1, USN.
Johnson, Thomas B., ET1(SS)–P2, USN.
Jones, Richard W., EM2(SS), USN.
Kaluza, Edmund J., Jr., SOS2(SS)–P1, USN.
Kantz, Thomas C., ETR2(SS), USN.
Kearney, Robert D., MM3, USN.
Keiler, Ronald D., IC2(SS)–P2, USN.
Kiesecker, George J., MM2(SS)–P2, USN.
Klier, Billy M., EN1(SS)–P2, USN.
Kroner, George R., CS3, USN.
Lanouette, Norman G., QM1(SS), USN.
Lavoie, Wayne W., YN1(SS), USN.
Mabry, Templeman N., Jr., EN2(SS)–P2, USN.
Mann, Richard H., Jr., IC2(SS), USN.
Marullo, Julius F., Jr., QM1(SS), USN.
McClelland, Douglas R., EM2(SS), USN.
McCord, Donald J., MM1(SS)–P2, USN.
McDonough, Karl P., TM3(SS), USN.
Middleton, Sidney L., MM1(SS)–P2, USN.
Muise, Ronald A., CS2, USN.
Musselwhite, James A., ETN2(SS)–P2, USN.
Nault, Donald E., CS1(SS), USN.
Noonis, Walter J., RMC(SS), USN.
Norris, John D., ET1(SS)–P2, USN.
Oetting, Chesley C., EM2–P2, USN.
Pennington, Roscoe C., EMCA(SS)–P2, USN.
Peters, James G., EMCS–P2, USN.
Phillippi, James F., SOS2(SS), USN.
Philput, Dan A., EN2(SS)–P2, USN.
Podwell, Richard (n), MM2–P2, USN.
Regan, John S., MM1(SS)–P2, USN.
Ritchie, James P., RM2, USN.
Robison, Pervis (n), Jr., SN, USN.
Rountree, Glenn A., QM2(SS), USN.
Rushetski, Anthony A., ETN2, USN.
Schiewe, James M., EM1(SS)–P2, USN.
Shafer, Benjamin N., EMCM(SS)–P2, USN.
Shafer, John D., EMCS(SS)–P2, USN.
Shimko, Joseph T., MM1–P2, USN.
Shotwell, Burnett M., ETRSN, USN.
Sinnett, Alan D., FTG2(SS), USN.
Smith, William H., Jr., BT1–P2, USN.
Solomon, Ronald H., EM1–P2, USN.
Steinel, Robert E., SO1(SS)–P1, USN.
Snider, James L., MM1, USN.
Van Pelt, Rodger E., IC1(SS)–P2, USN.
Wasel, David A., RMSN, USN.
Walski, Joseph A., RM1(SS)–P1, USN.
Wiggins, Charles L., FTG1–P2, USN.
Wise, Donald E., MMCA(SS)–P2, USN.
Wolfe, Ronald E., QMSN(SS), USN.
Zweifel, Jay H., EM2–P1, USN.

Men Who Perished With the Loss of *Thresher*—April 10, 1963

Krag, Robert L., LCDR, USN, Staff, Deputy Commander, Submarine Force, U.S. Atlantic Fleet.

Allen, Philip H., LCDR, USN, Portsmouth Naval Shipyard.

Billings, John H., LCDR, USN, Portsmouth Naval Shipyard.

Biederman, Robert D., LT, USN, Portsmouth Naval Shipyard.

Prescott, Robert D., Civilian Employee, Design Division, Portsmouth Naval Shipyard.

Charron, Robert E., Civilian Employee, Design Division, Portsmouth Naval Shipyard.

Guerette, Paul A., Civilian Employee, Design Division, Portsmouth Naval Shipyard.

Fisher, Richard K., Civilian Employee, Design Division, Portsmouth Naval Shipyard.

Whitten, Laurence E., Civilian Employee, Combat Systems Division, Portsmouth Naval Shipyard.

Beal, Daniel W., Jr., Civilian Employee, Combat Systems Division, Portsmouth Naval Shipyard.

Des Jardins, Richard R., Civilian Employee, Combat Systems Division, Portsmouth Naval Shipyard.

Critchley, Kenneth J., Civilian Employee, Production Department, Portsmouth Naval Shipyard.

Currier, Paul C., Civilian Employee, Production Department, Portsmouth Naval Shipyard.

Abrams, Fred P., Civilian Employee, Production Department, Portsmouth Naval Shipyard.

Palmer, Franklin J., Civilian Employee, Production Department, Portsmouth Naval Shipyard.

Dineen, George J., Civilian Employee, Production Department, Portsmouth Naval Shipyard.

Moreau, Henry C., Civilian Employee, Production Department, Portsmouth Naval Shipyard.

Corcoran, Kenneth R., Contractor's Representative, Sperry Corp.

Jaquay, Maurice F., Contractor's Representative, Raytheon Corp.

Keuster, Donald W., Contractor's Representative, Sperry Corp.

Stadtmuller, Donald T., Contractor's Representative, Sperry Corp.

FOREWORD

On April 10, 1963, while engaged in a deep test dive, approximately 200 miles off the northeastern coast of the United States, the nuclear submarine, SSN-593, the U.S.S. *Thresher*, was lost at sea with all persons aboard—112 naval personnel and 17 civilian technicians.

The Joint Committee on Atomic Energy, by law, is required to make continued studies of problems related to the development, use, and control of atomic energy. In compliance with this responsibility, as chairman of the Joint Committee, on being notified on April 10 of the loss of the *Thresher*, I immediately dispatched specially qualified staff members of the Joint Committee to New London, Conn., where the naval court of inquiry was scheduled to convene. The court of inquiry did convene in New London on April 11 and then on April 13 moved to the Portsmouth Naval Shipyard, the design and construction yard for the *Thresher*. The sessions continued at the Portsmouth Naval Shipyard until the court closed its inquiry on June 5, 1963. During this 56-day period, the court heard testimony from 120 witnesses, recorded 1,700 pages of testimony, and examined 255 exhibits. Throughout the entire proceedings, most of which were behind closed doors, the Joint Committee was represented through its staff who attended as official observers.

At the conclusion of the proceedings, a copy of the 12-volume record of the court, including its findings, opinions, and recommendations, was made available to the Joint Committee. Not until the court had officially completed its work, and after the court had submitted its report to the Navy, did the Joint Committee hold its own hearings. The committee did, however, receive regular progress reports from its staff during the court proceedings.

It was my expressed belief, in consultation with other members of the committee, that no outside investigation into the cause of the tragedy should be conducted until the Department of the Navy had been given an opportunity to complete its investigation.[1] Thereafter, the Joint Committee held its hearings in two parts.

During the first part on June 26, 27, and July 23, 1963, the committee received testimony in executive session from the Secretary of the Navy, the Assistant Secretary of the Navy (Installations and Logistics), the president of the court of inquiry, the Chief of the Bureau of Ships, and senior naval officers of operating elements of our naval submarine forces. During this initial phase, the committee received information on the design, construction, operation, and maintenance of nuclear submarines. Special emphasis was given to those elements of design and construction which, based upon the testimony and evidence obtained during the naval court of inquiry and the committee's own interrogation of witnesses, were deficient and in need of corrective action.

---

[1] See floor statement of Senator Pastore on April 22, 1963, p. 144.

One year later, on July 1, 1964, the committee again received testimony in executive session from the Office of the Secretary of the Navy and senior naval officers responsible for the design, construction, and operation of nuclear submarines in order to ascertain what actions had been instituted to correct the acknowledged deficiencies that existed.

Although there has been much speculation as to the cause of the *Thresher* loss, the committee must conclude from its own study of the facts developed that the specific cause is not known. It was important, therefore, that all aspects of the *Thresher*'s design, construction, and operation be reviewed to uncover whatever weaknesses may have existed at the time, whether or not they were the proximate cause of the accident.

Investigations revealed that in parts of the ship, practices, conditions, and standards existing at the time were short of those required to insure safe operation of the *Thresher*. Basically, the ship was built to two standards. The standards of design and construction for the nuclear powerplant were more stringent than for the rest of the ship. Of particular note is that the technical specification requirements were not greatly different, but that adherence to them was far more strict for the nuclear powerplant than for the rest of the ship.

It is also obvious that while nuclear power was revolutionizing the submarine as a weapons system during the past 10 years, the more conventional aspects of the submarine and its safety devices were not keeping pace with the more stringent performance requirements of greater endurance, higher speed, and deeper submergence. For example, the design and limited blowing capability of the deballasting system which might have been adequate for the World War II and postwar conventional submarines were inadequate as an emergency system for the larger, deeper diving, higher performance nuclear submarines. Similarly the use of the less costly method of joining metal piping systems by brazing is questionable for hazardous salt water lines subject to the tremendous pressures of deep depth as compared to welding which is a more expensive and time-consuming method. Corrective action is now being taken by the Department of the Navy in both of these areas.

It is extremely unfortunate that this tragedy had to occur to bring a number of unsatisfactory conditions into the open. The committee is favorably impressed, however, with the scope of the Navy's planned program to improve the quality and safety of new submarines and those already in the fleet. The program to bring about the necessary improvements is very costly and will take much time to complete. It now appears that the cost to upgrade our submarine program will be greater than if at the outset the higher standards comparable to those used in the nuclear powerplant had been adopted throughout the ship.

The lesson is obvious. There is no substitute for proper attention to quality of material and workmanship in the first instance. The initial extra costs which may be involved will eliminate much greater additional expense later on but much more importantly, it could mean the saving of the lives of the men who man our submarines.

For some time the Joint Committee has been concerned with the problem of the lack of continuity of military personnel in the management of highly technical programs. There is no doubt that a policy which requires military officers to be transferred every 2 to 3 years is not conducive to efficient technical management of complex technical projects which require periods of 6 or more years to complete.

For example, in the nuclear powerplant of the *Thresher* there was a continuity of technical management; Admiral Rickover has been in charge of the program from its inception. But in the nonnuclear parts of the submarine there were so many changes of personnel in responsible positions involved in the design and construction of the ship that fixing individual responsibility is impossible. **Unless there is a drastic change in the present military technical management concepts, whereby competent individuals will be assigned technical responsibility for time periods commensurate with the time required to complete a technical project without adverse effect on their promotion opportunities, the high standards of efficiency and safety required will be most difficult to attain.**

This committee, in light of its public safety responsibilities, has voiced concern on many occasions about the pressures to reduce the standards of selection and training that have been the hallmark of the naval nuclear propulsion program. The *Thresher*'s loss should reemphasize the need for continuing to uphold the high standards of selection, training, qualification, and requalification which is one of the keys to the long-term safety record in Admiral Rickover's program. **The committee reaffirms the position it has expressed previously that there must be no relaxation of existing procedures used in selecting, training, and assignment of nuclear propulsion personnel.**

A number of the recommendations made by the court of inquiry are still under study by the Navy Department. The Joint Committee has requested the Navy Department to keep it informed regarding future actions with respect to the recommendations which have been made.

The hearings held by the Joint Committe, of necessity, had to be in executive session because the testimony included classified defense information. However, it has been the long-established policy of the Joint Committee that it has a responsibility to make public as much information as possible consistent with the national defense security requirements of the United States. Accordingly, with the assistance and cooperation of the Navy Department, the hearing records were reviewed for classification and classified information deleted prior to publication.

The committee hopes that these hearings will be carefully studied by all who are engaged in military technical development, for they contain many lessons for which we have already paid a high price. If the lesson is learned that excellence in design, fabrication, operations, and training cannot be compromised in modern high performance military systems, the men of the *Thresher* will not have died in vain.

JOHN O. PASTORE, *Chairman.*
December 1964

CONTENTS

(A short subject index will be found on p. 191)

HEARING DATES

STATEMENTS OF WITNESSES

ADDITIONAL MATERIAL INSERTED IN THE RECORD

APPENDIXES

[These hearings were held in executive session. Classified security information was presented during the executive session. The hearing record was then reviewed and specific items designated by the Department of Defense and Navy Department as being classified information were deleted prior to publication.]

LOSS OF THE U.S.S. "THRESHER"

WEDNESDAY, JUNE 26, 1963

Congress of the United States,
Joint Committee on Atomic Energy,
Washington, D.C.

The committee met at 3:15 p. m. in room AE-1, the Capitol, Senator John O. Pastore, chairman of the Joint Committee, presiding.

Present: Senators Pastore, Jackson, and Curtis; and Representatives Holifield, Price, Aspinall, Morris, Hosmer, Bates, Westland, and Anderson.

Present also: John Conway, executive director of the Joint Committee; Edward Bauser, assistant director; and James B. Graham, technical adviser.

Present also: Ben Gilleas, staff member of the Senate Preparedness Investigating Subcommittee of the Committee on Armed Services.

Chairman PASTORE. The committee will please come to order.

I want to say this is a meeting of the full committee of the Joint Committee on Atomic Energy. On June 24, the Joint Committee received from the Secretary of the Navy a transcript of the testimony taken by the court of inquiry that investigated the loss of the U.S.S. *Thresher.* Also received by the Joint Committee on June 24 was a copy of the court's findings, including opinions and recommendations. I invited Secretary Korth to meet with the committee this afternoon to review for the committee the principal things that were wrong with the *Thresher* and what is being done to correct them.

At this point, right now, I might say, Mr. Korth, that I have very much appreciated the cooperation of the Navy Department and particularly the court of inquiry in permitting the Joint Committee staff to sit in the closed sessions, as well as the open hearings of the court of inquiry. On behalf of the Joint Committee, I want to thank the Department of the Navy and the president of the court of inquiry.

At the time the court was first formed I took the position that no congressional investigation should be conducted until the Navy Department had an opportunity to complete its investigation. I have held in abeyance any hearing until such time as the Navy had an opportunity to review all the facts and make its own determination.[1]

---

[1] See statement of Senator Pastore on the floor of the Senate April 22, 1963, app. 4, p. 144.

Since the Navy has completed its investigation and the matter has been reviewed within the Navy Department, I believe that now is an appropriate time for the committee to hold this meeting. Our meeting today, for the first time will give the committee an opportunity to hear directly from the Navy on this tragedy.

In arranging for this meeting I thought it best not to specify any particular individual or individuals as witnesses, but rather permit the Secretary of the Navy to bring with him whomever he wished. I would hope from the distinguished group of officers that Mr. Korth has with him, the committee will be able to receive a very thorough review of this matter.

In addition to the information developed by the court of inquiry, we hope we will receive whatever information was developed subsequently by the Navy. I also hope Navy representatives will be prepared to advise us on what actions have been or are being taken to assure that there will not be another tragedy.

Now before I begin, I would like to mention that in addition to the Joint Committee staff, Mr. Ben Gilleas, from the Senate Armed Services Preparedness Subcommittee is also present in accordance with previous discussions I have had with Senator Stennis. Senator Stennis addressed himself to the Navy Department, saying that he wanted a report and at that time the Preparedness Subcommittee of the Armed Services Committee would decide what they would do. I had a talk with Mr. Stennis last week, and I invited him to participate with us in a joint hearing if that were necessary, and he was very gracious about it, and he said that he would think that over but that in all probability he would either assign several members of his committee to come to these hearings ex officio, or that he would send a member of the staff.

I am glad to see that he has sent a member of the staff. I want the staff member to know that these are highly classified hearings and that I am glad to see that he has top secret and "Q" clearances so that there is no question at all about security. I want to welcome him here, and he can sit forward with us, in one of the chairs here, and make himself as comfortable as possible.

Mr. Korth, I leave it up to you to address yourself to this committee in any way you think is proper.

STATEMENTS OF HON. FRED KORTH, SECRETARY OF THE NAVY; VICE ADM. BERNARD L. AUSTIN, PRESIDENT OF THE NAVAL WAR COLLEGE AND PRESIDENT OF THE COURT OF INQUIRY ON "THRESHER"; AND REAR ADM. WILLIAM A. BROCKETT, CHIEF OF THE BUREAU OF SHIPS

Secretary KORTH. At the outset, let me say to you and to the members of the Joint Committee that I am very pleased that you have asked me to be present with you here today to discuss the findings of the court of inquiry, which looked into the circumstances surrounding the loss at sea of the U.S.S. *Thresher*. It may be helpful to you if I indicate some discussions which I have already had on this matter, and some of the actions, which are already underway as a result of this unfortunate incident.

I have, as a matter of highest priority, directed the Chief of Naval Operations to prepare a plan for establishment of a submarine safety organization as recommended by the court of inquiry. And various other steps are being taken within the Naval Establishment to profit as much as possible from this untimely occurrence and to reduce the possibility of any such future misfortune.

Accompanying me here today are Vice Adm. H. G. Rickover, Vice Adm. B. L. Austin, who conducted the court of inquiry, and whose permanent assignment is as President of the Naval War College, and Rear Adm. E. C. Stephan, the Chairman of the Navy's Deep Submergence Systems Review Group, and Rear Adm. J. H. Maurer, who is the head of the Submarine Warfare Division in the Office of the Chief of Naval Operations, Rear Adm. W. A. Brockett, Chief of the Bureau of Ships, and Capt. C. E. Bishop, who heads up the technical information group supplying the Chief of Naval Operations technical information on the search effort now underway to locate *Thresher*.

In that connection I should like to say that this morning at 8 o'clock the *Trieste* again submerged and searched for the *Thresher*. When we had the last report she was surfacing, and was about 600 feet from the surface, and I would say that perhaps by this very moment has surfaced. We have no information on what she may have found today.

These gentlemen whom I have mentioned, and their organizations, have in various ways taken actions as a result of the *Thresher* loss. Admiral Rickover has, as I understand, issued recently a new instruction concerning the operational procedures for nuclear propulsion reactors [classified matter deleted].

Admiral Rickover can, of course, amplify these remarks and respond to any questions which you may have in that connection. Admiral Austin has completed his thorough and objective investigation into the possible causes of the loss of *Thresher*. He, in addition to his duties as president of the Naval War College, has been serving as an expert source of information for all matters pertaining to events leading to and possibly causing the loss of *Thresher*.

Admiral Stephan, as head of the Deep Submergence Systems Review Group, has first assembled a group of recognized experts on matters of location, recovery, search, and operation of deeply submerged objects. Second, his group has nearly completed a documentary review of all existing literature on this highly involved subject. Third, they have solicited ideas from more than 200 industrial concerns, the scientific community, and other Government agencies. These comments and recommendations are beginning to flow in to Admiral Stephan's group.

Fourth, he has instituted a study of the ocean environment, itself, as it pertains to the practicality and feasibility of rescue and/or recovery of deeply submerged objects. Fifth, his group anticipates that on or about October 1 they will be prepared to report to me on, first, the Navy's current capability in this field, and, second, recommendations for short-term improvement, and third, recommendations for long-term improvement, necessary budget considerations, and a recommendation for the implementing organization to carry out the proposed plan developed.

Admiral Maurer, as head of the Submarine Warfare Division has monitored the operational practices of submarines and submarine systems, working closely with the Bureau of Ships and Admiral Stephan.

Admiral Brockett has established within the Bureau of Ships a Submarine Safety Task Group, with 10 separate tasks spelled out as they affect submarine design safety. He has established under Rear Adm. Andrew I. McKee, a retired officer called back to active duty, a separate ad hoc design study group to look into the design of the *Thresher* class submarine.

I might say here parenthetically, that the activities of Admiral McKee's group have been kept separate and distinct from the proceedings of Admiral Austin's court of inquiry, so that the result of Admiral McKee's group will be completely independent of any of the findings of the court.

Admiral Brockett, where specific material improvements were indicated as a result of the findings of the *Thresher* court of inquiry, has already caused corrective action to be taken in these areas. For example, the matter of the fail-safe position of the air blow valves—he has instituted a critical survey of system arrangement and testing as it applies to new ships, ships soon to be delivered and ships already in the fleet, to insure optimum benefit from the findings concerning the *Thresher* case.

Captain Bishop is serving within the Office of the Assistant Chief of Naval Operations for Development as a point of technical contact for those seeking to locate *Thresher*, and he has assisted in making available equipment and techniques which are currently employed to position, photograph, and to attempt to locate *Thresher*.

This has been a very brief highlighting of some of the things which have been done, or were already underway, and are related to the loss of *Thresher*.

I will be very pleased individually or collectively to discuss in more detail these or any other matters your committee desires. I think that it might be helpful, Mr. Chairman, to ask Admiral Austin at this point to explain how the court went about its work, and to highlight briefly the results of the court of inquiry, since I feel that this explanation could serve as a departure point for discussion of the actions already taken, and those which are contemplated as a result of this event.

Chairman PASTORE. Admiral Austin, will you oblige us by coming forward, please?

Representative HOLIFIELD. Mr. Chairman, this is a final rollcall on the Defense appropriation bill, and that includes the naval appropriations, I might add. Would you gentlemen excuse us while we go and vote?

(A brief recess was taken.)

NAVAL COURT OF INQUIRY

Admiral AUSTIN. Mr. Chairman, I appreciate this opportunity of appearing before you and giving you some of the background of this court, of whose report you have been furnished a copy, and the hearings. I would like first to say on behalf of the members of the court how much we appreciated your sending to us as observers such fine gentlemen who made it easier for us to cooperate with them.

We had a difficult problem to inquire into. [Classified matter deleted.] And so we had to explore the complete spectrum of possible causes. I think this was a blessing in disguise. It made for a long court, but it also caused us to look into things that probably would never have been looked into for some time to come had it not been under the impetus of this investigation.

UNSATISFACTORY CONDITIONS FOUND

We, of course, did find in our search of this entire spectrum of causes, things that were not being done as well as they could be done, things that needed to be improved, and manufacturing processes and repair procedures and quality assurance systems, in the method of operation of these ships, in the philosophy of their operation, and so on.

Many of these things, I am sure, would have been discovered in time, but I think that some of them might have been long in coming, and I think that some may never have been discovered except by such a process as this.

We looked into, first, the design of this ship. We looked into the construction of the ship, into the materials of which it was constructed, the processes by which these materials were fabricated, the tests by which the putting together of these materials was determined to be safe or unsafe. We also explored the personnel who manned the ship, to see whether or not there was a high probability of personnel failure. We also, of course, went into the shock tests of the ship prior to its going in for the overhaul which preceded its loss.

We found that the shock tests, for example, were no greater than those which had been given to other submarine hulls. [Classified matter deleted.] This is one of the many things we pointed out in our 166 facts, 54 opinions, and 20 recommendations.

We, of course, went into, very carefully, every job that was done by the shipyard during the long overhaul which preceded this ship's going to sea and being lost. We found, for example, in one case that a job of testing of a tank had caused the top of that tank to be ruptured due to poor supervision on the part of the man conducting the test. This of course raised the question as to whether or not this disruption of this tank top had in fact caused a high probability of a failure of some piping system that ran over this tank. In order to explore this thoroughly, we had two separate Navy yards conduct stress analyses of this particular piping system and we found that theoretically there would not have been a stress created by the 1-inch displacement of that tank top which would have caused a failure of a joint in a pipeline that ran over the tank.

This I cite only as an illustration of the way in which we went into the various job orders that were issued during the overhaul of the *Thresher* prior to its going to sea on April 9.

Then, of course, we went into the question of the processes and the instructions for doing various types of work on that ship. We found some of these processes in need of tightening up. We found that some of them were given as goals rather than as requirements, and this we point out in our findings.

I feel that many of the things which we found were valuable to us. [Classified matter deleted.] It was with this in mind that the court in its hearings only had open court when we were discussing matters which we felt were unclassified. [Classified matter deleted.]

But with that one limitation, we tried diligently, and I think succeeded fairly well in having as much open hearings as possible, because we realized there was much interest in this tragedy and that if we couldn't have a reasonable amount of the hearings in open court, it would cause the people of our country, and the press in particular, to feel that there was something that was being kept from them which they should know about.

I can assure you and the committee, sir, that this court sought the truth, the whole truth, and without any concern as to where the chips might fall. I hope that the recommendations of this court will accomplish what we hoped they would, and that is to make it safer to operate the submarines we already have built and to build greater safety into those yet to be built.

I would be happy to answer any questions which the committee might wish to address to me.

Chairman PASTORE. Before you do, I would like to address myself to the Secretary.

This group that you are assembling to report on October 1, what will be their function?

DEEP SUBMERGENCE SYSTEMS GROUP

Secretary KORTH. Their function will be, as I indicated, to explore into the deep submergence systems, that is the matter of location, detection, and possible bringing to the surface of deep submergence systems. What I would like to do is ask Admiral Stephan, who heads this group, unless you would prefer to ask Admiral Austin that question.

Chairman PASTORE. I think that our committee ought to ask Admiral Austin any questions if they have any, first.

QUALITY OF DESIGN

Representative HOLIFIELD. Admiral Austin, we have some questions which we think should be answered for our committee record, and I know you will understand the spirit in which they are asked.

Did the court attempt to learn from other shipyards that were building *Thresher* class submarines to the same Portsmouth and Bureau of Ships plans what they thought of the quality of the design work?

Admiral AUSTIN. Sir, we did get a certain amount of testimony regarding not only design but processes and test procedures from other yards, but I would point out, sir, that we did not address ourselves to a comparison. We focused our attention on the *Thresher* and the yard in which it was built, and therefore we would not pretend that our report would be a concise and full setting forth of the relative opinions and, shall we say, thoroughness of quality assurance and that sort of thing in various yards that built similar ships.

Representative HOLIFIELD. We have been informed that this yard has had trouble in meeting its quality standards.

Admiral AUSTIN. Yes, sir.

ROTATION OF KEY PERSONNEL

Representative HOLIFIELD. Another thing we wondered about was the transfer at one time of several of your top, key men away from this job when it was in the process of being done. Are the rules and regulations of the Navy so unchangeable that when you are engaged in a complicated job that the rule of transfer of responsible officers is absolute, and looking back upon it, wouldn't it have been better to have kept some of these men who were in top positions on that particular job until it was done? (See p. 87.)

Admiral AUSTIN. Mr. Holifield, I am not sure that I am the proper person to answer regarding that.

Secretary KORTH. I will answer the first part of it. Certainly the matter of whatever custom or rule there has been with reference to changing people or rotating people are completely within my purview to change, if that is indicated. I share the same concern that you do, Mr. Holifield.

Representative HOLIFIELD. I have run into this in other cases, where we were involved in some complicated problem in the military service, with a man that was eminently qualified or a group of men that were eminently qualified, and suddenly they were removed to completely different duties and men brought in to assume command in those areas that had to be, in essence, taught the trade of that particular function.

Secretary KORTH. This is an area that causes me concern, and I was discussing it this morning with Admiral Austin and others. I am going to talk with Admiral Smedburg, the Chief of the Bureau of Naval Personnel, to ascertain whether we cannot improve upon—and we can—upon the matter of rotation or moving out at critical time in the rework or overhaul of ships.

Representative HOLIFIELD. I think this is a basic thing that we ought to come to grips with. This is an old subject with me in another committee that I have—the Subcommittee on Military Operations of the House Committee on Government Operations—and time after time in investigating different situations, we have come across the succession of a man who was new to the problem—a very competent man who was new to the problem and the release of a man who had become competent in that field—and yet you lose accumulated knowledge in the field because of this necessity of rotation in relation to the man's own career advance.

Secretary KORTH. Mr. Holifield, actually I have not yet cleared up in my own mind really at what point, let us say, the commanding officer, if he is to be rotated and moved to another position, should be moved out.

In other words, he comes back with the submarine after the shock tests, and he perhaps knows more at that time about what failures or what shortcomings there are on the submarine, and he should perhaps stay on until those deficiencies have been corrected.

If someone else is to move on, he should move on soon enough so that he can be certain that a submarine, when it goes out, is in proper condition. In other words, it is so that he can supervise the work.

Representative HOLIFIELD. I was thinking of the situation of the men in charge of this.

Secretary KORTH. You are talking about the shipbuilding end of it?

Representative HOLIFIELD. That is right.

Secretary KORTH. In those areas, as well as in the areas of operations, I think we have to look at this very carefully.

Representative HOLIFIELD. Doesn't this apply in all specialized areas——

Secretary KORTH. That is right, sir.

Representative HOLIFIELD (continuing). Of operations, where you require specific and special competence which has taken a long time to acquire. It seems to me that, in this age of specialization, this whole problem ought to be looked at.

Secretary KORTH. It is, sir, and it will be.

Chairman PASTORE. If you will yield for a question on that point, you say on the return from the shock trip?

Secretary KORTH. I was using that as an example.

Chairman PASTORE. And then a transfer is made. What is the justification for it under the rules? What calls for it, Mr. Secretary?

Secretary KORTH. Actually——

Chairman PASTORE. Is a man limited just by calendar time or are there other considerations?

Secretary KORTH. Actually what happened here, as I understand it, Mr. Chairman, is that the old commanding officer, that is the commanding officer who was aboard at the time of the shock tests, was then put aboard a Polaris-type submarine, which was a promotion for him in effect. It was a new one that was building actually, but at the same time it was an advancement for him.

Representative HOLIFIELD. My remarks pertained to the ship superintendent——

Secretary KORTH. I am sorry. I did not understand.

Representative HOLIFIELD. The superintendent of the yard.

Secretary KORTH. This is likewise being looked into, yes.

Representative HOSMER. May I ask a question there? Wouldn't it be the superintendent of shipbuilding in a yard, and a particular superintendent of a hull—or is there a difference in this case?

Secretary KORTH. I don't precisely understand your question.

Representative HOSMER. You have some kind of an overall supervisor of all of the operations in the yard, and we have a submarine here and another ship there, and they are all in different stages of work. With one yard doing so many different jobs, you can't particularly tie a man who has an overall responsibility to one of the individual hulls in a yard.

Admiral BROCKETT. I am Admiral Brockett, Chief of the Bureau of Ships. Mr. Hosmer, I will build up the organization for you from the bottom. The ship superintendent will normally have one ship, particularly under circumstances such as existed in Portsmouth, and an assistant which was the case for the *Thresher*. His immediate boss is the repair superintendent who in turn reports to the production officer.

Representative HOSMER. We are talking about naval officers at this time or civilians?

Admiral BROCKETT. We are talking about naval officers. In the normal course of events, when you give a ship's superintendent a ship, you would expect him to stay with her from the day she begins until the day she completes. But occasionally there are things that upset the applecart. There are resignations and there are just distributions of shortages, as it were, and although I don't have the details on this case——

Representative HOLIFIELD. May I give them to you? There was a change in the *Thresher's* assistant ship's superintendent in November of 1962, and a change in the *Thresher's* chief superintendent in December of 1962. And in January of 1963 there was a change of the *Thresher's* chief executive officer and in the same month there was a change of the *Thresher's* commanding officer.

So there in a period of less than 90 days, four of your top people on this job were removed and this was during the time when as we understand it, when the submarine was in overhaul and where it would seem like to me the continuity of superintendents should have remained in the same people.

Admiral BROCKETT. I knew about the cases of the people being transferred but I have not developed, just having gotten access to some of the material, why it happened insofar as the shipyard was concerned.

I do know where these changes normally start from. Let us assume that there is a death or resignation. The latter is our biggest problem at the moment.

Representative HOLIFIELD. On the face of it, if I was doing a complicated job of construction I wouldn't want the four top men to be pulled out of it, and four strangers come into it to take on a job without a complete transfer of the background of experience and knowledge of those four men. It just looks to me—and I think it is probably a fault of the system which requires rotation, rather than continuity—as if this is a weak point.

Admiral BROCKETT. I would agree.

Secretary KORTH. I agree.

Chairman PASTORE. May I ask Admiral Austin, did the court place any emphasis upon this incident that we are discussing now, with relation to what the causes might have been?

Admiral AUSTIN. Mr. Chairman, we placed sufficient emphasis on it to pull it out of 1,700 pages of testimony and make it one of those 166 facts. We did not feel that it warranted an opinion on our part. We felt that the facts spoke for themselves.

Representative HOLIFIELD. I don't quite follow you on that, Admiral. It is either important enough, it seems to me, to require a recommendation of a change or it is unimportant. I am not competent to judge as to whether it is important or not.

Secretary KORTH. It is important enough for me to now look into this sufficiently.

Representative HOLIFIELD. Maybe I am in error. In opinion 53 of the court record, it says that:

A substantially contemporaneous transfer of *Thresher's* commanding officer and executive officer and ship's superintendent and assistant ship's superintendent in the final stages, was not conducive to optimum completion of the work undertaken.

So apparently you have rendered an opinion on that.

Admiral AUSTIN. I stand corrected.

Representative Holifield. I should have remembered that, but I didn't until my staff brought it to my attention just now.

Admiral Austin. I do recall that the court had considerable difficulty with this opinion, sir, and I was going on my memory and not recollecting that at a later date, on the insistence of certain members of the court, we did put in this opinion.

Chairman Pastore. Did you relate it at all to the tragedy?

Admiral Austin. Sir, not knowing exactly what occasioned the loss of the *Thresher*, it is impossible to say that any one thing or any one person or any one person's act or failure to act was directly responsible or contributed to the loss of that ship.

Chairman Pastore. Now, was this change of the four very top people a unique thing in relation to the *Thresher*, or did your investigation reveal that this is a common practice?

Admiral Austin. We sent for Admiral Smedburg as a witness, sir, and we looked into this as much as we felt we could. It is not a practice to remove the commanding officer and the executive officer, for example, at the same time. But he pointed out to us that in this case he had to place a competent officer in command of a new Polaris submarine, and that the most competent officer who was slated for such a billet was the commanding officer of the *Thresher* who had it since it had been built, and for a normal tour of duty.

The executive officer of the ship was needed on the staff of the deputy commander, Sublant, as the nuclear qualified officer on that staff. He was also the classmate of the new commanding officer, and it was deemed advisable, therefore, to make his transfer at the time that they brought the new commanding officer, a classmate of his, aboard, sir.

That was Admiral Smedburg's rationalization, and he said in view of that we left aboard Lieutenant Commander Lyman who was the engineer officer, and three other lieutenant commanders, in order to in part compensate for this breaking of two joints simultaneously.

I would say, sir, that this does happen due to the exigencies of the service more often than Admiral Smedburg probably would like, and I am sure more often than you would like.

DEVIATIONS FROM SPECIFICATIONS

Representative Holifield. On page 6 of the unclassified summary of events, it says that in general the ship was built in accordance with the specifications. (See app. 6, p. 151.) Yet the court record in your classified statement refers to finding 14 percent of the salt water joints tested being defective, frequent plugging or leaking of air-reducing valves, changes in design of the salt water system from the contract plans. Eight of the one hundred fifteen joints tested in the hydraulic system were found defective and so forth.

Now, in addition as reported in your classified summary on page 43, the court concluded numerous practices, conditions, and standards were short of those required to insure the thorough overhaul and safe operation of the *Thresher*.

So in view of those facts and that testimony, I ask you what does the phrase "in general" mean, that in general the ship was built in accordance with the specifications?

Admiral AUSTIN. "In general" there is meant in a very broad way, sir. The number of air bottles, for example, was in accordance with the specifications. The Bureau of Ships with the assistance of the Portsmouth Naval Shipyard developed the contract plans for the *Thresher*, but then the Portsmouth Naval Shipyard developed the detailed plans from which she was built. There were changes in these detailed plans from the contract plans.

Representative HOLIFIELD. Were these changes made with the approval of the Navy, or were they changes made by the contractor without approval?

Admiral AUSTIN. I would say with the approval of the Bureau of Ships, sir.

Representative HOLIFIELD. Did you have in the changing of these plans, competent analysis made of the requests of the contractor who changed them, or were they approved by minor officers as a routine?

Admiral AUSTIN. I would say, sir, from the viewpoint of the court, there needs to be a raising of the level of any change from a contract specification. Now, Admiral Brockett might have a different view on that.

Admiral BROCKETT. No; I agree that the deviations from the contract plans, so-called, which are those on which the ship is bid, as opposed to those working plans from which she is in fact built, will occasionally occur because there will be things in the contract plans which when you go to make them in detail do not work out the way you think they should.

Deviations from the contract plans would normally be referred to the Bureau of Ships, to the authority within the Bureau of Ships, but the level to which they would come, again in the normal course of events, and let us say prior to *Thresher*, might be lower than you would like to see them in the light of what has occurred in recent months.

Representative HOLIFIELD. In relation to this same problem, on page 11 in the unclassified summary of events. (See app. 6, p. 152.) I quote:

Portsmouth Naval Shipyard has authority to deviate from building specifications in certain areas, and is using the specifications as goals rather than requirements in certain cases.

This in itself is an indictment, it seems to me, of the shipyard's compliance with standards, and I would ask, were all of the deviations from specifications recorded? Does anyone really know what standards were actually meant in the construction of the *Thresher* and other Portsmouth submarines? Do they have authority to deviate and has that been delegated to local authorities in other shipyards?

I will take them one at a time, and I wanted you to get the full group of questions on that point. Were all deviations from specifications recorded?

Admiral BROCKETT. That I am not sure of yet, Mr. Holifield, but it is one of the areas in which we are working.

Representative HOLIFIELD. Does anybody really know what standards were actually met in the construction of the *Thresher* and other Portsmouth submarines?

Admiral BROCKETT. I think we do. Again the level of detail in which we will be able to develop this information remains to be seen.

I will say this, though [classified matter deleted] that it is going to be made perfectly clear that specifications are minimum requirements and not goals. This is in process in written form right now.

The big difficulty with having a goal, as you have suggested in an earlier question, is that you don't know where you are. If you set these up as requirements, one of two things should happen. Either you revise the specification, or you meet it.

Representative HOLIFIELD. And you record the deviation?

Admiral BROCKETT. As to the deviation, you don't waive them, you rewrite the specifications to meet a reasonable engineering target. [Classified matter deleted.]

In the other case, you should contract for the price that the ship is to be built for, and get your specifications across the board. This is good 20/20 hindsight.

Representative HOLIFIELD. Has authority to deviate from specifications been delegated to local authority in other shipyards?

Admiral BROCKETT. I am not entirely sure as to this statement, and I have to do some homework on it, which I have not had a chance to do yet.

Representative HOLIFIELD. As to any of these questions which are asked, I am sure it would be all right for you gentlemen to furnish us the answers to them.

Admiral BROCKETT. I would like to.

ULTRASONIC TESTING OF SILVER BRAZED JOINTS

Representative HOLIFIELD. I want to go back to the 14 percent of the salt water joints tested being defective, and I am relying on my memory now of the record. As I understand it, there was something like 3,000 silver-brazed joints in the vessel. That is in the salt water system. There were 145 ultrasonically tested.

Going back even further, I understand that originally there was no scientific way of testing a brazed joint. Then the ultrasonic system of testing was developed, and it was used on 145 joints. Of those 145 joints, 14 percent as I remember were found defective.

Now, at that point although there were several months of additional time in the shipyard, the team apparently was pulled off, I believe it was in November, and there was something like 3 months before the ship was in the water. Perhaps it was December.

And yet there is no activity shown in the record of a continuation of the ultrasonic testing during those 3 months, and there is an assumption therefore that something like 2,855 joints remained untested although there was a clear indication of 14 percent defectiveness.

Now, the question that occurs to a layman like myself is this: Why were not more joints tested, and why were not all of the joints tested when almost any one of those joints in the salt water system under great pressure could provide the reason for a catastrophe like this.

Chairman PASTORE. Does the Congressman mean to use the word "defective" or "below standard?"

Representative HOLIFIELD. I used the word "defective" because I would consider a joint was defective if it showed certain defects on a test. I don't know if the word is right. I would like to have it changed if it isn't right.

Admiral AUSTIN. Could I explain, Mr. Chairman? The word "defective" is questionable as being accurate.

Chairman PASTORE. Shall we substitute "below standard?"

Admiral AUSTIN. "Below standard" would be more accurate, sir, for this reason: The court found that there have been tests made, destructive tests, in which a pipe with only 10-percent bond in a silver-brazed joint, with proper geometrical distribution of that bond, stood up better than the pipe on which the brazed joint had been made.

Now, in the court's opinion, this was something which caused many people, not only at Portsmouth Naval Shipyard, but many people to think that the Bureau of Ship's standards were too high.

Actually, we do not think that they were too high. The method of testing which is now in use, ultrasonic testing, is not an exact thing. You have to allow for roughly 10 to 17 percent error in the answer that the test will give you. Now, if you have to have a 25-percent bond to allow for maldistribution of the metal that is bonding with the pipe, the silver brazing, then you have to add on to that the amount of your possible error of your testing equipment or your testing team, in order to be sure that you have a safe joint, sir.

This is why we said what we did about goals and requirements, because we found at the Portsmouth Naval Shipyard that their instructions on how to do silver brazing quoted the Bureau of Ships' requirements, but also belabored the fact that a 10-percent bond properly distributed would give you a safe joint.

Representative HOLIFIELD. But that would be a statement without the ability to check?

Admiral AUSTIN. That is right, sir.

Representative HOLIFIELD. Previous to your ultrasonic testing, then if there is an error in your ultrasonic testing as you have said of 10 or 15 percent, an allowance would have to be made for that either particularly down from what the test would show——

Admiral AUSTIN. That is right, sir.

Representative HOLIFIELD. And this still doesn't answer the question as to why the other 2,855 joints were never tested.

Admiral AUSTIN. The court had the same reaction which you have evidenced on this point.

Representative HOLIFIELD. But they didn't carry it forward. As I saw it, at that point they stopped in their questioning, and they didn't carry this point forward.

Admiral AUSTIN. No, sir; I believe you will find that we questioned exhaustively on this point, sir.

Representative HOLIFIELD. Perhaps I read this in the unclassified summary, I suppose.

Admiral AUSTIN. The unclassified summary, sir, I have not read, because that was prepared by other than the court.

Mr. CONWAY. If I may interpose here, my recollection is that the court did inquire and the commandant of the yard indicated that there were specific instructions from the Bureau of Ships that it should proceed during the entire availability period, if they found what might be considered a hazardous condition of these silver brazed joints. I think the Bureau of Ships also asked for comments and recommendations and results of this preliminary limited testing.

DECISION TO DISCONTINUE ULTRASONIC TESTS

Somewhere around November there was a decision made at the yard not to go further, and I think that they knocked off in December. And as I recall the testimony, no decision or no recommendation was sent to the Bureau of Ships, and the decision was made locally in the yard.

Admiral AUSTIN. Yes, and the court determined that this decision was made with the knowledge of the shipyard commander. It was not made by him, but it was made with his knowledge, and the court found that the shipyard did use poor judgment on not continuing those tests.

Representative HOLIFIELD. I understand that there was great difficulty in getting at some of these joints because they were involved in the hull and the structure of the ship, in order to make the tests. I understand that there was great difficulty.

But now what have you done since that time in order to prevent this from occurring again? Have you taken any action at all on silver brazed joints?

Admiral BROCKETT. I might give a little background on the *Thresher* joints in particular. As you have gathered, this ultrasonic method is fairly new, and it has been developed really within the last year. We have gotten it so that we have good confidence in the results that are obtained, and the way this has been done is to take ultrasonic pictures of joints, and then take them apart and see what is really there.

There has been refinement of it, and the *Thresher* looked like a good place to go and use it, and we said, "Put one team on the *Thresher* and work them all of the time she is in there and see what you find."

We have other test methods but they are not nearly as good in my estimation as the so-called "U–T." There are hydrostatic tests at 150 percent of working pressure, and hammer tests which seemed to be a good way to get into trouble and didn't prove very much, and a variety of things such as this. And finally we found a way we could test these joints.

I might add we have used silver-brazed joints in submarines for many years, but we have not contended with the pressures and depths we are contending with now.

Chairman PASTORE. Could I ask a question at this point? Did this question of 14 percent below standard on the examination that was made of the 145 joints come to your attention or come to the Bureau's attention?

Admiral BROCKETT. Not to my knowledge, Senator. I read the record here to the effect that the report was not made to the Bureau of Ships.

Chairman PASTORE. Did the court in its factual findings determine that this situation had come to the attention of any one of the agencies of the Navy?

Admiral AUSTIN. It was known to the commanding officer of the ship, Mr. Chairman. It was not reported any higher in the operational chain of command than the commanding officer of the ship, and it was not reported to the Chief of the Bureau of Ships.

Chairman PASTORE. Was the determination made by him that this 14 percent below standard was safe?

Admiral AUSTIN. By whom, sir? By the commanding officer?

Chairman PASTORE. By the commanding officer. I mean as I understand it there were 3,000 joints, and only 145 were examined, and out of the 145 examined there were found to be 14 percent under standard. Now, who assumed the responsibility to say, "This is safe," or "This is unsafe," or do nothing about it and let it be the way it is.

Admiral AUSTIN. The shipyard commander, in effect, assumed that responsibility, sir.

Chairman PASTORE. Did the court in its findings determine that he was right in that assumption?

Admiral AUSTIN. No, sir; we determined that he had used poor judgment.

Senator JACKSON. Might I ask a question there?

Chairman PASTORE. Mr. Holifield is going to raise all of these questions, and I know he doesn't mind if anyone wants to ask a question.

Representative HOLIFIELD. I am a little embarrassed that I am taking so much time.

ADEQUACY OF DESIGN TO MEET NEW USES AND APPLICATIONS

Senator JACKSON. I have one general question. The question I would like to ask is this: It is quite clear to me that when we move from conventional subs to nuclear subs, this automatically made new uses and new applications of the hull as a whole. I note that the World War II vessels had a depth capacity of 400 feet [classified matter deleted].

As we go down deeper, the flooding rate goes up and the discharge rate goes down.

It seems to me, and what disturbs me, Mr. Chairman, is this: Have we watched the design part of the overall boat carefully to meet these new uses and new applications that are entirely different than that in the case of conventional subs?

Isn't this what we boil down to? We can get into details, whether the silver brazed joints were the proximate cause of the difficulty or something else was the proximate cause of the sinking. But the real fundamental question, it seems to me, is that, have we been—and we all make mistakes—as careful and as prudent and as foreseeable as we should have been in contemplating the possibilities that are bound to occur when you make such heavy and diffuse uses when you put nuclear power into the boat?

Chairman PASTORE. We are trying to get there step by step. I realize that is the $64 question.

Senator JACKSON. But I want to know in general as to the design. This is on the whole question of the overall design of the nuclear boats. Did the Bureau go into this thoroughly in the matter of all of the floodings that have occurred in other submarines?

[Classified matter deleted.]

Secretary KORTH. I think Admiral Brockett had given you a general answer on this without precluding the development of the specifics.

Senator JACKSON. This is what I wanted.

Admiral BROCKETT. I think the answer to your question is that——

Senator JACKSON. I ask this not in a critical vein, but I want to know what happened.

Admiral BROCKETT. In retrospect the answer to your question is that we have really extrapolated the World War II fleet boats into the present ones, and I might also add that it is not nuclear power which is significant, it is the depth.

Senator JACKSON. I stated it a different way. The point is that for the first time we developed a true submarine, and we didn't have it before. We stayed submerged longer and we went deeper, and we just made more continuous use under more difficult circumstances, and we were in areas that were unknown before, and isn't all of this true once you put nuclear power into it?

Admiral BROCKETT. We were pushing the state of the art, and in the process of adapting to nuclear power we spent a great deal of time in some areas. We ran into difficulty, if you will remember, in the HY–80 steel.

This had been I think thoroughly explored. It had a great deal of attention paid to it, but some of the details fell in the crack in connection with hull design and fabrication. At the same time, we were not sitting still. We were going ahead on the silver brazing and the accelerations in process now. There are other factors in the boats which require a good hard look, and this is what we are trying to do now.

FAILURE OF SILVER BRAZED JOINTS

Chairman PASTORE. Of course, it goes beyond that, Admiral. Had you ever had an incident in any other of the submarines whereby a brazed joint had become loose?

Admiral BROCKETT. Yes, sir; the best known would be the *Barbel*.

Chairman PASTORE. Had that happened before the *Thresher* went out to sea?

Admiral BROCKETT. Yes, sir.

Chairman PASTORE. Had this matter been called to the attention of the commanding officer?

Admiral BROCKETT. It was common knowledge throughout the Navy; yes, sir.

Chairman PASTORE. You mean to tell me that this commanding officer who passed on the 14 percent below standard had known before this that one of the brazed joints had gone loose on one of the other submarines?

Admiral BROCKETT. I am sure that the *Barbel* was common knowledge throughout the submarine force.

Chairman PASTORE. Did the court determine that? We are getting at this question, it is true enough we are saying the man used bad judgment, and I don't want to be harsh with him because after all we could be wrong, but the important question here is this: Knowing of this defect, if we can call it a defect, or situation below standard, this man apparently gave the approval, and the big question here is, Did the Navy at that time know that these brazed joints were defective? Had they had this experience before? Was this the first time it ever happened?

Admiral AUSTIN. No, sir; there had been a number of cases, and they are set forth in the record, Mr. Chairman, and the most outstanding ones are all cataloged in the record and in the findings, I believe, you will find them nicely set apart. The commanding officer of the *Thresher* who accepted this condition and took his ship to sea was not available for questioning, sir, and we could not ask him whether or not he considered this a dangerous thing.

Chairman PASTORE. I am talking about the commandant of the yard who passed upon this.

Admiral AUSTIN. We did question him, sir, and he, in retrospect, admitted that he thought he should have looked into this more thoroughly, but at the time he did not consider it a dangerous situation. They were trying to meet a deadline date for the completion of the ship's availability, and to have gone further with the testing would have required unlagging of piping and delaying the ship and running up the cost of the overhaul and, you know, the many attendant things when you delay the ship.

Chairman PASTORE. Are the procedures of the Navy such that this man could make the final determination, and he could pass on the final judgment without consulting with the Bureau of Ships? Is that the procedure, and could he make that final determination?

Admiral BROCKETT. In the normal course of events we expect our people in the field to make decisions affecting the work that is in process in their shipyards. Again, the 20–20 hindsight on this is that it should probably not have been done and it should have been reported up the line.

Representative HOLIFIELD. Was not this known at the Bureau of Ships?

Admiral BROCKETT. It was not known——

Representative HOLIFIELD. Were there any telephone conversations?

Admiral BROCKETT. This is what I don't know, Mr. Holifield, or at least it didn't come to my attention. I was in a position not as the Chief of the Bureau of Ships, but I was one notch farther down the line, in the chain in which this information would have come.

Representative HOLIFIELD. Understand I am not trying to be a Monday morning quarterback.

Admiral BROCKETT. I was closer to it in November last than I am now, by one notch.

INADEQUATE PIPING INSPECTION

Representative HOLIFIELD. I notice that opinions 18, 21, and 22 state very plainly that the Portsmouth Naval Shipyard did not aggressively pursue the ultrasonic inspection of silver brazed joints as required by the Bureau of Ships letter of August 28, 1962, exhibit 115. The deputy commander of the submarine force, did not aggressively pursue the ultrasonic inspection, nor did the commanding officer of the *Thresher;* 21, that the management of the Portsmouth Naval Shipyard did not exercise good judgment in determining not to unlag pipes in order to continue the directed ultrasonic tests directed, after November 1962. That the Bureau of Ships improvement and corrective action regarding the silver brazed problem were not applied at the Bureau level or in the field with sufficient vigor, and then it continues along that line.

I refer back to the letter of August 28, 1962, which required ultrasonic inspections, and I am still unclear in my mind as to why the requirement was not continued after the first of December or thereabouts, and if this was a Bureau of Ships letter, what was the final determination, the response to that letter. (See app. 2, p. 134.) Was there a report required or not?

DELAY IN "THRESHER" PIPING REPORT

Admiral BROCKETT. There was a report required.

Representative HOLIFIELD. And the report was presented to the Bureau of Ships?

Admiral BROCKETT. The report was presented.

Representative HOLIFIELD. After the termination of inspections?

Admiral BROCKETT. It was in process and it was received after the 11th of April.

Representative HOLIFIELD. After the 11th of April?

Admiral BROCKETT. Yes, sir.

Representative HOLIFIELD. They terminated it the first of December and you did not receive it at the Bureau of Ships until April?

Admiral BROCKETT. That is right.

Representative HOLIFIELD. Do you have any explanation for that?

Admiral BROCKETT. No, sir; except I don't believe it was considered to be a matter of priority. This condition of the joints in the *Thresher* within a matter of percentage points was probably not much different than other submarines, as we have found out since. Now of course you take a different tack. Then we made a check on a certain number of them, and found them not deficient in the sense of not having any material in them, but they would be below the 50-percent bond, which incidentally we have now raised to 60. We were working up to this knowing that joints have been made for many years and probably not under the best kind of conditions. But by working on this and giving people instructions in how to make them properly and instituting tighter controls——

Chairman PASTORE. There is a vote in the Senate, and I will have to go, and the vice chairman will take over, and we will be back as soon as we can.

TIGHTER INSPECTION AND DESIGN STANDARDS

Mr. CONWAY. I want, so the record may be accurate and so there may not be a misinterpretation, to indicate how vital this was considered to be, the letter from the Bureau of Ships of 28 August 1962 (see app. 2, p. 135), it stated as follows:

The significance of gross failures of silver-brazed joints in vital submarine systems is such that the Bureau considers it a matter of urgency that inspection program be developed for these systems.

Admiral BROCKETT. Developed, and this was one team. Let us see what we have in *Thresher* approach.

Representative HOSMER. You were getting into this business?

Admiral BROCKETT. It was a part of the developmental process.

Representative HOSMER. And there were probably half a hundred other things with respect to getting them done within the time that the ship was scheduled, about which there were judgments to be made, whether or not to do this or that or what to pursue and some of them had to come out and some of them had to stay in, is that right?

Admiral BROCKETT. It was part of the developmental process, Mr. Hosmer, and as I started to mention, the standards that we were in the throes of establishing, and we are up to now requiring 60-percent bond.

Representative HOLIFIELD. I note in your recommendations, No. 6 and No. 7, you have really tried to correct this situation. In No. 6, you state that in hazardous piping systems of submarines [classified matter deleted], silver brazed joints of more than 2 inches in inside diameter be replaced by welded joints when replacements are required. I don't know what the "when replacement is required" means, but that is your wording.

No. 7—

that for new construction submarines, welding piping joints will be specified for joints of more than 2 inches in inside diameter in hazardous systems.

I notice that you have taken corrective action there in that area. Now, had there been any substantial questioning of brazed joints on the part of members of the Navy.

Admiral BROCKETT. Well, the Bureau of Ships and the Navy in general have questions. The *Barbel* incident which was the bad one, highlighted this whole thing. But silver braze didn't get so much of a downcheck as the operation of the pipe shop in Portsmouth, as I remember that case. They have gone a long way since then in Portsmouth to correct their practices within the shop. At the same time, we did not have, until recently, an honest to goodness inspection process. We have it now, in a nondestructive test.

DEPTH LIMITATION ON EXISTING SUBMARINES

Representative HOLIFIELD. What are we going to do about all of these submarines that have silver brazed joints, and that are supposed to go [classified matter deleted]. Is it the intention of the Navy to gamble with these silver brazed joints, or are they going to be changed?

Admiral BROCKETT. The process that we are contemplating is this: The first is a matter of philosophy. You set a goal, what in the engineering sense is the reasonable thing to do in these ships for the [classified matter deleted] depth. Once you have done this, then you, in turn, have several different problems to consider, and several different groups of ships as Secretary Korth mentioned. You have those that are in the 1963 building program, and they haven't laid the keels yet, and those in the current construction program. We have required that after May 1, those ships which are being built now, every silver brazed joint that is made over 1 inch will be ultrasonically tested and meet the 60-percent requirement. We have the depth limitation as you know, on the ships that are in operation. On those we do not plan to back off one iota from the goal.

Representative HOLIFIELD. From the goal of what?

Admiral BROCKETT. Of the ultimate ship, the ultimate method, or the ultimate engineering that we want to do on the ones that are just beginning. But we realize we are going to have to program to this. You are not going to be able to do it overnight. So there is going to have to be a trade-off on depth and the degree to which this has been accomplished.

Representative HOLIFIELD. The trade-off on depth will be more or less permanent until you have confidence that the situation is corrected in these ships that are now operating.

Admiral BROCKETT. Yes, sir; and there are other things in here beside the piping system. The blow rate is part of this picture.

Representative HOLIFIELD. As far as this No. 9 is concerned, that is a permanent trade-off that will not be changed until you have done enough corrective action.

Admiral BROCKETT. Until we find out where we are.

Representative BATES. How long do you think that will take, Admiral?

Admiral BROCKETT. We haven't programed it yet, in the sense of setting dates on it. We are considering different ships, now, as they come up, and what has to be done to them before we want them to go to sea below restricted depths. We are being conservative as you might expect.

REINSPECTION OF EXISTING SUBMARINES

Representative BATES. This means then unlagging and checking all points?

Admiral BROCKETT. This means going through the entire ship in essence on this point.

The program is underway right now, and there has been quite a bit of work done already.

Representative BATES. Might I ask one question there?

In reference to the commanding officer who was advised as to this condition, what is the source of that information?

Admiral AUSTIN. There was a documentary proof of that. He got a copy of the report which was submitted by the quality assurance people in the Portsmouth Naval Yard, asking for a decision and reporting what they had done and asking for a decision as to whether or not they should unlag and continue, and he got a copy of that.

Representative WESTLAND. You are speaking of Harvey when you say the commanding officer?

Admiral AUSTIN. No, sir; this was Axene, then, at the time the memo was written. Now, whether or not Harvey actually saw that or not, I don't know, sir. But Axene was the commanding officer at the time that memorandum was written from the quality assurance division of the yard to the production or design department asking for this proceeding.

Representative WESTLAND. So you do not know whether or not Harvey knew that there was this 14-percent deficiency as a result of your tests?

Admiral AUSTIN. It is difficult to determine what he did know, sir.

Representative HOLIFIELD. Now, I might recall in relation to your question on page 18, of the classified section, where it says:

The commanding officer, Axene, evaluation of the first year of operations contained in his letter, serial No. 16 November 1962, called *Thresher* the best ASW submarine afloat today.

FLOODING DANGER IN "THRESHER" POINTED OUT

In pointing out *Thresher's* deficiencies, he highlighted her overcomplexity in certain areas [classified matter deleted] and the vulnerability of her auxiliary seawater system.

He stated:

In my opinion the most dangerous condition that exists in *Thresher* is the danger of salt water flooding while at or near test depth.

Now, he gave this report as he was leaving and as Harvey was his replacement, Harvey must have known about this; did he not?

Admiral AUSTIN. It would be presumed, Mr. Chairman, that he did know about it, but, of course, we can't be certain.

Representative HOLIFIELD. You cannot be sure. Then in the Bureau of Ships August letter (see app. 2, p. 134) as to the instructions—you said that the intent of the Bureau is that the inspection directed by this letter shall serve as a pilot test of silver-brazed piping inspection in operating the ships, which were conducted without benefit of present-day quality controls. A similar pilot test is contemplated for silver-brazed piping which will be conducted by another shipbuilding activity. The results of these trials and inspections will be of service as a basis for a Bureau instruction which will have as its purpose a step-by-step program of certifying vital submarine piping systems as meeting minimum Bureau acceptance standards in ships constructed prior to the current quality control program. To this and Portsmouth Naval Shipyard is requested to forward comments, suggestions, and recommendations, based upon their experience as a result of this pilot test. This was signed by R. L. Moore, Jr., Deputy Chief of the Bureau.

As far as the record shows, then, you had no response to this request for comments, suggestions, and recommendations based upon their experience in the Bureau of Ships; is that right?

Admiral BROCKETT. That is right, sir.

Representative HOLIFIELD. Do you not consider that it was the job or responsibility of the Bureau of Ships to follow up upon that letter?

Admiral BROCKETT. I will have to guess on this, and I don't like to do it, but the way we would set it up, we expected it to continue right up practically to the completion of the ship, which would be April, and I don't suppose anyone was heckling for the letter. Normally you would expect to get this after the ship had completed and left. Whether or not any of my boys down the line realized it had been stopped in November or December, I am not sure. Did you develop any testimony along that line?

Admiral AUSTIN. Yes, the report which the shipyard submitted was in response to a jig as it were, from your Bureau. I do not remember offhand the date that they queried them but it was in response to a specific request for a report.[1]

Admiral BROCKETT. I remember the letter coming in because it was after the *Thresher*, and that is why I was sure it was after the date. Of course, it had a big red flag on it.

Representative HOLIFIELD. I am not quite clear what the step-by-step program means, because it would seem to me that if this had determined to be a hazardous situation, that you would not let a submarine go to sea on a step-by-step basis, but until the whole thing was corrected.

Admiral BROCKETT. You see, it is a question of the deficiency or defect versus standards. We were still in the process of setting standards. As I say, the silver-brazed fittings had been used for years. The *Barbel* incident, to get into the technicalities of the matter just a little bit, was essentially not due to silver brazing per se, but because the wrong material was used in one of the entering pipes. And you don't make a bond with stainless, when the brazing material is for copper-nickel piping.

PREVIOUS PIPING FAILURES IN "THRESHER"

Representative HOLIFIELD. You had two failures in *Thresher*. During the first builder's trials, a salt water vent line failed, and a joint in trim system failed, so you had warning on the *Thresher* that those joints were not reliable; did you not? (See app. 1, p. 133.)

Admiral BROCKETT. This is not unusual, sir. With the multiplicity, and we speak of 3,000, but there are about 16,000 piping joints all told on that ship, and 24,000 on an SSB(N).

---

[1] For discussion on this point, see p. 24.

Representative HOLIFIELD. Do you not think what Senator Jackson said is true, that we have gone to those depths with older methods which were satisfactory at shallower depths, and suddenly we find [classified matter deleted] it becomes very hazardous [classified matter deleted]?

Admiral BROCKETT. Plus some assurance from the fact that we have had many excursions to depths in *Thresher* and other ships.

Representative BATES. We have no record of who called off this inspection?

Admiral BROCKETT. The shipyard commander knew about it and it was a question of going only so far. They were trying to get the ship finished and at that time I am sure that the philosophy was, "this is as good as any other ship." The 14-percent deficiencies below standard does not mean that these were bad joints in the normal sense. They were tight joints and they held 150 percent of the normal working pressure. [Classified matter deleted.] These hydrostatic tests were made.

Representative BATES. Was this a Bureau of Ships team or a shipyard team?

Admiral BROCKETT. A shipyard team.

Representative BATES. They were still there at the yard, but they went on to something else?

Admiral BROCKETT. They put them on something else.

Representative BATES. And these other tests that you gave, by prior standards and by prior tests, do they coincide pretty much with the ultrasonic tests here?

Admiral BROCKETT. The basic test has been hydrostatic test.

Representative BATES. And you did simultaneous tests?

Admiral BROCKETT. They would show up tight but a joint would show up——

Representative BATES. My question was, did you run tests simultaneously, on the same joint, and did you apply this system and that system?

Admiral BROCKETT. The whole system got the normal hydrostatic tests; yes, sir.

Representative BATES. So on these that you found fault with you also tested on the others, and how did the tests compare? Did they indicate they were below normal?

INADEQUACIES OF PIPING PRESSURE TESTS

Admiral BROCKETT. No, there were no failures from the hydros, as far as I know. In the normal course of events, I would say you have a few weeps, and you go back and remake those joints. But a hydrostatic test unfortunately shows you just one thing, that at that particular instant of time, that that system would take 150-percent pressure.

Representative BATES. Why do you have the variation?

Admiral BROCKETT. The variations in what does this joint in fact have as a bond between the pipe and the fitting? It can be almost chewing gum in a sense and still hold its pressure. But the submarine works; it rotates and it compresses, and this applies forces to the piping system throughout the hull. This is why we felt that we had to have more bond and we were still trying to find out how much.

This is where we come to a 10-percent joint.   It will hold but it is not a good joint.

Representative BATES. And a test in a shipyard is not the same test as you would have in the sea [classified matter deleted].

Admiral BROCKETT. Over a period of time, in particular, or on just shallow dives, you see, your boat works.

Representative HOLIFIELD. In other words, you are saying your utilization of that brazed joint, while it may respond to a test at the time it is finished and tested, the constant working of the submarine, the expansion and prop rotation and vibration of those joints will develop fatigue in that kind of a joint, if you want to call it that, and possibly cause it to become unreliable later on.

Admiral BROCKETT. It is not quite a fatigue phenomenon in the technical sense, but your assurance of maintaining it under working conditions, without a separation between the silver braze material itself and the base pipe—your assurance that it is going to continue to hold when there is only just enough metal in there to seal it, shall we say, is not great. This is why we were working up to more and more bond, feeling that this would be the answer. But again, for many years and at other depths [classified matter deleted] we had only a minimum of serious difficulties. One of them, the *Barbel*, as I say, was pinned down to the use of wrong material. So one of our first approaches was a careful material control program. That is on the piping itself, and also on the brazing material.

Representative HOSMER. You never had a real red flag on this?

Admiral BROCKETT. Well, the *Barbel* was a red flag, but it flagged the material problem.

Representative HOSMER. It flagged something else, and it was not a lack of bond?

Admiral BROCKETT. There are two schools of thought on silver brazing in general.

REDESIGN AND WELDING OF PIPING

Representative HOSMER. And you are working out on the new ships, and you are taking it out?

Admiral BROCKETT. Not necessarily; this is a recommendation of the court. We have another design group which was mentioned also working on this. My personal inclination, although I don't have all of the technical facts, is to weld whenever we can.

Representative HOSMER. Is there any thought of redesigning the whole system and cutting some of this piping out?

Admiral BROCKETT. This has been done, and as a matter of fact on the ships that are in the 1963 program, there has been development of those plans to eliminate joints. One of the best ways to have a good joint is not to have any at all. So efforts have been bent in this direction.

Representative HOSMER. Was that before this event?

Admiral BROCKETT. This design is 2 years old.

Representative HOSMER. And in other words, it was recognized that these joints were something desirable to get rid of?

Admiral BROCKETT. In any system, get rid of the joints.

Representative HOSMER. And to work out a design that would cure it.

Admiral BROCKETT. That is correct.

Mr. CONWAY. I would like for the record to go back to the point about the yard submitting its report on the silver brazing after the loss of the *Thresher*, which you mentioned was in response from a jig of the Bureau of Ships. I think that if you will check the record, the jig from the Bureau of Ships went out 2 days after the *Thresher* was lost, April 12, so that the jig did come but not until after the *Thresher* had been lost.

Admiral BROCKETT. If I may comment on our mail system, it was probably written a week before.

PREVIOUS SUBMARINE CASUALTIES

Representative PRICE. Mr. Chairman, in the classified report, though, you are talking about the *Barbel* investigation, and you say that the inadequacy of assurance dated back prior to 1961? That is on page 34. Was there any action taken then to set a limitation on the depth, and so forth, until you solved this problem? (See app. 1, p. 133.)

Admiral BROCKETT. No, sir; there was not.

Representative PRICE. And yet also on page 34, it says that several submarines had suffered casualties which nearly resulted in their loss.

Now, the *Barbel* was one, and what were the other ones?

Admiral BROCKETT. There were several nonnuclears in that list. [Classified matter deleted.]

Admiral AUSTIN. One cause was flexible hoses and the *Thresher* had a silver brazed joint failure.

Representative PRICE. At what depth was the *Thresher* on that occasion?

Admiral AUSTIN. The *Thresher* on that occasion, sir, was on its builder trials and that was a second builder trial so it went to test depth at that time. [Classified matter deleted.]

Representative PRICE. Do you know what depth it was when it had the silver brazed joint failure?

Admiral AUSTIN. It went fairly deep before they called it off.

Representative PRICE. That could not be one that you considered to be in danger of being lost, then?

Admiral AUSTIN. Well, I would say, sir [classified matter deleted] the pressure is pretty great, and I would say that you do have some danger of losing the ship if you have a failure.

Representative PRICE. The *Skate* was also a 2-inch silver brazed failure [classified matter deleted]. It would seem to me that you had enough of those instances at the time to be alarmed, and it appeared that maybe some precautionary action should have been taken.

Admiral BROCKETT. Yes, we were alarmed, but again in retrospect probably not sufficiently alarmed. The reaction on these things is to go in and find out what is wrong and institute a program to correct it. The question of depth of course is very important to the operating characteristics of the submarine and what it can do. I would say that neither the Bureau of Ships nor the operational forces felt that this was symptomatic of a basic deficiency which should cause restrictions on the operating depths of these boats.

Representative BATES. How did this compare with problems that you might have had on conventional ships before?

Admiral Brockett. Well, to my mind, Mr. Bates, it is a situation that Senator Jackson pointed to, the fact that as you go to the greater depths your problems don't go up in direct proportion, they go up in some kind of a curve. We have treated them as a straight line sort of thing. [Classified matter deleted].

STATISTICAL APPROACH TO QUALITY CONTROL

Representative Holifield. On page 14 of the summary of events, it is noted that the court recommends a statistical approach to quality control. (See app. 6, p. 153.) Wasn't this approach that got the *Thresher* in trouble in silver brazing? It was a statistical approach or is there some difference that I don't understand there?

Admiral Austin. The court felt, sir, that we were not referring to the sequence of events regarding the silver brazed joints on the *Thresher* only here, but we found, for example, that in many cases the individual failure was reported on an individual ship that went to a fairly low level in the shipyard.

Now, we felt that had the whole picture been brought as a complete whole to the attention of the shipyard commander and he had been asked for a decision based on the whole complex of all of these little slips of paper, he might have clicked much better than he did, sir.

Representative Holifield. In other words, an accumulation of the statistical events to give you a sense of the number of events that there were, and therefore the judgment as to their importance.

Admiral Austin. Yes, sir.

Representative Holifield. Of each separate event, whether it was an isolated event or a series of events.

Admiral Austin. That is correct, sir.

Representative Holifield. Well, I wondered how you could use statistics on that kind of a thing when the failure of one of these joints of course could sink a ship, unless you did have them together and could take a course of action which would be corrective as a result of accumulation of the statistics. Is there any difference in the control work of the reactor part of the ship from the control over work in the other areas of the ship?

Admiral Austin. Yes, sir.

REACTOR COMPARTMENT MORE STRINGENT

Representative Holifield. As I understand it, there were no silver brazed joints in the reactor area of the ship.

Admiral Austin. There were when the ship came in for this overhaul, and they were all changed to welded joints during the overhaul period.

Representative Holifield. But the rest of the ship was not considered as important as this. Was that because of the danger of leaks of radioactive material in the reactor part?

Admiral Austin. It is because of the requirements for the reactor compartment, sir, and the requirements for the rest of the ship were not that stringent.

Representative Hosmer. Where do these requirements come from with respect to the reactor portion of the ship? Do they come out of code 1500?

Admiral Austin. Yes; Bureau of Ships.

Representative HOSMER. And the others come out of other codes in the Bureau of Ships?

Admiral AUSTIN. Yes, sir.

Representative MORRIS. What is this code 1500?

Representative HOSMER. That is Admiral Rickover.

Secretary KORTH. I think Admiral Brockett and then perhaps Admiral Rickover should both speak to this feature.

REACTOR COMPARTMENT SPECIFICATIONS ENFORCED

Admiral BROCKETT. I would like to say that the reactor compartment is unmanned, for one thing, and this means that which is done therein, and I am sure, I hope, Admiral Rickover will support me in this, is of particular significance. Secondly, I must say this in all fairness, that the work done in connection with the reactor compartment and that system meets its specifications, and this basic difference that I mentioned earlier of the specifications as a goal as opposed to a requirement does not apply to Admiral Rickover's work. The specifications are met and the builders are held to it. This is exactly what I have in mind for the remainder of the ship. The specifications may not be the same, but they will be met.

Chairman PASTORE. May I interrupt at this point?

I do not know what the plans of you gentlemen may be, and I do not want to impinge upon those plans, and I was wondering, it strikes me that it would be for the benefit of all of us if we did meet again.

Secretary KORTH. Absolutely, whenever you say so.

Chairman PASTORE. And I want to make it mutually convenient, and I do not know what the desires of the committee might be, but it is 5 o'clock now, and we could go a little longer, but certainly we could not conclude. I would like the advantage of the other members coming back. This has been a busy day on the floor of the Senate. Today is Wednesday. Next Monday we start our civil rights hearing before the Senate committee.

Representative HOLIFIELD. I am wondering on the question of Admiral Austin, if there are other questions to give him in regard to the court's actions. Personally, I don't have any further questions in regard to the court's function. It seems like to me you have had a very fair and complete hearing as far as the court is concerned. You are up at Newport at the War College, not here in Washington.

ACCEPTANCE OF SHIP AS READY FOR SEA

Representative WESTLAND. I would like to pursue a matter one step further, on page 10 of the summary of events, you say that all work undertaken by the shipyard during the *Thresher's* post-shakedown availablity was reported as having been completed satisfactorily, and the commanding officer expressed his concurrence that the work was completed. I would expect that that would be the case.

Now, how did the commanding officer express his concurrence? Was it in writing when he accepted the ship as ready for sea? (See app. 6, p. 146.)

Admiral AUSTIN. It was in a letter to his immediate superior in the chain of command, stating that he was ready for sea, that everything was tested out all right.

Representative WESTLAND. And this is Commander Harvey?

Admiral AUSTIN. That is correct, sir.

Representative HOSMER. Will you yield on that? That actual matter of practice, I don't suppose that is given too much substantive weight, if the commander is really upset about something of a major nature.

Admiral AUSTIN. We thought we ought to look into that a little bit and we inquired into the type of man that Harvey was, and every indication was that he was the type that would not have hesitated to say a ship wasn't ready to go if it had not in his opinion been ready to go.

Representative HOSMER. A nagging doubt about whether or not some silver brazing was the right way to put these joints together wouldn't have prevented him from signing that letter, would it?

Admiral AUSTIN. Well, of course, he might have had doubts about the process itself, but certainly I don't think he felt he was taking an unsafe ship to sea.

Representative BATES. Do you know he actually saw this?

Admiral AUSTIN. No, he is the one who took it to sea.

Representative HOSMER. The report went to the previous commanding officer and do you know whether Harvey in fact was aware of this problem with reference to the silver brazing.

Admiral AUSTIN. We do not know, sir, whether Harvey actually ever saw the ship's copy of the report about the number of joints that had failed to meet specified requirements. We do not know that. But it was on the ship. I would think that Axene would have turned over something like that to him, but this I cannot answer definitely.

Representative HOLIFIELD. It wasn't really Harvey's responsibility to know this.

Representative BATES. It was when he signed he was ready to go to sea.

Chairman PASTORE. It is now 10 minutes past 5, and these men have been sitting here since 3 o'clock. We will recess until 2 o'clock tomorrow.

Secretary KORTH. Mr. Chairman, as I say, I am not contributing a great deal here, and if I find that it is impossible tomorrow afternoon personally to return, because I do have another hearing, unfortunately, which I am preparing for, could I be excused?

Chairman PASTORE. Why do you not leave it this way, that you are excused.

Secretary KORTH. And I will try to be here in any event.

Chairman PASTORE. And if you feel it convenient to come, you come back, but you are excused.

Secretary KORTH. I hope you don't think that I am placing the importance of one committee over another.

Chairman PASTORE. You are a busy man and we know that.

(Whereupon, at 5:10 p.m., Wednesday, June 26, 1963, the committee was recessed, to be reconvened at 2 p.m. the following day.)

LOSS OF THE U.S.S. "THRESHER"

THURSDAY, JUNE 27, 1963

U.S. Senate and House of Representatives,
Joint Committee on Atomic Energy,
Washington, D.C.

The committee met at 2 p.m., in room AE–1, the Capitol, Senator John Pastore presiding.

Present: Senators Pastore (presiding), Aiken, Bennett, Curtis, Hickenlooper; Representatives Morris, Anderson, Holifield, Bates, Price, and Hosmer.

Also present: John T. Conway, executive director; Edward J. Bauser, assistant director; George F. Murphy, Jr., professional staff member; James B. Graham, technical adviser; and Jack Rosen, staff consultant.

Witnesses: Secretary of the Navy Korth; Vice Adm. Hyman G. Rickover, Assistant Chief (Bureau of Ships) for Nuclear Propulsion; Rear Adm. John H. Maurer, Director, Submarine Warfare Division, Naval Operations; Rear Adm. William A. Brockett, Chief, Bureau of Ships; Rear Adm. Edward C. Stephan, Chairman, Deep Submergence Systems Review Group; Capt. Charles Bishop, Office of the Chief of Naval Operations (in charge of technical information group of search effort); Capt. M. G. Bayne, naval aide to Secretary Korth; Capt. S. E. Robbins, Director of Congressional Investigations; and Lt. Comdr. LeRoy E. Hopkins, Navy Legislative Liaison.

Chairman Pastore. The committee will be in order.

This afternoon we resume the second session of our hearing on the loss of the *Thresher*. We are happy to have you back, Mr. Secretary, and the other representatives of the Navy.

I understand, Mr. Secretary, that you may have to leave before our session is over this afternoon. Therefore, I would like to get in some of the areas in which you have special interest. To start with I would like to find out what the new depth limitations mean to our ships—tactically or strategically. Then I would like to get into the administration aspects of assuring that future shipyard work is satisfactory, and what the Navy specifically plans to do to clear up unsatisfactory conditions which were uncovered as a result of the investigation of the loss of the *Thresher*.

Those are three points. No. 1, this new depth limitation—How is it fixed and why and what does it mean?

No. 2, What are we going to do about future work at the shipyard to make sure that it meets the highest quality of standards?

No. 3, What are we going to do with relations to our own nuclear propelled submarine contingent because of this?

STATEMENT OF FRED KORTH, SECRETARY OF THE NAVY—Resumed

Secretary KORTH. Mr. Chairman, at the outset, let me give you this word of information or news; that the *Trieste* went down again this morning at 11 o'clock and has not yet completed her search or surfaced. There is no information as to what she may have found; actually, no information that she has found anything of interest is a better way of putting it.

With reference to your first question——

Chairman PASTORE. How about the expedition of the *Trieste* yesterday?

Secretary KORTH. No results, sir. Nothing was learned. Nothing was discovered of any significance.

Senator AIKEN. Are we continuing with the cameras that you have used previously?

Secretary KORTH. I don't know whether that is being done in the last couple of days or not.

Captain BISHOP. No, sir. While the *Trieste* is operating none of the other ships are in the immediate area.

Senator AIKEN. Are we going on with the *Trieste* exclusively at this time?

Secretary KORTH. At this time; yes, sir. But we will continue to search with all available means. With reference to your first question, I think it best that I call on you, Admiral Maurer, to speak with reference to the depth limitation.

OPERATING DEPTH LIMITATION

Admiral MAURER. [Classified matter deleted.] It must be recognized that this limitation is one that we consider temporary.

It will be lifted just as soon as possible in all ships. The limitation specifically, was chosen to assure that we had a depth from which all of these ships could recover, recognizing the most serious flooding casualty that we could visualize with a certain margin of error involved.

[Classified matter deleted.]

At the present time, all of these ships have these restrictions imposed. They have not been modified or lifted from any of them. This restriction will not be lifted until we are assured that each ship has been examined individually to determine that the necessary modifications to its piping system, to its blow rate capability, the necessary changes to the operating procedures, the necessary indoctrination of the people in modifications to the operations of the nuclear plant have been introduced and all of the ship's company is thoroughly cognizant.

Chairman PASTORE. [Classified matter deleted.] You mean the entire nuclear-propelled submarines contingent?

Admiral MAURER. Yes, sir. All nuclear-propelled submarines [classified matter deleted].

Chairman PASTORE. How many submarines do we have in use at the present time?

Admiral MAURER. We only have two *Thresher*-type submarines, the *Permit* and the *Plunger* on the west coast.

We have approximately 16, I believe, attack type [classified matter deleted]. All of the SSBN's in commission except the first five, are [classified matter deleted] built on the same basic design as the earlier nuclears [classified matter deleted].

MORALE EFFECTS

Chairman PASTORE. Have we been using these subs in regular routine fashion without hindrance? Has there been any slowdown, loss of confidence [classified matter deleted].

How have things been going since the *Thresher* disaster?

Admiral MAURER. Our operations have been generally routine, but there are restraints in training [classified matter deleted]. From a training standpoint, it is unsatisfactory because our people should be accustomed and should have the confidence in normal operations of taking their ships down to the deeper depths. Not necessarily to test depth, but in the vicinity of test depth.

Chairman PASTORE. Are you in a position to tell us what the morale has been since then?

Admiral MAURER. It has been quite high. There have been no ill effects as far as we can see, other than the natural feeling on the part of all of the members of the submarine organization that they would have in the face of a tragedy of this scope.

But from the point of view of any shaking of their confidence it has not been noted.

In fact, we have had several of the skippers that said immediately after the tragedy that they would have no hesitation of taking their ships down to [classified matter deleted] test depth today.

Chairman PASTORE. Have you any way of giving us statistics since the time of the disaster [classified matter deleted] the number of hours our submarines have been submerged at that depth? In other words, what I am trying to get at here is what has been our experience as to accidents since this accident [classified matter deleted] and what volume of operations we have had. [Classified matter deleted.]

Have we gone on normally just as if it had not happened? In other words, are we in a position to say that we are in a pretty safe position with our submarine fleet [classified matter deleted].

Admiral MAURER. Yes, sir, I think we are. I have heard of no casualty of note since the *Thresher* incident insofar as flooding is concerned.

Chairman PASTORE. Our operations have been normal?

Admiral MAURER. Yes, sir, our operations have been normal. I am sure that the forces have no hesitancy to operate at depth. In fact, there have been recommendations from the forces afloat to please relax this as soon as you can.

The Commander, Submarine Force Pacific, has asked that we extend the restriction [classified matter deleted] so that he can perform certain tests that he has in mind [classified matter deleted.]

Chairman PASTORE. Before we get to what this means tactically and strategically, I think I would like to ask if there are any questions.

Senator AIKEN. I wonder if you feel that the accident to the *Thresher* might have happened [classified matter deleted] if it had not gone lower.

Admiral MAURER. Might have happened [classified matter deleted].

Senator AIKEN. Yes.

Secretary KORTH. And resulted in her loss?

Senator AIKEN. Yes.

Admiral MAURER. There is always a possibility, sir, that an accident could have occurred [classified matter deleted] which might have resulted in her loss.

If a piping system of the maximum diameter that is installed in the ship carried away [classified matter deleted] you probably would have had the same extreme situation you might have had with the maximum diameter pipe that was computed for this particular casualty.

Secretary KORTH. Mr. Chairman, I would like for Admiral Brockett, if he will, to speak to that, also.

Admiral BROCKETT. I might say this : We are postulating in answering this question [classified matter deleted].

DEBALLASTING

So there are two things. One is how fast does the water come in through a leak, and how fast can you blow out your ballast tanks. In both cases, they are working against you as you go deeper.

But if you come up [classified matter deleted] you do get an assurance factor [classified matter deleted]. Although I haven't seen the calculations I will estimate that with the size which the court of inquiry mentions [classified matter deleted] that recovery of the ship might well have been possible [classified matter deleted].

Senator AIKEN. Thank you.

Chairman PASTORE. Could you give us the factor of the freeze element with reference to deballasting [classified matter deleted] ? [1]

Admiral BROCKETT. That would be substantially the same, the possibilities of this happening.

Chairman PASTORE. Two to one ?

Admiral BROCKETT. No, because you get this drop in temperature immediately when your upstream pressure is two times or more greater than your downstream. You reach a so-called critical flow situation. your temperature drops down well below freezing. Depth is not significant insofar as freezeup is concerned.

Chairman PASTORE. Have we ever had trials before with relation to deballasting at those depths? That is, actual experiments?

Admiral BROCKETT. What has actually been done in the past under testing conditions is to demonstrate that you can in fact blow, but it is not carried through to the exhaustion of the air banks or the complete deballasting of the tanks. Specifications in this respect, as I answered Senator Jackson's question the other day were really those which have been carried through from World War II insofar as the amount of air that you carried which was the primary thing addressed by the specifications.

Representative HOSMER. May I ask, Mr. Chairman, why hasn't there been an increase in deballasting capability, considering these depths and so forth?

Are you just going on the theory that you are going to ride the thing through on power and planes?

Admiral BROCKETT. The dynamics of the situation are important, and in the normal course of events—and I think you can check me on

---

[1] Subsequent to the loss of *Thresher*, dockside tests were conducted of an identical high-pressure air system aboard the *Tinosa*, sister ship to *Thresher*. The *Tinosa* was nearing completion at the Portsmouth Naval Shipyard. The purpose of the high-pressure air system is to provide air in order to displace water from the ship's ballast tanks thereby increasing buoyancy. During the tests, ice formed on the screen-type wire strainers in the air piping system cutting off air flow to the ballast tanks. Also see pp. 35, 37, 108, and 112.

this—if you do get in trouble you want to have way on and you get much faster reaction from your planes and get out of trouble, as it were, in a hurry.

Secretary KORTH. I think Admiral Maurer should speak to that as an operator.

REQUIREMENT FOR HIGH SPEED DURING TESTS

Representative HOSMER. As I understand it, the policy is not to keep very much on during the tests.

Admiral MAURER. Doing that is an error in judgment on the part of the operators. Most of these commanding officers of these high-speed ships feel that their primary ability to recover lies in the fact that they have this tremendous power available.

I think that this tragedy has emphasized the absolute requirement that we either have it or we have the ability to recover from it as soon as possible. [Classified matter deleted.]

Representative HOSMER. I was speaking as a matter of routine during tests.

As I understand it the operational instructions were to proceed at a very slow speed, maybe 3 knots or something.

Admiral MAURER. This was not specified, no, sir.

Representative HOSMER. That was the skipper's discretion.

Admiral MAURER. At the commanding officer's discretion. Unfortunately, as a result of this it has come out—and that is one of the things that has already been passed out to the forces afloat. [Classified matter deleted.]

There is always a balance in this situation [classified matter deleted]. The commanding officer has weighed the two situations and has usually come up with some sort of compromise. [Classified matter deleted.]

ADVANTAGES OF OPERATING AT DEPTH

Chairman PASTORE. Mr. Morris?

Representative MORRIS. What are the advantages of operating at various depths?

Admiral MAURER. There is an offensive advantage in that you are in a position to take advantage of sound channels within the ocean spectrum. It could well be that [classified matter deleted] that you would have a layer which is a dividing line between waters of different densities and different sonar propagation characteristics. So if you were below the [classified matter deleted] position you would not hear a target.

Or if you were above it, you would. The vagaries of the ocean are such that if you have the ability to go above or below these separations in the ocean spectrum, you can select at will, you can conduct a much more effective search for targets.

Contrariwise, it is of tremendous value from a defensive standpoint in that the destroyer types that might be seeking you out or enemy submarines that might be seeking you out would be above that layer and you could be below it, you would be much less susceptible to detection, also. [Classified matter deleted.]

There is the added advantage if the ship is constructed for a [classified matter deleted] test depth in the intermediate range you have a tremendous strength factor from the point of view of damage control. I think these, in general, are the advantages. [Classified matter deleted.]

Can you think of any others that would be pertinent?

Admiral BROCKETT. The only other one I can think of is increase in the total envelope.

Captain BISHOP. One other factor is that added depth gives you more of a third dimension to operate in so if you do have a problem involved with control at high speeds you have more of a safety factor for pull-out.

DEEP-DIVING EXPERIMENTAL SUBMARINE

Chairman PASTORE. Are we designing or planning anything that might go deeper?

Admiral MAURER. Yes, sir.

[Classified matter deleted.]

Admiral BROCKETT. Yes, sir. That ship is in the design and construction phase at Portsmouth.

Representative HOSMER. Let us ask about that ship.

So far, you have explained that these are like Douglas airplanes, you have a model and you get a faster and deeper model. This [classified matter deleted] ship of yours, is this an entire new approach to something, or are you just magnifying your own ships?

Admiral BROCKETT. It is an experimental ship. It involves a good deal of research to go with the [classified matter deleted] depth.

Representative HOSMER. What I am asking, is the total concept where you have to design or redesign the inside as well as the hull and put together a weapon system more or less of a different nature than that which you have?

Admiral BROCKETT. It is fundamentally a new hull concept—in the fabrication of materials, the use of materials, the kind of materials. [Classified matter deleted.]   For propulsion, we have gone, in a sense, a step back. We have the silver zinc battery type, much like the *Albacore*, with electric propulsion.

Representative HOSMER. But the envelope you have there is not the kind that you could shove in all of this equipment that you put in the *Thresher* hulls?

Admiral BROCKETT. No, it has very little payload. It is an experimental submarine. It is a deep *Albacore*, if you want to think of it that way.

Representative HOSMER. Once you get a depth of that nature you would essentially have to redesign the rest of the ship?

Admiral BROCKETT. It is a complete new structural design.

Representative HOSMER. I mean the geometry and volume and whatever else is involved.

Admiral BROCKETT. Yes, sir.

Senator CURTIS. Are the orders to a submarine communicated from the shore?

Admiral MAURER. Yes, sir; they are.   [Classified matter deleted.]

Chairman PASTORE. Are there any other questions on this point? Mr. Bates?

MALOPERATIONS OF DEBALLASTING AIR SYSTEM

Representative BATES. Admiral, have we tested the valves on other submarines as we did on the *Tinosa*?

Admiral BROCKETT. Is this the blowdown, Mr. Bates?

Representative BATES. That is right.

Admiral BROCKETT. Yes, sir.

Representative BATES. Full time?

Admiral BROCKETT. Yes, sir.

Representative BATES. We did that since the *Thresher* went down?

Admiral BROCKETT. Yes, sir.

Representative BATES. How did that work out?

Admiral BROCKETT. All right.

Representative BATES. No freezeup?

Admiral BROCKETT. No, sir.

Representative BATES. Do they have strainers in them?

Admiral BROCKETT. The strainers were removed.

Representative BATES. Before the test?

Admiral BROCKETT. Yes, sir. After the *Tinosa* and the difficulty with those strainers and the restrictions that were involved, those have been removed. (See pp. 32, 37, 108, and 112.)

Representative BATES. You didn't try any with the strainers at sea after the *Tinosa?*

Admiral BROCKETT. No. This has all been done alongside the dock. Your freezing will occur. It is a matter of pressure differential.

Representative BATES. There is no variation in that. All strainers are out?

Admiral BROCKETT. Yes.

Mr. CONWAY. My recollection on the *Tinosa*, after you took the strainers out, it ran long enough just to blow half your tanks which was way under what the standard specs call for.

Admiral BROCKETT. That is right.

If you will remember on that one there was a lot of garbage in the system and when this was cleared out there was some difficulty with the control valve. With this cleared out, she blew OK.

Mr. CONWAY. She met the specifications?

Admiral BROCKETT. Yes, sir.

FULL CAPACITY TEST OF AIR SYSTEM NOT MADE

Representative HOLIFIELD. Maybe there was garbage in this other system that had not been cleared out.

As I understand it, you had never completely blown out your air supply.

Admiral BROCKETT. That is right, sir.

Representative HOLIFIELD. There were only momentary blowouts close to surface. Was there ever a complete blowout [classified matter deleted]?

Admiral BROCKETT. Not that I know of. I know there was a test depth requirement that I mentioned earlier during trials with the valves open to make sure air went through that that was about it. As soon as you got a bubble you stopped.

Representative HOLIFIELD. You had a high pressure but your reducers pulled it down [classified matter deleted], is that right?

Admiral BROCKETT. Yes, sir.

Representative HOLIFIELD. Why was this adaptation made? You had a lower pressure in your conventional submarines, didn't you?

Admiral BROCKETT. Yes, sir.

Representative HOLIFIELD. Here you went to a depth where the factor of danger was greater than the one would be at that normal depth, and yet you had not designed the equivalent air system to take care of that additional hazard. You assumed that additional hazard, it seems, with only the power that you had [classified matter deleted]. The thing that looks funny to me as a layman is this: There are two. One is, that you put in reducers, which in itself could be a factor of trouble. I can't see why you went to a high pressure and then used it at a lower pressure unless you wanted a longer blow. Yet you never exhausted the time period of a [classified matter deleted] blow in tests.

I don't understand those things.

Admiral BROCKETT. Two reasons. At the same volume you can get more air [classified matter deleted] if you follow me. You have more pounds of air in your system in the same size bottles.

Representative HOLIFIELD. I understand.

Admiral BROCKETT. Space is something you are always looking for.

Secondly, the [classified matter deleted] criteria was something that had been carried on, granted, from the other boats. But, as I recall, the question of the ability of the ballast tanks to take the sudden [classified matter deleted] air pressure is a design problem which we are now thrashing with because we want to bypass that reducer.

But we are not quite ready to do it until we are sure we can make the ballast tank structure itself strong enough to take that immediate application [classified matter deleted] of pressure. It can be dissipated some, but these are still things we are looking at.

[Classified matter deleted.]

TESTING OF AIR REDUCER VALVES

Representative BATES. Didn't you ever test these reducer valves for the higher pressure? Weren't those ever tested, or did you presume originally that you had a maximum considerably in excess of the design?

Admiral BROCKETT. I fell off the track.

Representative BATES. You used the same valves [classified matter deleted]?

Admiral BROCKETT. Downstream from your reducer.

Representative BATES. The same ones?

Admiral BROCKETT. That is right.

Representative BATES. Did you ever make that test to see whether or not they were adapted to the greater pressure?

Senator BENNETT. They had a reducer between them?

Admiral BROCKETT. It was [classified matter deleted] downstream from the reducer. The reducer is the first thing you see. Downstream from it [classified matted deleted].

Representative BATES. I am talking about the valve itself. Did you use the same valves to reduce this pressure?

Admiral BROCKETT. No.

Representative BATES. They are different valves?

Admiral BROCKETT. It is a different valve [classified matter deleted].

Representative BATES. I thought somebody said the other day it was the same one.

Mr. CONWAY. Downstream they are the same valves.

Representative BATES. The pressure is the same. I thought you meant the initial ones.

Mr. CONWAY. Apropos of Mr. Bates' question, did you ever check these Marotta reducing valves to see whether they could handle the full load [classified matter deleted] with a full tank. Were they ever fully checked out? I refer to the ones that froze up.

Representative BATES. These are the ones I am talking about.

Mr. CONWAY. I know.

Admiral BROCKETT. Yes, that is the Marotta reducers. From my own knowledge, I don't know.

Mr. CONWAY. I gather from the testimony of the court they never did.

Admiral BROCKETT. This is my impression, too. But from my own knowledge that I cannot—I can quote here, I don't know.

TESTING OF BLOWDOWN ON OTHER CLASSES OF SUBMARINES

Chairman PASTORE. What have we done on the remaining fleet afloat [classified matter deleted]? Are we safe with regard to all of them?

Admiral BROCKETT. In regard to the blow, Senator?

Chairman PASTORE. Yes.

Admiral BROCKETT. Yes. We have gotten rid of the strainers and we have run several time tests alongside the dock and this would indicate whether or not there is a freezeup. The opposing pressure merely means that you equalize earlier.

It is a more stringent test in a sense so far as freezing is concerned to dump your banks at the surface because your opposing pressure is less.

Consequently, you bleed further down. With the system clean and with the strainers out, this has worked out and we have a complex of data on this. We have had it all come in by message and are assembling it. The last one I saw was within the specifications.

Chairman PASTORE. Has any test been made at depth to blow it out completely since the disaster?

Admiral BROCKETT. Not that I know of, sir.

Chairman PASTORE. Why not? Don't you think that would be the best criteria?

Admiral BROCKETT. I am not sure.

Chairman PASTORE. We may be confronted with another incident. I am wondering now with all of these submarines afloat with a limitation [classified matter deleted] why we don't get an actual test on this blow [classified matter deleted].

Admiral MAURER. Mr. Senator, if I may speak to that, sir, we have had ships [classified matter deleted] prior to the time of this incident that blew their tanks dry—completely dry—[classified matter deleted].

Chairman PASTORE. Without trouble?

Admiral MAURER. Without trouble; yes, sir.

Representative HOLIFIELD. That is what we have been trying to find out.

Representative BATES. That is the first I have heard that.

Chairman PASTORE. With or without the filters?

Admiral MAURER. That was with the strainers; yes, sir.

Representative HOLIFIELD. And they didn't freeze up? (See pp. 32, 35, 108, and 112.)

Admiral MAURER. No, sir.

Representative BATES. On this kind of ship?

Admiral MAURER. No, sir, it was the previous *Scorpion* class.

Representative HOLIFIELD. You didn't have reducer valves?

Admiral MAURER. I think we have to remember on this class of ship we have three of these ships right now. The *Thresher* was the first of the class, and there are only two others, the *Permit* and the *Plunger*, and I think both of them are currently in the yard on the west coast at the present time either for possible shakedown availability or other availability.

Representative HOLIFIELD. I am going to ask a question——

Secretary KORTH. Could the Admiral finish?

Representative HOLIFIELD. I thought you finished. Excuse me.

Admiral MAURER. I think your point is very well taken on have we done this, and if we have not why we have not done it. I think the "why" we have not done it is because we just have not arrived at that stage yet where we have had to and where it is necessary to take a ship out to perform these tests. In other words, Admiral Brockett's examination of the faults in the blow system and so on, the capacity, the modifications to the blow system to do an effective job are still in the stage of formulation and completion of the examination of those faults.

I think we should all feel assured that before we send one of these ships out to operate we are going to have definitive tests which will satisfy all of us that there will be no complications on the ability of the ship to blow its tanks completely dry without any freezeup.

Chairman PASTORE. Admiral, you are talking about the *Thresher* type, is that right?

Admiral MAURER. Yes, sir.

Chairman PASTORE. I am talking about the ships afloat now that are being ordered to navigate at [classified matter deleted] depth. May we run into trouble on a blow on those? A full blow? I am not talking about the *Thresher* type now. I am talking of these other ships that are afloat, the *Polaris* and so on, that have the same kind of system. Have these been fully tested from a very practical realistic way?

Admiral MAURER. The 14 others have. The *Polaris* has not.

Admiral BROCKETT. No, not that I know of. The *Polaris* has much more air capacity and better blow rate, the ones they are finishing now. [Classified matter deleted.]

NEED FOR COMPLETE BLOW SYSTEM TEST

Chairman PASTORE. Wouldn't it be good to have a test blow? If the *Polaris* goes down with 16 missiles on it, we are in trouble.

Secretary KORTH. There is no question about it, it will be done.

Representative HOLIFIELD. I will ask my question, if you are finished.

My question is that we are going to deballast a submarine at any depth if you get in trouble, and you want to come to the top and emerge in an emergency situation, if you are going to go deep, why don't you find out [classified matter deleted] if you can make a full deballast against the pressure at that depth? As I understand it, it never has been done.

Admiral MAURER. That is right, sir.

Representative HOLIFIELD. It would seem to me you would want to deballast it every 100 or 200 feet down. If you are going to get into a position deep, it seems to me you should know not as a matter of theory but as a matter of actual operation what you can do with that in case of an emergency.

Admiral MAURER. I quite agree.

Representative HOLIFIELD. There, as I understand it, you [classified matter deleted] are working against a much more powerful pressure [classified matter deleted].

Valves, whatever there might be, pipes, anything might develop with that load of pressure.

You talk about being in the developmental stage. It would seem to me that this would be a basic test that you would make theoretically first and practically after you get the submarine off the dock. I think this would be one of your basic tests that you would make without delay.

Admiral MAURER. You are right, sir. Your point is very well taken. I assure you that it will be done.

Representative HOLIFIELD. I know it will be, but why hasn't it been?

Admiral BROCKETT. We are in the phase of starting alongside the dock. This part is being done. We start on the surface, as you suggested.

Representative HOLIFIELD. Are you talking about the *Thresher* class?

Admiral BROCKETT. No, I am talking about the others, too.

Representative HOLIFIELD. You are further than that on these others. Nuclear submarines have been running since 1955 and going at depths lower than conventional depths since that time. That is 8 years.

Yet you tell me that you have not made these tests. I can't understand why you have not made them during the 8 years.

Admiral BROCKETT. Admiral Maurer says they have blown at depth to his knowledge.

Admiral MAURER. Yes, sir. [Classified matter deleted.]

FUTURE DEBALLASTING SYSTEM TESTS

Representative HOLIFIELD. You never have gotten around to the point of testing them at a deep depth?

Admiral MAURER. May I say, sir, that I accept your thesis completely. Let us accept this as being something that we have learned from this disaster, and we will do it.

In other words, this is one of the many lessons we have learned, sir. The fact that we did not blow those tanks in the first ship that came out and make a definitive test at test depth was an error. We should have done it; yes, sir.

Chairman PASTORE. Which is also an error, too, Admiral, that since we have had the *Thresher* that we have not done it yet. You are promising now that you will do it.

The thing that amazes me that since you have had the experience with the *Thresher* and you had these ships afloat [classified matter deleted] why shouldn't you have done it up to now since the *Thresher?* That is the thing that surprises me.

Secretary KORTH. Captain Bishop?

Captain BISHOP. What you say is certainly true as far as the desirability to test the ballasting capability. There are other factors involved in recovering a submarine from emergency.

Our basic training when we get in trouble is first speed, then angle, and then ballasting. I think our primary reliance has been, and I think this covers the nuclear submarines as the older ones, when you get in trouble, the first thing you crank up speed, get an up angle on the boat and deballast.

Mr. CONWAY. The ballast system is the most critical emergency system? If it is that much of an emergency system, the question would be, Why hasn't it been tested? It is the most emergency system you apparently have.

COMMANDING OFFICER OF "SKYLARK"

Senator HICKENLOOPER. I want to get into a little collateral discussion for a moment, if I can.

I have been interested since the information came out the first few days of the hearing and recently running through the reports, it seems that a substantial issue has been made about the *Skylark's* commanding officer failing to transmit all of the so-called information that he had, and a specific criticism was made of that man on page 6 of the report I have here. It says that he failed to notify our higher authority of all the information available to him pertinent to the circumstances attending the last transmission received by *Skylark* from *Thresher* on the 10th of April, as it was his duty to do—this is the significant thing in an official report—but then they go ahead and say, it did not contribute anyway to the loss of the *Thresher* and was not materially connected therewith.   (See Navy news release, app. 6, p. 148.)

The thing that has been intriguing me throughout this hearing I have not seen one word of criticism of any other higher authority or commanding officer or anybody else who failed to explain why when they discovered 14 percent deficiency in the silver braze joints on that ship and did not test the rest of them, the sampling of 140 tests that they made and found 14 percent deficiency, the rest were not tested. No criticism of anybody who failed to see whether this blow system would work at depths even though it was equipped to operate at such depths.

I have not seen any criticism of the failures that occurred in the Portsmouth Navy Yard. I wonder why this young fellow is singled out for criticism which maybe he has coming as a disciplinary action, but especially in view of the fact that even under the finding it had nothing whatsoever to do with the loss of the *Thresher*. Is he being made a patsy?

Secretary KORTH. Certainly not.

Senator HICKENLOOPER. I think there is evidence from which one might argue that he is.

I am not saying that he is. But it is rather significant that higher authority is not being condemned or criticized in any way.

Secretary KORTH. No action has yet been taken, you are absolutely correct.

Senator HICKENLOOPER. It is rather interesting. But a great deal has been made of this fellow commanding the *Skylark* and I understand the evidence shows that he didn't even have working sonar equipment on this thing that could enable him to receive and identify locations. He had to get locations relayed back originally from the *Thresher*. I wonder what is happening to this fellow.

Secretary KORTH. I can't answer that.

Senator HICKENLOOPER. I have no connection. I don't know who he is and nobody has spoken to me about him on his behalf except I have been reading the reports.

This seems to crop up. I don't excuse anybody from not doing what he is supposed to do. That is not the point. Here is something that had absolutely nothing to do with the loss of a hundred-some lives. It had nothing to do with the loss of the ship. Yet some issue is being made of it here and no issue is being made about any other derelictions that might have occurred.

It is rather difficult for me to kind of dovetail that.

Secretary KORTH. Senator, I don't consider that this commanding officer will be made a patsy in this instance. Actually, the report itself——

Senator HICKENLOOPER. I would like to see his service record a year from now.

Secretary KORTH. He may well not be on this same ship, I will say that. But, at the same time, and we must take these individually rather than balancing one against the other, the action has not yet or no action has yet been taken with reference to the commanding officer, Portsmouth Naval Shipyard.

Senator HICKENLOOPER. Maybe it shouldn't be.

Secretary KORTH. I don't say it should be, either, sir. This report has not yet been acted upon. Actually, it has come into my possession only for the last week or so.

It has been reviewed, is being reviewed by the Judge Advocate General's department of the Navy. I have not talked with the Chief of Naval Operations or the convening authority, Admiral Smith.

Senator HICKENLOOPER. I am not after anybody. I am not suggesting that anything happen to anybody. That is not the point.

I am only calling attention to what, to me, seems to be a rather significant and rather unexplainable reason why this situation has been given some prominence here even at the outset. Suddenly somebody is blamed for something, although it didn't have anything to do with the loss of the ship.

Secretary KORTH. I suppose more than anything else, Senator, is the fact that there was a failure to disclose something even though it was not material. It was irritating. It was irritating to me to learn that this fellow had the information and I didn't know about it.

Senator HICKENLOOPER. That was put in the press release. I understand he was not even consulted for a couple days out there. He was just kind of given a good letting alone.

Representative HOLIFIELD. The log was not even called for by his immediate superiors until the court of inquiry requested it.

Senator HICKENLOOPER. The log was not called for.

Here is a fellow sitting on the ocean with an ineffective sonar.

Secretary KORTH. He did not transmit the information.

Senator HICKENLOOPER. That is true.

It had nothing to do with the loss.

Secretary KORTH. He was made an interested party. He was subsequently released from that category.

Chairman PASTORE. Mr. Secretary, can you say equivocally that no disciplinary action has been taken against the commander of the *Skylark?*

Secretary KORTH. Not that I am aware of.

Representative Holifield. How about some of you other gentlemen?

Secretary Korth. Has disciplinary action been taken against him?

Admiral Maurer. Not to my knowledge.

Chairman Pastore. We are not his advocate. We are resting this upon the fact, Mr. Secretary, you said that no action has been taken as yet because this report is being reviewed.

Secretary Korth. That is right, sir.

Representative Holifield. He was relieved of his command?

Admiral Maurer. No, sir; he was not.

Representative Holifield. Is he still on the *Skylark*?

Admiral Maurer. Yes, sir.

Senator Hickenlooper. I raise no brief for or against anybody. Except the interesting significance of this thing which has cropped up so many times in this hearing. I can't find any instances of where any other person has been singled out.

Secretary Korth. For similar treatment?

Senator Hickenlooper. I don't know. As I say, I am not advocating that anybody be chastised under any circumstances one way or the other unless the facts warrant it. I expressed it a moment ago and the question in my mind is the guy being made a patsy, that is all.

I hope not. (See p. 121.)

Secretary Korth. He certainly isn't.

Senator Hickenlooper. It is hard for me to understand why this has crept in here so significantly even in the news releases that came out.

Secretary Korth. I think only because he was made an interested party, Senator. That is the reason for prominence, more prominence was given to it than with the others.

Mr. Conway. Admiral Palmer was also an interested party.

Admiral Brockett. And remained one. (See p. 119.)

[Classified matter deleted.]

Representative Holifield. May I ask a question of Admiral Brockett in regard to his testimony of yesterday, Mr. Chairman?

Chairman Pastore. Yes, of course.

DIFFERENCES IN SPECIFICATIONS FOR NONNUCLEAR PORTION OF SUBMARINE

Representative Holifield. You stated yesterday that the specifications of the nonnuclear portions of the submarine were different from those utilized in the nuclear portion of the ship. Will you elaborate on what these differences might be? I know from the testimony that there were no silver-brazed joints in the nuclear portion. There were these silver-brazed joints in other parts. I don't quite get this. You said the specifications will differ from those used in the nuclear portions. You mean they did differ, and will in the future?

Admiral Brockett. They did and they will, yes, sir.

Representative Holifield. But that does not mean that you are going to keep those differences the same as they are now? In other words, you raised one on your silver brazed to a 60-percent tolerance. That is one difference that will be changed. What other changes do you plan to make at this point?

Admiral BROCKETT. What I was addressing myself to really was the piping system, because that seemed to be the primary subject of conversation yesterday, if you will remember. The requirements in the nuclear reactor compartment preclude the use of silver brazing now. They did not originally. The portions which are part of the nuclear plant circuits, the piping associated directly with the plant, the primary and secondary, have been all welded from the beginning.

Senator BENNETT. Do you have any ships now operating with silver-brazed joints in the nuclear compartment?

Admiral BROCKETT. I am not sure whether they have all been changed or not. For instance, I know the *Thresher* was built with silver-brazed joints in the nuclear reactor area. As a matter of fact, during her postshakedown availability these were changed to welded.

Representative HOLIFIELD. Because there was one leak in the *Thresher* during its shakedown?

Admiral BROCKETT. Yes.

Representative HOLIFIELD. It was at that point that there was a change?

Admiral BROCKETT. It came along before that, at Admiral Rickover's insistence. It is very difficult to weld the copper nickel and Monel pipe. She was in the yard, if you will remember, from July until April, and a great portion of that time was spent remaking a dozen joints in the reactor compartment to get one which would successfully pass radiography. It becomes particularly difficult with smaller sizes to weld them. This is a variation. I don't think at this point that we are in any position to, and I don't think we should go to a requirement that all piping be welded. This is the first reaction you might get. But at the same time, you have to build these submarines, and with this advent of the ability to use the ultrasonic test successfully, at least down to the 1-inch size, we are reviewing the bidding on where we want to start welding. You might know on the *Thresher* the specifications that existed at that time required all welding between the hull and the backup valve, the first large valve inside of the hull valve. All of that was welded. It is a very tortuous and difficult process.

I might also say this, that we have learned a lot about doing this. We are much more able to weld these pipes than we were even a year ago. So when I mention differences in the specifications, I feel that the requirements are different, and that we have to make our judgments on these with all the knowledge that we have, and with our best engineering judgment, and the advice from the best people we can talk to.

SILVER BRAZED VERSUS WELDED PIPING

Mr. CONWAY. I think the court in its recommendations had two recommendations on this point. One in hazardous piping systems of submarines designed to operate deep, silver-brazed joints of more than 2 inches in inside diameter be replaced by welded joints when replacement is required.

Do I understand you still have that under consideration?

Admiral BROCKETT. This is correct. We have not yet implemented it. When I mentioned I had a series of studies this is one of them. The whole question of silver brazed versus welding. I am not convinced yet because I have not acquired all the information as to how good a silver-brazed joint is, and what the significance of 60 percent is. I know this is a lot better than 10 percent.

Mr. CONWAY. Another recommendation is that for new construction submarines welded piping joints be specified for joints of more than 2 inches in inside diameter in hazardous systems. This was another recommendation. This also has not been adopted?

Admiral BROCKETT. It has not been implemented; no, sir.

Chairman PASTORE. Are there any other questions?

POSSIBILITY OF RADIATION RELEASE

Representative HOSMER. Yes. I had another Member who contacted me before I came over today. He did not know I was coming. He called about the rumor that there is a radiation release out there. I just wanted to make sure—that my assurance to him—that there was no radiation release is correct.

Admiral MAURER. I can assure you there is no radiation there.

Representative HOSMER. Was there any suspicious activity on the part of the Soviet motorship and trawlers that were supposed to have gone in the area the other day?

Secretary KORTH. Do you want to comment on that, Captain?

Captain BISHOP. Yes, sir; there was one Soviet ship that passed within 700 yards of the search ship that was in the area at the time, but moved on through.

Representative HOSMER. Is it a fact that the Russians have claimed that there has been a radiation release in the area?

Captain BISHOP. Not to my knowledge.

Secretary KORTH. I think they raised the possibility.

Chairman PASTORE. Do you have radiation instruments on the *Trieste*?

Secretary KORTH. Yes, sir.

Captain BISHOP. Yes, sir.

EFFECT OF DEPTH LIMITATION

Chairman PASTORE. I would like to ask now the question that we started out to ask. This limitation [classified matter deleted], what does that mean tactically and strategically?

Admiral MAURER. I don't think we will feel any long-term ill effects on this thing, this restriction, from the point of view of our tactics. At least if it does not go on too long so that we get our people set in their ways and thinking that [the limitation] is the maximum depth to which they can operate safely.

Chairman PASTORE. A lot of us have been saying that our Polaris submarine system is the first line of defense. Is it still the first line of defense?

Admiral MAURER. There is no question about that, sir. [Classified matter deleted.]

Yes, sir; I was saying that we would have no hesitation today in the event of conflict to immediately lift that restriction and send our ships to sea with their optimum operating depths reinstated. We certainly can't in peacetime remove these restraints until we are reassured that each ship is able to recover. We will never be able to build in enough safety in these ships so that you can make them completely foolproof. But we can build these ships so that if the commanding officer and the crew react properly and in the most timely fashion that they will be able to recover from almost any casualty that might take place.

SUBMARINE SAFETY TASK GROUP

Chairman PASTORE. What are we doing now, and what have we done since the time of the disaster to assure ourselves that the work at these shipyards is satisfactory?

Admiral BROCKETT. First of all, there have been developments, as I mentioned, in several areas. If I might, Mr. Chairman, I again mention the submarines' steering safety task group, which has been set up in the Bureau of Ships. I would like to read you the projects that we have. These are broad categorical titles, and under each one of these there are a series of tasks. I think it might help to bring together some of the questions that have been asked about various things in the submarines.

I will address myself to your question directly as I get toward the end of this list:

Task No. 1 is the sea water system subjected to submergence pressure. [Classified matter deleted.]

No. 2. Fabrication methods, materials, and test procedures for hazardous piping systems. This is not only salt water, but high pressure air and hydraulic systems.

No. 3. Machinery components in hazardous sea water systems. These are your condenser heads, for instance, your salt water pumps that see sea pressure.

No. 4. The mandatory use of class plans and components in vital systems. This is an argument with the shipbuilders. We feel once we draw a set of plans, they should be followed across the board by everybody.

No. 5. High pressure air systems which include the question of blow rate and air capacity.

No. 6. Submarine readiness for builders and sea trials. This is to have a certification that they are ready to go.

No. 7. Protection from sea water of electrical systems.

No 8. Submarine pressure structure penetration, a review of this. We think we are all right, but we have to take a look at it as well.

No. 9. Consolidation of information for damage control sections of the ship's information book, so that the ship has a ready place to find the various methods of operation and what to do if a particular casualty happens.

No. 10. Ship control system. This is the question of the planes.

No. 11. Habitability versus safety. In making the ships nice to live on, have we possibly introduced some things which are not good from a damage control standpoint. Access to control valves, for instance, those that are not normally used, but you might want to get to them in a hurry.

No. 12. A submarine test tank. This is a proposal which is quite interesting. It seems a little far out when you first look at it. That was my first reaction. The more I read it, the better I liked it. This is the idea of having a tank which can pressurize, put a full-sized submarine in, and put on the pressure to see what you have.

Representative BATES. That is like a drydock.

Admiral BROCKETT. A big circular drydock. We have a contract to see what this might look like and see how much it would cost to build one or two.

No. 13. The evaluation of the diving trainer which is mentioned in the report. The improvement of existing capabilities. We would help out on this.

No. 14. Submarine shock test procedures before and after, and the level of shock.

ENFORCEMENT OF STANDARDS

And finally, the submarine safety program task to revise and institute an expanded quality assurance program. One of the things that we find is no matter how many pieces of paper we produce in Washington, you do not always find they are observed in the field. As a result, we are sending out audit teams to find out how well the instructions are being carried out. Our first team is at Ingalls right now.

This quality control problem is a difficult one. If I can philosophize on that, the pride of workmanship of the individual mechanic is not enough even where it exists. It is too bad, but it is so. We have the hardest time trying to convince people of this fact. I knew it took me a long time to believe it, and I finally became convinced of it about 4 years ago. You talk to shipbuilders and you get their pride of workmanship routine. Then you can go around and point out to them some things which certainly warrant improvement. It is a difficult thing to sell. You have to have it, and you have to have an active program of inspection. Quality control of material, and audit to make sure that those who are supposed to be assuring the quality are in fact doing it, this is our attack.

Representative BATES. That is what these two fellows were telling me in Portsmouth. We tell everybody but they don't care. We have some pride in our work, but they don't care. The more I hear about this, the more I think these fellows have something.

Chairman PASTORE. Who doesn't care?

Representative BATES. The man they reported to.

Chairman PASTORE. They did not mean the Navy?

Representative BATES. The same as what the admiral is saying. Here they have some pride in their work, realization that they are going to sea. This is what they told me in 1960. Here is the admiral saying the same thing. They don't care up there. Let it go.

Representative HOLIFIELD. This is happening throughout America in our industrial plants as we mechanize and automate. The pride of craftsmanship of the old trained artisan is gone. The young men are not going into these difficult artisan craftsmanship jobs to learn. They don't have to. They join a union, and if they stay there so long somehow or other they get stepped up and they get to the point where they are drawing journeymen's wages without the skills they had in the old days. We might as well face it. I don't know what the fault is. Maybe it is the fault of our civilization. I find that in my own business in California. I hire a man and pay him top wages, and I don't get the resultant craftsmanship.

Admiral BROCKETT. I want to make this clear. This is not a shipyard phenomenon. This is a national phenomenon.

Representative HOLIFIELD. I just got through saying it happened in every area in America. I went into the Hart, Schaffner & Marx plant in Chicago a while back, and as I look back where these tailors were working making clothes, craftsmen, most of them were old men, many of them past 70 years of age that served their apprenticeship and became real skilled craftsmen. I talked to the man in charge of hiring these men. He said:

We don't get this kind any more. The young people won't come in and go through the years of apprenticeship necessary to make themselves skilled craftsmen, and as a result we are turning more and more to machine work, and we are turning more and more to workmen that cannot do the things older men can do. As each one of these men dies we can't fill their places. We don't have anybody coming up to fill their place.

Secretary KORTH. That is true.

Representative HOLIFIELD. The same thing in the watchmaking industry, and many of the industries that require really skilled training and long periods of training, you are getting less and less men.

Senator BENNETT. May I go off the record?

(Discussion off the record.)

INSPECTION IMPROVEMENTS

Chairman PASTORE. What are we doing to make sure our inspection procedures are of the highest quality, Admiral?

Admiral BROCKETT. I think we may have given too much emphasis to silver brazed joints, but I will address myself to that because it happens to be a good example.

Every joint made after the first of May in the ships we are building has to be inspected with this UT device that is 1 inch or better. We can't get down to the half-inch size, but these joints are not the problem to begin with that the larger ones are. They make up easier. If they fail, they don't present the problem that a larger one does.

The first thing you would have to do is to inspect your inspectors.

Senator HICKENLOOPER. Do you have anything to say about your inspectors, or do they just hand them to you?

Admiral BROCKETT. We hire them and qualify them and they get a ticket that they are qualified to make the inspections. This is also true in the private yards. This is going forward right now. These inspectors inspect every joint that is made after the first of May. Then we have a requirement to inspect all of those joints which are between the hull and backup valve which have a high level of danger. This is the most hazardous spot you have. [Classified matter deleted.]

The quality control aspects, as I say, are being audited. They have been emphasized. In the private yards we certify that they do, in fact, have adequate quality assurance procedures. We require them to make the inspections. We really check on the procedures as opposed to the individual joints.

In the Naval shipyards the quality control groups in Mare Island and Portsmouth, which are the submarine yards, are quite large and have been increased in number. It is hard to come by good quality assurance people, I might add. It is a new business.

Representative HOLIFIELD. Insurance or assurance?

Admiral BROCKETT. Quality assurance. It is difficult to find really good quality assurance engineers as opposed to technicians. We have had considerable difficulty in hiring people of this nature in civil service. But I believe that fundamentally our quality assurance organizations are strong and getting stronger, plus the fact that we have put in their hands those things which they are supposed to look for. We have not had this in the form we would like to have had in the past, because in many cases we didn't know.

Chairman PASTORE. This information that you are giving us now with reference to the new procedures, is this considered classified secret, official, or what?

Admiral BROCKETT. No, the new procedures I would think would be unclassified of themselves. In connection with the *Thresher*, I would recommend some discretion, because they always come back and cause conjecture. They are wide open. We have had a week-long meeting at Mare Island with the quality assurance people, welding people and management types, going into the question of how do we put pipe together so that everybody is doing the same thing. This has been another difficulty. The different interpretations in the different shipyards.

DEPTH CERTIFICATION

Mr. CONWAY. Does this mean that all of your submarines that you have worked prior hereto will have to be rechecked under these new procedures?

Admiral BROCKETT. We will have to go back through and our aim is the ability to certify that a particular system is ready to go to sea [classified matter deleted]. For the moment we are going to have to say this system has been checked [classified matter deleted]. Then what we hope to do in connection with the studies being made on flooding rates and the modification to the blow systems, which are being made, is to certify this ship is good for x number of feet [classified matter deleted]. We are going to have to work our way back to test depth.

Representative HOSMER. I wonder if Admiral Stephan wishes to speak?

Secretary KORTH. I was going to say that at some appropriate point, I would like Admiral Stephan to make a few brief remarks here, and subject himself to such questions as you may have.

Chairman PASTORE. Are you through with these gentlemen?

USE OF COMMUNICATIONS RECORDERS

Representative BATES. This is on an unrelated point, but do you recall some time ago when the airplanes got into trouble and cracked up, and there was no recording what the last messages were, particularly since there has been so much controversy what was the message that actually came to the *Skylark?* There was no recording at all, I presume, of this?

Admiral BROCKETT. As I remember, there was only a communications log.

Representative BATES. I wonder if it would be advisable particularly if you are on trials like that——

Secretary KORTH. Let him answer the first question.

Admiral MAURER. All of the ASR's are equipped with recorders now. This is since the incident. At that time they did not have recorders.

In addition we have beefed-up their communication capability [classified matter deleted]. There was a delay of a couple of hours when they were trying to get the message across.

Representative HOLIFIELD. Has there been anything done to tie up the relationship between the escort ship and the submarine that is going through the test? We had some testimony that it is not at all unusual for them to lose track of each other for several hours and things like that.

Admiral MAURER. Yes, sir.

Representative HOLIFIELD. Has there been anything done along that line?

Admiral MAURER. Yes, sir. Of their own volition the commander, submarines, Pacific Fleet, and Atlantic Fleet, have had ad hoc groups reexamining the test procedures in their entirety, including the interrelationship between the ship being tested and the escort ship, the communications, the positions that they take, the interchange of information prior to the time that they conduct the tests.

Representative HOLIFIELD. It seems to me if you have the power to go down to them and up to your escort ship, that in a case like this if you did have a full report on everything that they were doing, you might have a much more complete record to analyze to prevent something happening in the future.

Admiral MAURER. They are reexamining on the basis of putting the two in such relative positions during the conduct of these tests that they will have optimum communications by sonar between the two.

Representative HOLIFIELD. And that will be recorded?

Admiral MAURER. Yes, sir.

CRUISE RECORDER

Representative BATES. Now, my second question was on those occasions when they are operating alone, and they send messages, will those be recorded?

Admiral MAURER. Investigation is being made now to the installation of the black box type of concept where there is an automatic recording of what is transpiring within the submarine, and in the event of disaster you would be able to recover that box, similar to an aircraft.

Representative BATES. I mean when they are not in company with escort ships.

Secretary KORTH. Routine operational messages?

Admiral MAURER. No, sir.

Representative BATES. In any airplane what is the situation today? Everything is recorded?

Secretary KORTH. I can't answer that. I don't think we have any aircraft experts here.

Representative BATES. If it is important enough when they are on trials and you have an escort vessel to record it, there are also situations that will develop when they have trouble when they are alone that they might want to send messages.

Admiral MAURER. They would have to be on or very near the surface to do this. They would have to be at the proper depth and on the surface, and under those circumstances, I doubt seriously they would be in extremis. If they are submerged and in trouble, they are not going to get that message out.

Representative BATES. You don't know. You can be socked. You can be coming up. When we were on one of them we almost hit a fishing vessel. A lot can happen near the surface and you can go down. [Classified matter deleted.]

Admiral MAURER. There are no steps to automatically take down all of the messages that are received from sea, no, sir.

Chairman PASTORE. Admiral Stephan, would you please come forward?

Secretary KORTH. You want him to speak about what he is doing?

Chairman PASTORE. Yes.

DEEP SUBMERGENCE SYSTEMS REVIEW GROUP

Admiral STEPHAN. I am Adm. E. C. Stephan. On the 24th of April I was relieved of duties as the Oceanographer of the Navy, and commander of U.S. Naval Oceanographic Office, and assigned to be Chairman of the Deep Submergence Systems Review Group.

The objectives of this group, and my responsibilities, are to review the current plans for location, identification, rescue and recovery of large objects from the deep ocean floor. To recommend changes to these plans for expeditious improvement. To recommend changes for a longer term improvement, and to develop a 5-year program to improve toward a maximum capability our ability to locate, identify, rescue, and recover large objects from the ocean floor.

I am also responsible for recommending the means and the organization required to implement this program. I am specifically directed to not become involved in the current operations in the location of the *Thresher*.

In carrying out these assignments, I am to be sure that we familiarize ourselves with all in-house programs in the Navy, with programs in other agencies of Government that are interested in this oceanographic field, and to insure that the scientific community, industry, individuals, and interested citizens, all have a full opportunity to put their ideas into this problem. [Classified matter deleted.]

At the present time, we are facing the problem of locating and identifying and rescuing, if that is required, and recovery of something as large as a Polaris submarine. [Classified matter deleted.]

Our progress to date has first been the large effort toward staffing. In staffing we have recognized at the same time that this sort of study group was going on, the Bureau of Ships and other agencies within the Navy were heavily involved in the *Thresher* operations, and in the restudy of submarine design, such as Admiral Brockett has mentioned. So my staffing has primarily been obtained from people, civilians, Reserve officers, retired officers, and others from industry, and from the scientific community.

I think it might be well to mention just a few of the names. I think some of the people who are involved will be familiar to you.

From the scientific community, Dr. Vine, Dr. Snyder, Dr. Hersey, Dr. Moore, Dr. Spies, director of Scripps.

From industry, we have Mr. Ed Link, the inventor of the Link trainer, who has transferred his interest to the field of oceanography.

Captain Arnold, retired, who is director of research with United Aircraft. We have Dr. Behnke, who is probably one of the outstanding submarine rescue and medical problems men. Captain Welham, Commander Workman, Captain Hendrix, who is very prominent in the field of military oceanography.

We have assembled, I think, as fine a staff as you could assemble. To date we have had a series of briefings by the bureaus; the Bureau of Ships, Bureau of Medicine, Yards and Docks, Chief of Naval Operations—particularly with emphasis on the *Thresher* problem—the Atomic Energy Commission, and a number of other agencies that have an interest.

We have sent out some 200 letters to industry soliciting their help in arriving at ideas in this area. We have sent letters to the scientific community. We have assembled through a machine run by the Defense Documents Agency some 60 studies that have previously taken place, or papers on this subject to be reviewed by the group. We are getting the help of the Library of Congress on other papers on this subject. We have gone out to foreign countries. The British have recently set up a similar group in connection with the same problem. We are trying to conduct a patent search to see that we do not overlook some old ideas that were not feasible then, but are since the new technology.

We have been staffed and in existence a little over a month and a large part of the background material has now been reviewed, and we are meeting daily and considering the technical approaches to the problem.

In the instructions setting up my office I was required to make my best estimate of when we would finish, and I made an estimate of the 1st of October. I think it was a guess, but at the present time I have no further information to change that guess. This is where we stand today, Mr. Chairman.

Chairman PASTORE. Are there any questions?

DEBRIS IDENTIFICATION

Senator HICKENLOOPER. This is a general question which has occurred to me frequently. It is nothing original with me, I am sure. I am wondering in cases like this, is it feasible or is there a practical reason why all of the equipment, for instance, on a particular submarine such as the *Thresher* should not be frequently marked with a name or indisputable identification mark of that particular vessel so that in case of disaster or something of that kind, there would be no question about identifying debris or anything of the sort of any major size or proportion that might result. There might be some practical reasons why it should not be done. I don't know. In case of disaster things float up, and they say it is estimated that this must have come from some place. Would there be any reason why there could not be frequent identification on the equipment of a particular vehicle or submarine or ship or something like that?

Admiral BROCKETT. We could do it. For instance, the picture that was in the paper the other day of the air or gas bottle. (See fig. 1A, p. 52.) I suppose that might have had *Thresher* on it. The loose gear, I don't know.

FIGURE 1A

Senator HICKENLOOPER. If you standardize gear and it is interchangeable among vessels, it would present some problems.

Secretary KORTH. That is the problem.

Senator HICKENLOOPER. I don't know. Maybe it is utterly impractical.

Secretary KORTH. I think it certainly deserves further looking into.

Senator HICKENLOOPER. A number of times in the past we will find airplane wrecks that apparently have been there a long time. They are not quite sure it was this plane or that plane that was lost. There is not necessarily identification in the equipment of the plane that does survive to indicate with positiveness whether it is that plane or not. It would seem to me a lot of major equipment of a ship, even though it costs a little bit more money and a little more trouble, if it were specifically marked—we don't want any disasters—if we had a disaster it would merely help in more positive identification.

Admiral BROCKETT. The only objection I can see to it would be psychological.

Admiral MAURER. May I mention, sir, that if you go to war, then you would immediately be forced to unmark it.

Senator HICKENLOOPER. There is that enemy identification and all that sort of stuff.

Secretary KORTH. It is something we ought to look at anyhow.

LOCATION OF "THRESHER"

Representative BATES. In view of your knowledge of oceanography and currents and that type of thing, how far could the *Thresher* be now from where she actually went down?

Admiral STEPHAN. In looking at this, first of all in considering the oil slick, and where it could be due to currents from where it appeared, we felt that the resultant current from the 8,500-foot depth to the surface was insignificant in terms of the navigational error. In other words, we calculated some 10 minutes for this to rise from the bottom. The currents don't all flow in the same direction. It is the resultant current that affects it. We felt that this was insignificant. There are estimates as to the velocity with which the *Thresher* from the time she was out of control and was sinking out of control, that she could obtain that are engineeringly sound, that indicate she could have been going as fast as 160 knots when she hit the bottom. This is an extreme and the lowest estimate is about 15 knots.

Secretary KORTH. Going straight down.

Admiral STEPHAN. Yes, sir. This means in any event there would not have been much time for her to have been affected by the currents. But the aspect at which she was going at this speed might have taken her well away. In other words, if she goes straight down, there will be very little displacement from where she was on the surface. If she goes down at a 60° angle, she could have quite a bit of displacement.

Representative BATES. What would you guess as to angle?

Admiral STEPHAN. We have tried. This is why we are so very interested in seeing her. We want to see what sort of distortion there has been, how close she came to what she most probably would have done, nose over and go down bow first because her propellers were the principal drag. If she is badly enough distorted, this won't be the case.

Representative BATES. Wouldn't she be practically submerged now? What is the ocean bottom, how soft?

Admiral STEPHAN. Computing the bearing strength of the ocean floor as best we can from the cores that we have taken of the ocean bottom, had she been going at this velocity up to 160 knots, and not knowing how much she would have broken up on impact, her nose could have been as deep as 500 feet into the ocean bottom. She probably can take that sort of angle. Had she gone in what we consider the most favorable position, again using that ocean-bearing strength, we think she would be some 10 feet below. In other words, the keel would have gone some 10 feet farther into the ocean. It would have forced its way down that far.

Secretary KORTH. But still leaving a sufficient amount above.

Admiral STEPHAN. Yes, sir.

Representative BATES. Summing this up, from the point where she might have gone down, what would be the maximum you would guess that she would be from the point she went down, the maximum angle at 160 knots?

Secretary KORTH. She would not go at 100 knots.

Admiral STEPHAN. If she is at a 30° angle, and she drops 8,000 feet, she will be 4,000 feet from you. If she goes down 60° from the horizontal or 30° from the vertical, she will be displaced 4,000 feet.

Representative BATES. Haven't you pretty well covered that area that you know about?

Admiral STEPHAN. I think they have covered it, and I think they have very good information that the submarine is in fact in the area that they are covering.

Representative BATES. That is the first time I have heard that. What information would bring you to that conclusion?

Admiral STEPHAN. The wreckage, the debris.

Representative BATES. What have you found now?

Admiral STEPHAN. This is not an area of my responsibility. I think you should speak to someone else.

Representative BATES. What do you have right now that you can say is absolutely it?

DEBRIS IDENTIFICATION

Secretary KORTH. We have some things here to show you that we believe came from it.

Chairman PASTORE. They showed us some pictures. You mean the tank and the bottle.

Representative BATES. Do you know that is the *Thresher*?

Secretary KORTH. No.

Representative BATES. We were assured by the newspaper that this was the *Thresher* and we found it was not.

Secretary KORTH. There was complete error.

Representative BATES. What do we have today?

Captain BISHOP. The most positive evidence is two things. One is these rings that you have seen pictures of in the paper. These were dredged up from the ocean floor. There are 19 pages of O rings. (See fig. 2A, p. 55.)

FIGURE 2A

Representative HOLIFIELD. What?

Captain BISHOP. O rings. They are gaskets that are used in submarine hydraulic piping. These were retrieved from the ocean floor in the area in which we believe *Thresher* lies. There are three different types of O rings in that group, and all three of these types of O rings were known to have been in the spare parts kit aboard the *Thresher*. Two of the types were also common to other types of ships. So this is not positive proof that these came from *Thresher*, but it is a very high confidence level.

The Portsmouth Naval Shipyard people and the supply people have all verified that these were in fact the type carried in the *Thresher*.

One other piece of positive evidence which I did not bring with me which is fragile in nature is a piece of submarine battery grid which is about the size of my hand, and badly banged up. This has been identified through chemical analysis as having the same chemical constituents as the battery grids of nuclear submarines, which are different from the battery grids of the diesel boats or from regular commercial batteries. They are peculiar to nuclear submarines. The Exide battery representative has measured the geometry of the grid and identified it as one from the *Thresher*. (See fig. 3A, p. 56.)

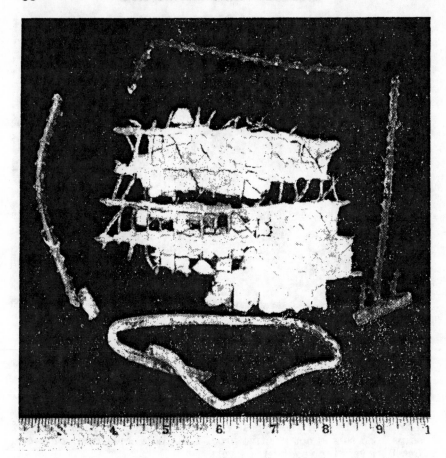

FIGURE 3A

This has been reported to the board of inquiry as evidence as coming from the *Thresher*. These articles were all found in the area in which the *Trieste* is now diving.

RADIOACTIVITY SURVEY

Representative BATES. There have been expressions of concern about radioactivity. Do we have any indication at all of any radioactivity in this area? Are there any samplings?

Captain BISHOP. There have been numerous measurements made. There have been no measurements made by them which differ significantly from what the normal background radioactivity is in that area. These measurements include aviation planes where they surveyed the whole area, samples taken from various depths of actual captured water which were then taken to the shipyard and analyzed by representatives of various laboratories doublechecking by different measurement teams.

Radioactivity measuring devices were lowered from one of the ships and towed in the area. This was only through a small part of the area. There has not been a complete survey throughout the whole area yet. In other words, samples have been taken as a spot check. There have been bottom cores taken in various places throughout the area, and the mud has been analyzed, and just background radioactivity was present.

The *Trieste* has aboard her three separate radioactivity measuring instruments so that if she does in fact locate the hull or a major part of the hull of the *Thresher*, she should be able to determine whether there is any radioactive effluent from it.

Representative BATES. How close does she have to be to get a reading?

Captain BISHOP. This depends on the strength of what is coming out, and whether the reactor compartment is open. If the reactor capsule is intact, she practically has to hit it to get a reading.

Representative BATES. Is there such a possibility?

Captain BISHOP. I believe so.

Secretary KORTH. Possibility of what?

Captain BISHOP. That the reactor is still intact.

Secretary KORTH. Absolutely. Certainly Admiral Rickover thinks so.

Captain BISHOP. The major capsule in which the reactor is located, the core itself, if it did not shatter on impact with the bottom.

Representative BATES. Still, if all the piping is banged away, you would be getting water contaminated in the area.

Captain BISHOP. You would expect there would be some, yes, sir.

Chairman PASTORE. Are there any further questions?

LOCATION OF "THRESHER"

Representative HOSMER. I would like to ask this: It seemed everybody figured they would find the ship within a couple of weeks at least. It is a great big hunk of iron. How do you explain the vast difficulties that have been encountered in locating it? I hear so many things about locating nuclear explosions in Russia and so forth.

Captain BISHOP. If you like, I can run through the operation to date to give you a feel for what the problem is.

Representative HOSMER. I didn't mean the technical question. I meant a short feel for the thing.

Secretary KORTH. I will say this. I will stick my neck out a little bit, because I have confidence in the people I have talked with. I am confident that we are going to find the *Thresher*.

Representative MORRIS. What are you going to have after you find it?

Secretary KORTH. We are not going to have very much.

Representative MORRIS. What are you going to prove after you find her?

Secretary KORTH. I think we have to find her.

Representative MORRIS. What advantage can you possibly get from it after you find it? No question but what it is lost.

Secretary KORTH. You might be able to get some indication of where the implosion occurred which might in turn indicate to you where the flooding was. These are all possibilities or "mights."

Chairman PASTORE. Unless, gentlemen, there are any more questions, I want to thank these gentlemen for coming. We are going to explore this further, but I don't think we are going to bring you up as a group. With your kind permission, we would like to call on any one or any group of people to come up here as this hearing progresses at a time that would be mutually satisfactory.

Secretary KORTH. That is fine, Mr. Chairman. I assume that the committee will at an appropriate time get into the reactor end of the operation here, and have Admiral Rickover up to testify. It would be helpful to us if, for instance, Admiral Brockett or Admiral Maurer or both of them could be present and hear this testimony at the time, unless there is some objection on the part of the chairman.

Chairman PASTORE. I will take that up with the committee. I see no objection to it.

Secretary KORTH. Only in an effort to be helpful to the committee.

Chairman PASTORE. We will consider that.

Secretary KORTH. Yes, sir.

Chairman PASTORE. Gentlemen, thank you very much.

Secretary KORTH. Thank you.

(Thereupon at 4 :35 p.m., Thursday, June 27, 1963, a recess was taken subject to call of the Chair.)

LOSS OF THE U.S.S. "THRESHER"

TUESDAY, JULY 23, 1963

JOINT COMMITTEE ON ATOMIC ENERGY,
CONGRESS OF THE UNITED STATES,
Washington, D.C.

The Joint Committee on Atomic Energy met, pursuant to call, at 2 p.m., in the committee room, the Capitol, Hon. Chet Holifield (acting chairman) presiding.

Present: Senators Clinton P. Anderson, Henry M. Jackson, Wallace F. Bennett and Carl T. Curtis; Representatives Chet Holifield, Melvin Price, Wayne N. Aspinall, Thomas G. Morris, William H. Bates and John B. Anderson.

Committee staff present: John T. Conway, executive director; Capt. Edward J. Bauser, assistant director; Jack Newman, staff counsel; George F. Murphy, Jr., professional staff member; James B. Graham, technical adviser, and Maj. Jack Rosen, staff consultant.

Representatives of the Department of Defense: Hon. Kenneth E. BeLieu, Assistant Secretary of the Navy (Installations and Logistics); Vice Adm. H. G. Rickover, Assistant Chief, Bureau of Ships (Nuclear Propulsion); Vice Adm. L. P. Ramage, Deputy Chief, Naval Operations (Fleet Operations and Readiness); Rear Adm. William A. Brockett, Chief, Bureau of Ships; Rear Adm. Robert V. McElroy, Chief, Office of Legislative Affairs, Navy; Capt. M. G. Bayne, naval aid to Secretary Korth; Capt. S. E. Robbins, Director of Congressional Investigations; and Comdr. Walter M. Meginniss, assistant to Admiral McElroy, Office of Legislative Affairs.

Atomic Energy Commission representatives: Hon. James T. Ramey, Commissioner; Robert E. Hollingsworth, Deputy General Manager; Robert Panoff, Assistant Manager for Submarine Projects, Naval Reactors Branch, RD Division; I. Harry Mandil, Chief, Reactor Engineering Branch, Division of Reactor Development; David T. Leighton, Assistant Manager for Surface Ship Projects, Naval Reactors Branch, RD Division; Clifford K. Beck, Division of Licensing and Regulation.

Observer from Preparedness Investigating Subcommittee of the Committee on Armed Services, Senate: Ben Gilleas, professional staff member.

Representative HOLIFIELD. I think we will start the meeting. Senator Pastore asked me to preside until he could arrive.

Today we continue our executive hearings on the loss of the nuclear submarine *Thresher*.

This is the third hearing we have had on the *Thresher* incident. The first two hearings were held on June 26 and 27, at which time Secretary of the Navy Korth gave a general review of the overall investigation and plans for further investigations. Also testifying at the hearings were Vice Adm. Austin, president of the *Thresher* court of inquiry, who reviewed the proceedings of the court; Rear Adm.

Brockett, who reviewed the *Thresher* design, construction, inspection, and overhaul procedures; and Rear Adm. John H. Maurer, who summarized nuclear submarine operations and restrictions imposed on the operations of our Polaris missile and attack submarines after the loss of the *Thresher*.

Secretary of the Navy Korth was scheduled to testify today, but he had to appear before the McClellan committee. I am happy to say, though, we have Assistant Secretary Kenneth BeLieu here today to represent the Navy. I recall that the last time Assistant Secretary BeLieu appeared before the Joint Committee was on March 31, 1962, in our hearing aboard the nuclear aircraft carrier *Enterprise*. We are very pleased to have Mr. BeLieu with us again.

We have also asked representatives of the Atomic Energy Commission to be here since the subject we are scheduled to cover is the nuclear propulsion plant. I understand Commissioner Ramey——

Mr. HOLLINGSWORTH. Mr. Ramey has not arrived yet.

Representative HOLIFIELD. Mr. Hollingsworth, we welcome you and the other members of the Commission staff who are here.

We will proceed with the first witness, Admiral Rickover.

Admiral RICKOVER. Mr. Chairman, before I start I must say that I have not had time to present my prepared testimony to the Department of Defense for clearance because we were notified relatively just a short time ago that I would testify. So I would like to have it understood this testimony has not been cleared by the Department of Defense.

Representative HOLIFIELD. You understand that this is a classified hearing.

STATEMENT OF VICE ADM. HYMAN G. RICKOVER, ASSISTANT CHIEF, BUREAU OF SHIPS (NUCLEAR PROPULSION)

Admiral RICKOVER. Yes, sir.

Mr. Chairman, I am pleased that you have asked me to testify before the Joint Committee concerning the loss of the *Thresher*.

During the numerous times I have appeared before this committee in the last 15 years I have never used a prepared statement to present my views. However, because of the implications of the loss of the *Thresher* and the large amount of speculation as to the cause of her loss, I considered it desirable to set down my thoughts in some detail so there will be minimum risk of misinterpretation by those who may study the testimony given at these JCAE hearings. My sole objective in what I am going to say is to help bring about improvement in the way we design and build ships.

My staff and I have spent considerable time reviewing the testimony presented before the *Thresher* naval court of inquiry, particularly as it bears on nuclear propulsion, to insure that every possible lesson to be learned is applied. We have similarly studied the testimony given to your committee on June 26 and 27, 1963.

The findings of facts, opinions, and recommendations of the court, together with statements made in testimony presented to the court and to this committee are based on suppositions and judgments which can lead to incorrect conclusions. Unfortunately, in postulating what happened to the *Thresher* on the morning of April 10, too heavy a reliance has been placed on the [classified matter deleted] computer studies directed by the court. Based on these, statements have been made that [classified matter deleted] the ship lost propulsion. Such statements cannot, in my opinion, be substantiated and may cause us to lose sight of the basic technical and management inadequacies that must be faced and solved if we are to do all we can to prevent future *Thresher* disasters.

It is not the purpose of my testimony here today to prove that the nuclear powerplant did not contribute to this casualty. When fact, supposition, and speculation which have been used interchangeably are properly separated, you will find that the known facts are so meager it is almost impossible to tell what was happening aboard *Thresher* at the critical time. When you do not know the specific failure which caused the accident, then the only thing you can do is to examine your designs, fabrication techniques, inspection criteria, training programs, and operating procedures to see if there are further improvements that can be made. There is much we can do and will do in the nuclear power area.

In the testimony I am about to present, I will analyze some of the statements previously made to you regarding performance of the *Thresher*'s nuclear propulsion plant so that this committee may judge the issues for itself. I will then present what I consider to be the real problems. Finally, I will offer suggestions on possible remedial steps that could be taken.

I would like to emphasize that it is not my purpose to question the action of any individual because, as I will attempt to show, the real lesson to be learned is that we must change our way of doing business to meet the requirements of present-day technology. [Classified matter deleted.]

Representative MORRIS. Admiral, will you please comment on the reason why the same high degree of reliability required in the nuclear portion of the ship was not called for in the non-nuclear portion.

Admiral RICKOVER. I cover that part substantially very soon. I do have that covered in my testimony.

As I mentioned before, we have been studying intensively the record of the court. This is no small task. However, I want to be sure that we glean every possible lesson from the facts available.

STANDARDS OF DESIGN FOR NUCLEAR COMPARTMENT

The record of testimony indicates that higher standards of design, fabrication, quality control, and administrative control have been used in the nuclear powerplant as compared with other parts of the ship. Yet nowhere in the findings of fact, opinions or recommendations of the court is this pointed out. I do not say this in the vein of seeking credit for this difference; I did hope that the court would recognize that these higher standards are equally important for the rest of the ship. The high performance required of these ships, the exotic materials being used, the pushing of older materials to greater limits—all this, in my opinion, means the Navy cannot afford not to use higher standards throughout.

Senior people, when questioned by the court about the use of nuclear power standards versus their own standards, generally replied that the higher standards could not be accepted without subjecting the Navy to tremendous increase in cost of construction and tremendous increase of time to produce ships.

I am answering your question right now, Congressman Morris.

Representative MORRIS. I see you are.

Admiral RICKOVER. I find such statements difficult to accept. Perhaps the fastest the Navy has built warships since World War II has been our nuclear submarines. The aircraft carrier *Enterprise* was built faster than required by her contract; in fact she was operational before two conventional carriers authorized in the two previous fiscal years to the *Enterprise*. The destroyer leader *Bainbridge* was built as fast as our modern conventional frigates. As for "tremendous" cost increase for use of nuclear propulsion standards, I wish to point out that the reactor plant installation in a POLARIS submarine represents a small percentage of the ship's weight and of the shipbuilder's fabrication cost.

Does that answer you, sir?

Senator ANDERSON. Will you stop just a second while we take a look at that?

Admiral RICKOVER. The point made by senior Navy officers is it would take longer to build them and they would cost a lot more if my standards were used. I am pointing out to you that this is not necessarily so.

Senator ANDERSON. I don't follow that last sentence. You say, "As for 'tremendous' cost increase for use of nuclear propulsion standards, I wish to point out the reactor plant installation in a Polaris submarine represents a small percentage of the ship's weight and of the shipbuilder's fabrication cost."

Admiral RICKOVER. Shipbuilder costs usually price out at so many dollars a pound. [Classified matter deleted.] What these figures mean is that the installation cost per unit weight is just about the same as for the other parts of the ship.

Senator ANDERSON. I am not questioning that. However, in order to prove the cost question which Congressman Morris raised, you might tell us whether or not building a whole ship to the same standards as the nuclear portion of it would increase the cost by x percent, 10 percent, 15 percent, or 20 percent.

Admiral RICKOVER. I think it could decrease the cost of the ship. Do you want to hear why?

Senator ANDERSON. Now you really have me confused.

Admiral RICKOVER. You run a business too. You know if you have a lot of inefficient employees and you have to do the work over again, you might be better off to hire one good clerk rather than two poor clerks.

Senator ANDERSON. I am making a capital investment in types of IBM equipment and so forth which does cost me more money. Are you trying to say that the initial construction cost would not be higher?

Admiral RICKOVER. It might not be higher. I will tell you why. A nuclear submarine or any warship today costs a lot of money. However, when you are working in a submarine you are working in crowded quarters. If you have to do work over because the initial work was faulty, that is where the cost goes up. If you have good procedures, good specifications, and good people you will save money. That is the point I am trying to make. But I say that even under existing conditions there is about a 2-percent difference; this isn't a "tremendous" increase in cost.

Senator ANDERSON. You took me over the *Triton* when it was in drydock and they were putting in new wires and everything. Is that the sort of thing you are referring to?

Admiral RICKOVER. Yes. For example, if you have poor welders on a ship and the radiographs of the welds show the welds are not good, it may cost you more money to repair the welds than it took to make them the first time. If you had trained people, if you laid out the welds properly, if you had proper inspection and insisted on it, even though you paid the good welder more money you would save a lot of money. This is being found out right now. I will refer to this later on.

I have tried to inculcate some kind of discipline in the yards by insisting that specifications be met and procedures adhered to in the nuclear areas. Meeting specifications has not been required in other areas. I have insisted on meeting these standards. In some nonnuclear work the answer was to lower the standards.

Representative ASPINALL. Will the Senator yield?

Senator ANDERSON. I have just one final question.

Representative ASPINALL. I just wanted to know what would be the situation if you had the same capable people to build both kinds of ships?

Admiral RICKOVER. You would save money.

Representative ASPINALL. You would save money on which one?

Admiral RICKOVER. You would save money on anything by doing it properly in the first place. If you buy one really good suit, it is better than two cheap suits. It is that sort of saving.

ENFORCEMENT OF STANDARD

Representative ASPINALL. Did others in the Navy consider that you had equal competence in both areas?

Admiral RICKOVER. In the shipyards we use the same fabrication shops for nuclear work that do the nonnuclear work, except in my area I have my own representatives, and I have insisted that standards be met. In other areas they do not insist that standards be met. That is the crux of the problem.

Senator ANDERSON. Could we agree on this much? If there is any increase in cost—and personally I think there might be an increase in cost if there was an increase in standards—do you think that increase in cost, whatever it might be, would be justified?

Admiral RICKOVER. Yes, sir.

Why are you appropriating for Polaris submarines or for any warship or airplane? You are appropriating money so it can get on station and do its job. If it is necessary to do the job, as far as I know, every Member of Congress would appropriate all the money that was necessary to have a good ship. Even if you had to pay two times as much for the *Thresher* you would have appropriated that much if you knew it would have saved the ship.

You know, Senator Anderson, you and I are getting along fairly well in years and we know there are a lot of things you can't buy for money. You can't buy love, for example, and you can't always buy good workmanship for money, either.

Senator ANDERSON. It would be your testimony even if it cost more it would be worth it, but you don't think it would cost substantially more.

Admiral RICKOVER. I do not believe it would, sir.

Representative HOLIFIELD. Can you help me reconcile some of these figures? I understood you to say the reactor plant installation represents a small percentage of the ship's weight and of the cost. Could we compare that with the conventional propulsion weight of a conventional ship and conventional cost?

Admiral RICKOVER. The cost of a conventional plant is much less than the cost of a nuclear plant.

Representative HOLIFIELD. Then the percentages do not necessarily tell the whole story.

Admiral RICKOVER. It does for the installation in a Polaris submarine.

Representative HOLIFIELD. If the conventional is compared to the reactor for the nuclear [classified matter deleted] you could honestly say then that the nuclear propulsion submarine part cost twice as much as the conventional part. If you then conveyed that same care to the other part of the ship, it would figure out that the whole ship would cost twice as much.

Admiral RICKOVER. I believe you misunderstand, sir. I believe you are also including the cost of the propulsion plant equipment. I am talking only about the installation cost. There is a slight increase in doing nuclear plant installation over the nonnuclear installation but not any great increase. That is the point I am making.

COST OF SILVER BRAZING VERSUS WELDING

Senator JACKSON. May I ask one question? Aren't there two factors of cost involved here? When you apply the same high standards of excellence to the nonnuclear portions that you apply to the reactor compartment, your costs may go up but you will get better material and better structural design. The initial capital investment may be higher, but you may save money by using better skill and judgment. For example, this is similar to what you did in changing from silver brazing to welding.

Admiral RICKOVER. It was more expensive.

Senator JACKSON. Silver brazing was more expensive?

Admiral RICKOVER. Initially I think it was more expensive to weld than to silver braze.

Senator JACKSON. Is it now more expensive to weld?

Admiral RICKOVER. I think if you learn to weld well, it will not cost you much more than silver brazing.

Mr. PANOFF. Aren't these things rapidly approaching each other?

Admiral RICKOVER. They are approaching each other. Because you have to increase your inspection expense to make sure the silver braze is good, you will find that the two approach each other.

DESIGN ADEQUACY

Senator JACKSON. I am wondering if we have made the changes necessary in the nonnuclear part of the submarine to make it possible for that submarine to withstand the severe stresses that would follow with the use of nuclear power. It is obvious with nuclear power we have been able to go deeper and faster and to operate more continuously. I just wonder whether or not we have projected all of those factors into the design and structural effort of the nonnuclear portion that went into the nuclear portion.

Admiral RICKOVER. Do you wish me to answer?

Senator JACKSON. Yes.

Admiral RICKOVER. In my opinion, no. Again it is not anyone's particular fault. I am developing that point in my testimony.

I think the worst thing that could happen would be for this committee to get off on a sidetrack and think the real issue in the *Thresher* was this silver brazing versus welding. This could be a diversion which would cause us to lose sight of the true lesson of the *Thresher*.

The lessons from the *Thresher* go far deeper than silver brazing, and I am coming to that.

Senator JACKSON. Doesn't it go in part to the idea I have just expressed?

Admiral RICKOVER. Yes. It seems to me that this is so clear that it should have been at least in part foreseen.

I lectured at the Naval War College before the *Nautilus* was in operation and I remember telling the officers this was a brandnew weapon. I made no impression.

The Navy referred the question of nuclear-powered submarines to their Weapons Systems Evaluation Group and they came up with the figure that a nuclear submarine was worth about 1.4 of conventional submarines. That is what the Navy came up with. This is the sort of thing we had to fight at that time to get nuclear power into the Navy. As you well know had it not been for the Congress— for this committee—we could not have gone as far as we have. If you are talking about not being able to see far ahead, you have that not only in nuclear power; you have it in many things.

Senator JACKSON. I hope you will be able to catalog at some point— not right now because I have to leave for a little bit—the changes that were made in the design of the nonnuclear part of the submarine as a result of the introduction of nuclear power. What real effort has been made to take care of the new intended use with the advent of nuclear power?

Representative HOLIFIELD. What Senator Jackson has brought up is quite important. I can remember back in 1910 the first automobile which I saw. It was an internal combustion engine installed in a buggy. It was a vehicle that was very similar to a buggy except it had a shaft and a bar to guide it, but it had regular buggy wheels. This may be going to some extreme, but you might say to some extent what we did with the submarine was to put a new type of motor in a buggy.

Possibly the biggest lesson we can learn from the *Thresher* is that the hull and the rest of the nonnuclear part of the submarine must be brought up commensurate with the improvement in the propulsion engine.

Admiral RICKOVER. I agree with you.

May I proceed, sir?

Representative HOLIFIELD. Go ahead.

Admiral RICKOVER. I think I have covered the cost part. Was that satisfactory, sir?

Representative MORRIS. Yes, Admiral.

Admiral RICKOVER. I can't give you an exact figure, but it is not considerable.

Representative MORRIS. I wasn't trying to get exact figures. I just wanted to know whether it was cost or what the reason was that they were not able to do it.

COMPLIANCE WITH SPECIFICATIONS

Admiral RICKOVER. I am on page 22, sir.

Another erroneous impression I tried to straighten out in my testimony before the court but which still persists, is that I raised all fabrication standards. What I have actually done in the nuclear program is primarily to insist that everyone concerned meet the Navy specifications—specifications which had been in existence for many years. It is only when I required people to comply with these specifications that I uncovered the carelessness, looseness, and poor practices that have obtained in our shipbuilding business.

It took me many years to get a full and realistic view of just how bad the situation was. As I testified before the court, to get nuclear power work done properly in the environment that exists in our shipyards—I mean both private and Government yards—I was forced to set up my own organizations, use separate inspectors, have separate quality control; I had to use my own representatives to see to it that our work was done in accordance with specifications. Today, in many respects, our standards are higher because, when it was uncovered that the shipyards were not meeting specifications, some of those responsible for the nonnuclear portion of the ships tended to reduce their requirements.

Another issue I discussed with the court was quality control. Basically, the kinds of materials we used during the war and prewar years, the low limits to which we were then pushing these materials, and the basic simplicity of the designs, made our ships reasonably "workerproof." The less exotic materials then being used could withstand some deviation from design, inexactness of fabrication, and improper inspection. However, such conditions cannot be tolerated in modern ships such as the *Thresher*.

We are sitting on a quality control precipice where slight deviations can result in unsatisfactory or unsafe products. No longer are the materials we use in our ships "workerproof." No longer will these materials take the abuse of inexpertise or lack of attention to detail. We have reached the point where every designer and every workman must know what he is doing and do it well. No longer is there room for the unskilled or the untrained. In my opinion, failure to realize this new situation is the main reason for the *Thresher* testimony being replete with many examples of poor design, violation of plans, poor fabrication, poor workmanship, incomplete inspection. Although it has been claimed the Navy cannot afford to adopt higher standards throughout, I hope it is now realized we cannot afford not to.

I believe, Senator Anderson, that answers your question.

Drastic action must be taken to upgrade our design activities and shipyards so that design, fabrication methods, and inspection techniques are commensurate with the high-performance materials being used and the increased performance being demanded of our ships.

I know that the Joint Committee has kept itself informed on the *Thresher* inquiry. I could tell from reading the testimony of June 26–27 that you are familiar with silver brazing, ballast blow systems, fabrication standards, and other facts contained in the *Thresher* testimony. The poor silver brazes, the improper ballast control systems, the overcomplication that has crept into our ships—all of these are subject to some correction. But these are only symptoms; they are not the problems themselves. We must beware that not only the symptoms are treated; we must be sure to recognize and treat the disease itself. If we are to glean every iota of experience from the loss of the *Thresher* these symptoms must be traced back to their causes. It was to this course of action I hoped the court would address itself. In my testimony I made points which, had they been followed persistently, would, I believe, have uncovered the basic underlying weaknesses in our ship design and construction.

TESTIMONY BEFORE COURT OF INQUIRY

Representative MORRIS. You are speaking now of your testimony before the court of inquiry?

Admiral RICKOVER. Yes, sir. I always use the word "committee" when I talk of testimony here.

At this point I believe it will be of help to your committee if I quote to you the salient parts of the testimony I gave in closed session to the court of inquiry on April 29, 1963:

WITNESS. Admiral Austin has asked me to appear before this court to tell you what I know, which might be pertinent to the loss of the *Thresher*. I believe I can be of most help if I am specific. I will give examples, but it should not be concluded that the particular examples I mention are unique. Rather they are illustrative of practices which have grown up in the naval shipbuilding industry over many years. In fact, the major point I want to make is that the conditions which possibly led to the loss of *Thresher* exist throughout the submarine design and construction program. We may never learn the specific failure which was the immediate cause of the *Thresher's* sinking, but we may be able to reach an understanding of the underlying conditions which made such failure possible, and then do everything possible to prevent recurrences.

The first item I will take up is silver-brazed joints; the problems asociated with silver brazing of sea water systems provide a specific example of what I am talking about. Over the last several years several submarines, both nuclear and conventional, came close to being lost, due to failures in silver-brazed salt water systems, resulting from design, workmanship, improper use of materials, and inadequate quality controls.

I understand that the Bureau of Ships has calculated that in a *Thresher* class submarine at test depth the ballast tanks blow system can only compensate for a small leak. [Classified matter deleted.] I believe this calculation is based on the assumption that the ship is leveled off at test depth and has no downward motion. Thus, in a *Thresher* class ship, the quality of each of the several hundred silver-brazed joints in sea water systems is of critical importance. Each of these joints is part of the hull and should, therefore, have high integrity.

In assessing integrity of silver-brazed systems now installed in our submarines, it should be borne in mind that the large diameter silver-brazed joint which failed in a salt water system in the *Barbel*, did not fail until after 2 years of operation, despite the fact the joint had been made with the wrong material and had been assembled incorrectly. There have been other cases of silver-brazed joints which have passed many hydrostatic tests and diving cycles, yet subsequently failed completely and without warning. Following the failure of a [classified matter deleted] silver-brazed joint in the trim system of the *Thresher* in May 1961, I decided I could no longer depend on silver brazing for high-pressure systems.

I therefore took the following action for systems under my cognizance:

(1) All systems exposed to salt water would be fully welded, regardless of pipe size. Welding and its inspection would be in accordance with established reactor plant welding and nondestructive testing standards.

(2) Salt water systems would be fabricated to the same standards and quality control as the rest of the reactor plant.

(3) In addition, I required that joints and sea water piping passing through the reactor compartment also be welded, even though this piping was not under my cognizance.

In the *Thresher*, this work was all completed before she last went to sea.

The operating forces have also been concerned over failures in submarine sea water systems. The deputy commander, submarines, Atlantic Fleet, sent a message to the Bureau of Ships in September of 1961, with copies to the Chief of Naval Operations, the Commander in Chief of the Atlantic Fleet, and commanders of the Atlantic and Pacific submarine forces. The subject was "Submarines salt water piping systems." (See app. 1, p. 133.) This message referred to several submarine flooding incidents of 1960 and 1961, and said in part:

"Recent instances of flooding in submarines because of defective sea water piping or flexible hoses, are cause for grave concern. We have been fortunate thus far in that casualties have been handled promptly and correctly, and that, except in one case [classified matter deleted] electrical apparatus has not been involved. Continued dependence upon such tenuous and unfortunate circumstances, particularly when considering additional hazards imposed under wartime conditions, is obviously unacceptable. It is considered that urgency of problem and inherent danger of disaster must be brought more forcibly to the attention of all concerned, and that corrective preventive action must be pursued, even more aggressivly than has been done * * *."

I do not know what action is planned for silver-brazed joints in systems not under my cognizance. I do know, however, that inspection of a small percentage of these silver-brazed joints in several operating nuclear submarines, built by different yards, has shown a number of them to be defective. For example, last week a survey of but 36 silver-brazed joints in one submarine revealed that 7 joints had less than 40 percent bond. Two of these [classified matter deleted] joints had 10 percent bond or less * * *.

I have just learned that during the recent stay of *Thresher* at Portsmouth about 5 percent of her silver-brazed joints were ultrasonically inspected. These joints were in critical piping systems, 2-inch diameter or larger. The inspection revealed that about 10 percent of those checked required repair or replacement. If the quality of the joints so inspected was representative of all the *Thresher*'s silver-brazed joints this means that the ship had several hundred substandard joints when she last went to sea.

Representative HOLIFIELD. Our figure on this is 14 percent.

Admiral RICKOVER. The figures may have changed because more accurate information has been made available. I am merely pointing out a principle, sir. Not only on this ship but on other ships they would test a sample. They would find a percentage wrong in a sample. Then they would only repair those they found wrong in that sample. That is the point I am trying to make here. You may be quite right about the actual percentage.

Senator ANDERSON. One percent is high. Wouldn't you say even if 1 percent is wrong that you ought to go over the rest of the ship and see how many joints were defective?

Representative HOLIFIELD. What is being done on the *Tinosa?*

Admiral RICKOVER. I believe a great deal is being done.

Admiral Brockett, who recently became Chief of the Bureau, is handling this. He is requiring ultrasonic testing of silver-brazed joints.

Representative HOLIFIELD. What is happening with the sister ship, *Tinosa?*

AVAILABILITY OF WELD RADIOGRAPHS

Admiral RICKOVER. I think on that ship they have found that they didn't have all the radiographs of the hull welds so they have had to go back and do a lot of reradiographing. The *Thresher* has forcibly pointed up a large number of inadequacies which the Navy is attempting to correct. You can't take a ship, however, that is already designed and built and correct everything on it. You can't do that. You have to do all you reasonably can. You have to weigh the need of the ship as compared to what you have to do on it. If I were in the top position, I would do what I possibly could and then send the ships at sea. I am not advocating we lay up these ships or anything of that sort. I repeat, sir, I am not really trying to get at the specific instances of the *Thresher*. I am only citing these examples to show the sort of thing that has been going on for a long time and will probably continue to go on unless Congress takes a hand.

Representative HOLIFIELD. We have a fleet of submarines out now with silver-brazed joints that were constructed before this ultrasonic method of testing was developed. They are out on duty. Is it possible this same thing can happen to any number of ships?

Admiral RICKOVER. Mr. Chairman, of course, you are up against a practical situation. We would not have a Navy unless there was a reason for it and we have to take chances. As long as we try to get everything we can fixed as rapidly as we can, I don't think we can do any more.

Representative HOLIFIELD. I recognize you can't put them all in drydock and build them over. I recognize that point, but certainly there has to be limitations——

Admiral RICKOVER. There are limitations on depth——

Representative HOLIFIELD. There must be a program of intensive checking now going on of all of these that have been constructed and remedial methods being taken with respect to those that are in construction.

Admiral RICKOVER. There is a program and there have been limitations placed on operating ships. [Classified matter deleted.] The silver-brazed joints are being ultrasonically tested. The Bureau of Ships has started a program to look into the hydraulic systems to see if there is overcomplication. Some of this is being done. That still does not solve the problem I am addressing myself to. I am talking more about how do we go about doing the Navy's shipbuilding business. I am not talking about correcting the obvious errors we uncovered.

DEFECTIVE WELDS, POOR RADIOGRAPHY, AND INCOMPLETE INSPECTION RECORDS

I am still on page 28.

The next item I will discuss is welding. Another source of concern to me is the situation that has become evident in our yards over the last few years in the areas of pipe welding, radiography and quality control.

When I first started in nuclear power, I had no reason to assume that welding and the associated nondestructive testing used in our yards was other than adequate. My reason was that since these yards had been building and repairing ships for a long time they must have developed the skills to the required degree, and that the necessary specifications had been established and were being met. When I use the word "yard" I mean both private shipyards and navy yards. However, I have found from experience that the Bureau's pipe welding and nondestructive standards and specifications, while of good quality, were incomplete. Further, I gradually came to realize that these standards and specifications were not generally complied with. As a result, for nuclear propulsion work I had to prepare comprehensive welding and nondestructive testing specifications, and to make sure that the yards met these requirements. These specifications, while more complete—by these I mean the ones I just referred to as those I had prepared—these specifications, while more complete than existing specifications, required essentially the same quality of work the yards were supposed to be doing all along.

It has been difficult and time consuming to insure that shipyards met the specification requirements in the area of pipe welding under my cognizance. In many instances we had to overcome the prevalent attitude that specifications were merely a goal to shoot for, and did not need to be taken literally. This was aggravated by the opinion, also prevalent, that the quality of welding and inspection required by the specifications was unnecessarily stringent. There-fore, in order to insure satisfactory welding in areas under my cognizance, I found it necessary to set up my own welding and radiography inspection teams. These teams audited all yards doing nuclear work, to determine if our specifica-tions were being complied with. Weaknesses and noncompliance were found in practically all yards, although some yards were better than others. Defective welds, poor radiography and incomplete inspection records were typical. Following such inspection the management of the shipyard and the Chief of the Bureau of Ships were advised of the deficiencies found. I took corrective action for work in my areas.

Representative MORRIS. Mr. Chairman, I have one question.

You state, "Defective welds, poor radiography and incomplete in-spection records were typical." Does that mean they were the rule rather than the exception?

Admiral RICKOVER. Yes, they were the rule. Shortly after the war we took in some of the subs we used in the Pacific and took off the superstructures. Lo and behold, people wondered how those ships could have stayed alive with some of the welding they found in the hull. It is my considered opinion that some of the subs we lost during the war by depth charges was because they had defective welding. I think they just couldn't take it. Of course we don't know what really happened since the ships did not come back. What I say is from what I have seen and what I have learned. It shows that in a submarine you can't afford to have defects of design and workmanship any more than you can afford them in an airplane.

We found poor workmanship all over. I actually had to start teaching people in the shipyards how to read the radiographs. I worked for 2 years with the manufacturers and the shipyards and got up new specifications on how to read them. There was no common standard so you could have two people reading them and get two dif-ferent results. I had to go to that extent. This new standard is now used for nuclear work. I had to train the people in the shipyards who were doing the nuclear work. I also trained some people who were doing work other than nuclear. I think you can understand why I have such strong feelings on this subject.

I also found it necessary to set up schools to train my own radiographers to monitor the reactor plant welding of the shipyards. Further, I assisted the Bureau in training some of the personnel in naval shipyards and supervisor of shipbuilding offices. In addition, I established requirements for the qualification of inspectors for nondestructive testing. Also, I set up a special group in our naval reactor laboratories to guide and monitor all phases of the reactor plant welding in the yards.

I have special teams that go around constantly checking both private yards, Navy yards and the factories that make our material. My own teams go around and require them to demonstrate to us they are welding and testing properly.

As a consequence of what we found I have been inspecting and correcting, as necessary, welds under my cognizance in all nuclear plants built before we learned that specification requirements were not being met. This is being done by reviewing radiographs and repairing substandard welds as the ships become available. In those instances where the inspection records are not adequate, or where satisfactory radiographs are not available, new radiographs of the welds in question have been and are being taken.

In the case of the *Tinosa*, being built here at Portsmouth, the number of sub-standard welds and radiographs were so great that correction of the defects led to a delay in the scheduled completion of the ship. This delay was reported by the Chief of the Bureau of Ships to the Chief of Naval Operations as being due to the need for repairs to reactor plant welding.

This is what got me going on this subject. Instead of reporting that the real reason was the poor quality of all the welding on the ship, they reported the delay as being due to repairs to the reactor plant welding.

I was concerned that the full implications of these defects were not recognized; therefore, I sent a memorandum to the Chief of the Bureau of Ships. This memorandum stated that I could not understand how in the same yard, using the same specifications, the same welders, the same radiographers, the same film readers, the welds under my cognizance could be in poor condition while the welds in the rest of the ship, in areas equally critical, such as the hull, the salt water and steam systems were considered to be satisfactory. About 6 months after this event the Bureau relaxed pipe welding specifications for the nonnuclear portions of the *Tinosa*, and all other nuclear submarines.

LOSS OF "TINOSA" RADIOGRAPHS

Mr. CONWAY. Admiral, the committee has been informed the *Tinosa* has not gone to sea as scheduled; that is the sister ship of the lost *Thresher*. We understand the reason is because radiographs have been lost. No one can find them.

Admiral RICKOVER. I believe that is correct. They are being done over again.

Mr. CONWAY. Have they lost any of the radiographs of the reactor plant?

Admiral RICKOVER. No, sir.

Mr. CONWAY. Yours have not been lost?

Admiral RICKOVER. No, sir; not mine.

Mr. CONWAY. But the others are lost.

Admiral RICKOVER. I believe that is correct, but since Admiral Brockett is here I think he probably has the answer to that.

Admiral BROCKETT. Yes, sir; they are missing and this is why we docked the ship. These are of hull welds of the HY 80 structure and they are being retaken.

Admiral RICKOVER. Not the reactor plant, sir. We now require our radiographs be kept for 7 years. We used to keep them for only 3 years as required by the regular Navy specifications.

Senator ANDERSON. When were these radiographs made of the *Tinosa?*

Admiral BROCKETT. They were made some months ago.

Senator ANDERSON. Before the loss of the *Thresher?*

Admiral BROCKETT. Yes, sir.

Senator ANDERSON. After the loss of the *Thresher* they became lost.

Admiral RICKOVER. They were found missing after the *Thresher*.

Admiral BROCKETT. When a ship is ready to go one of the things that has to be certified is that all radiographs have been taken and have been reviewed. Then the ship is certified by the shipyard commander or the supervisor of shipbuilding as the case may be. In this case when we came up to that point some of them were quote missing unquote.

Senator ANDERSON. I realize that. I am trying to find out why they are missing.

Admiral BROCKETT. We are trying to find out too, Senator Anderson. The Deputy Chief is up at Portsmouth, N.H., right now.

Senator ANDERSON. Good. The point is they were made prior to the loss of the *Thresher* and then they turned up missing.

Representative BATES. How do you know they were ever made?

Admiral BROCKETT. We don't.

Senator ANDERSON. You just finished saying they were lost.

Admiral BROCKETT. I said they were missing; not lost.

Senator ANDERSON. I asked you whether they were made before the *Thresher* incident and you said that they were.

Admiral BROCKETT. The general radiographing of the hull would have occurred over this period. These are not all the radiographs of the hull.

Senator ANDERSON. Do you have any for the *Thresher?*

Admiral BROCKETT. Yes, sir.

Senator ANDERSON. Are there any missing?

Admiral BROCKETT. Not that I know of, sir.

Senator ANDERSON. Have you looked?

Admiral BROCKETT. No, sir. I have not.

Senator ANDERSON. Wouldn't it be almost time to check?

Admiral BROCKETT. I assume they are there, but I accept the suggestion.

Admiral RICKOVER. Let me say there are no missing radiographs for any part of the reactor plant. I see to it that we have those.

Senator ANDERSON. I would think somebody would be a bit curious about the *Thresher* as to whether those pictures were properly made and if not, whose fault it was.

I want to say, Admiral Brockett, that I do not want you to associate my remarks with any criticism of you because I certainly intend none. I do believe it would be very helpful if somebody would look and see if those radiographs are available on the *Thresher* and what they reveal if available. Could you try to have that done for us?

Admiral BROCKETT. Yes, sir. I think the subject is addressed in the court of inquiry——

Senator ANDERSON. The court might not be as anxious as this committee to try to find out what might have happened. It might be. I don't know.

Representative HOLIFIELD. In any event, will you make a search and report to this committee on that? (See p. 103.)

Representative BATES. Mr. Chairman, do we understand that the court of inquiry did not have somebody examine these?

Admiral BROCKETT. No; I say I am quite sure the court of inquiry did, but I cannot testify to this here because I have not gone through it. There is some 60 pounds of material.

Representative BATES. I don't see how they could possibly not check into it.

Admiral BROCKETT. That is one of the first places you would look.

Representative HOLIFIELD. Proceed, Admiral.

Admiral RICKOVER. I will read this letter which I sent to the Bureau of Ships in February 1962. I think it is quite important and epitomizes this whole problem.

Senator ANDERSON. Mr. Chairman, at this point could we put in the record another inquiry which was addressed to this same subject. Mr. Conway wrote a letter to the Navy trying to find out about the *Tinosa*. He received in reply what might be called "gobbledegook." (See p. 155.)

Senator BENNETT. A brushoff.

Senator ANDERSON. Yes. I ask that the letters he wrote and the replies he received be made a part of this record.

Representative HOLIFIELD. Without objection that will be done.

Senator ANDERSON. Thank you.

(Copies of the following correspondence are attached to and considered part of this record: Ltr JCAE to Dept of Navy 6/14/63, (app. 7, p. 155); Ltr fm Navy to JCAE with press release 7/1/63, app. 6, p. 147, and app. 7, p. 155); ltr fm JCAE to Navy 7/6/63, (app. 7, p. 156); and ltr fm Navy to JCAE 7/23/63, (app. 7, p. 156.)

DEVIATION FROM SPECIFICATIONS

Admiral RICKOVER. I supplied a copy of this memorandum to the court and I will read it because I think it is an important memorandum.

Ser 1500 M–1504.
13 FEBRUARY 1962.

MEMORANDUM

From: Code 1500.
To: Code 100.
Subj.: *Tinosa* (SS(N)606)—Delay due to welding problems.
Ref.: (a) BUSHIPS ltr (SS(N)593C1/4760, Ser 525–308 of 2 Feb 1962.
  (b) PNS ltr Ser 100 SS(N)606/4760 of 16 Jan 1962.
  (c) PNS ltr Ser 300 SS(N)606/9670 of 18 Jan 1962.

1. In reference (a), you advised CNO that the *Tinosa* would be delayed due to welding difficulties in the reactor plant systems. I was given no opportunity to comment on reference (a) prior to its release. Although I have no basic argument with the facts contained in reference (a), the letter is misleading by virtue of omissions.

2. Reference (a) implies that the only welding problem existing at the Portsmouth Naval Shipyard in connection with completion of the *Tinosa* is reactor plant welding; in my opinion that is not the case.

a. The reactor plant piping for *Tinosa* was radiographed and welded in accordance with MIL–STD–271A which is the very same specification that applies to the nonnuclear portions of the ship, most important of which are the steam and saltwater systems.

b. The very same radiography activity of the shipyard took the radiographs for both the reactor plant piping and for the other piping system welds in the ship.

c. The same radiography activity of the shipyard interpreted the radiograph films for the reactor plant piping welds and for the welds in the nonnuclear systems of the ship.

It is therefore difficult for me to understand how it can be concluded that only reactor plant welding is in trouble.

3. In reference (c) the Commander, Portsmouth Naval Shipyard, reports that:

"In the radiographs of nonnuclear pipe joints, the requirements of reference (a), particularly as to sensitivity, have not been met. It has been the exception rather than the rule when the 2T hole in the penetrameter could be seen." Penetrameter is the instrument which is used to judge radiographs. "Also, in some cases, approximately 20 percent of the total, either the wrong penetrameter or no penetrameter was used. The film processing was in many cases not of the best. In spite of these many deficiencies, it is considered that the radiographs were readable and only minor defects would be missed as a result of the lack of conformance to reference (a)."

Thus, reference (c) admits that the radiographic requirements of ML–STD–271A have not been met, but nevertheless concludes that the radiographs were readable and those that were not readable would only contain minor defects. The conclusions of reference (c) have not been borne out by our experience with the reactor plant welding and radiography at Portsmouth. The Portsmouth radiographs obtained were of extremely poor quality—worse than those of any other shipyard;[1] therefore I cannot understand how the conclusions can be reached that they were readable. We have found it necessary at Portsmouth to reradiograph reactor plant welds in order to ascertain their condition. Where reradiography was done, about 30 percent of the welds required repair work since they were below the minimums prescribed, not only by Navy specifications, but even by the more relaxed *commercial* standards Therefore the basis for the shipyard's conclusions on the adequacy of welds in nonnuclear systems is not evident.

---

[1] EDITOR'S NOTE.—See app. 15, p. 183, for report on quality of radiographs.

4. Reference (c) cites the additional cost and time delay involved as a justification for not meeting the Navy's standard welding requirements. It seems to me that Portsmouth has taken it upon itself to make a decision that rightly belongs with the Bureau of Ships. I consider it is the responsibility of the Bureau of Ships to set standards of quality for construction or repair of all ships. This is not a responsibility which, to my knowledge, has been delegated to the Bureau's field organizations. It appears that Portsmouth in nonnuclear areas of the ship has decided to set its own standards and is acting as the final judge whether these standards should be met. I consider this to be wrong, for it indicates that the Bureau is abdicating its headquarters responsibility. As is the case in any technical issue where the field organization feels that standards set by the Bureau are not proper, these should be argued on a technical basis. Until the issue is resolved, it is the responsibility of the field organization to comply with the Bureau standards.

5. I am concerned about the increasing difficulty of obtaining high quality work in our shipyards and of obtaining compliance with standards established by the Bureau. This is especially the case where one portion of the Bureau is attempting fully to comply with Bureau standards, while in areas under the responsibility of other portions of the Bureau local option is permitted, and the requirement for adherence to standards is not enforced.

6. Insofar as *Tinosa* is concerned, I do not see how the problem of its nonnuclear pipe welding can be lightly set aside. High integrity steam and salt water systems are equally as important in a submarine as the nuclear systems; all involve safety of the ship. Based on experience with the reactor plant welding, I recommend the shipyard be required to comply with applicable Bureau welding specifications.

H. G. RICKOVER.

CC. 400
    600
    700

Representative HOLIFIELD. That was in February of 1963.

Admiral RICKOVER. No; 1962.

Representative HOLIFIELD. In 1962 and it was April of this year when the tragedy occurred. This was about 14 months before the loss of the *Thresher*.

Senator CURTIS. Is it oversimplification to ask why the work is of such poor quality?

Admiral RICKOVER. No; I think that is quite a logical question. I think people just did not believe that adherence to the specifications was necessary.

Senator CURTIS. Was it a careless attitude on the part of the workmen?

Admiral RICKOVER. Careless attitude, in my opinion, on the part of all concerned. I don't believe you can blame the workmen alone. All of the workmen have a man over them. There is a foreman. There are officers in the field. If I have a job to do and it doesn't get done well, I am not going to blame the workmen.

Senator BENNETT. You have an inspector over the workmen.

Admiral RICKOVER. You have inspectors. You have all sorts of people. Suppose the inspectors think the standards are not necessary. And this is actually the case.

(Off the record discussion.)

Senator ANDERSON. One of the reasons I insisted we have an additional hearing on this is the warning 14 months ahead of the occurrence that something might be done wrong.

Admiral RICKOVER. There were many other warnings too.

Senator ANDERSON. I just believe, regardless of what may have happened, the refusal to take a look at this might have had some bearing upon it. It might not.

Admiral RICKOVER. Senator Anderson, the difficult position this puts me in is that it might appear I am acting in a very holy manner—that I am the only one who does good work and everyone else does wrong. I want to assure you my attitude in this is far different. I am concerned about the United States and the Navy and not about any particular individual. It has bothered me to present this testimony to the committee. I just do not know how else to bring it out without stating facts like this. I do not know how else to do it. I repeat I have to do it and I do not know any other way.

Senator ANDERSON. My interest is about the same. While I was chairman of the Joint Committee, members went on the *Nautilus* and enjoyed a wonderful trip. After we had this first trip and landed it was Senator Knowland from the opposite side of the aisle who began pressing for a larger nuclear Navy. I would not want you to think it was done on a partisan basis. Bill Knowland put his whole power behind this program and it was tremendously helpful to us.

However, let two or three incidents like the *Thresher* take place and people will begin to agitate against the building of these dangerous submarines. I think that would hurt the country immeasurably. That is my only interest.

Admiral RICKOVER. Yes, sir.

Representative BATES. Did you ever get a reply to this communication?

Admiral RICKOVER. Not as far as I know.

Of course, there is another question you can ask me. "Why in light of this didn't you do something? Why didn't you come to this committee when with a strict interpretation of the law the committee is to be kept fully and currently informed?" You might ask me this. I will tell you why. The issue had been raised with my superior in the Navy. I can't come to a congressional committee with every technical issue I have. A congressional committee is not the best forum to air technical issues because you will get experts who will argue both sides of the issue convincingly. I did everything I could to point this out. At the same time I did everything I could to keep my own areas out of trouble. That is all I could do.

Senator ANDERSON. Your letter went from code 1500 to code 100——

Admiral RICKOVER. My Bureau of Ships code number is 1500, sir. Code 100 is the Chief, Bureau of Ships. The other officers to whom copies of this letter went were the head of the Design Division, the head of the Shipbuilding Division and the head of all technical codes.

Senator ANDERSON. Who is code 100 and why didn't he reply?

Admiral RICKOVER. Code 100 was the Chief of the Bureau of Ships, Admiral James at that time.

Senator ANDERSON. I wish you would please say, "not the man who is here now."

Admiral RICKOVER. Oh, no. It is not Admiral Brockett.

Incidentally, the present Chief of Bureau of Ships and I served together on the U.S.S. *New Mexico*. I was a lieutenant and he was an ensign. I ran the legs off him. I think he will admit he learned a lot. He did a very fine job on the *New Mexico* and I am very happy he is the Chief of the Bureau of Ships. On the *New Mexico* I treated him the same way we treat contractors. [Laughter.]

I think we are very fortunate to have somebody like Admiral
Brockett as Chief of Bureau of Ships.   I know he will do everything
he possibly can.
   Senator ANDERSON. I tried to say a moment ago any criticism I had
made has not been directed to him.   I have heard nothing but the finest
things about him and his record.
   Admiral RICKOVER. No, sir.   This is not directed toward him at all.
   Representative HOLIFIELD. Go ahead, Admiral.

CRACKING OF WELDS IN HY–80 HULL STEEL

   Admiral RICKOVER. I will now continue with the testimony I gave to
the court:

   The next item I will discuss is HY–80 hull steel. Cracking of welds in the
HY–80 hull has long been of concern to me. I know this is a controversial
statement, but in light of the loss of the *Thresher*, I believe that this bears
further investigation. The primary structural material of our submarines
is susceptible to considerable weld cracking. It is also more susceptible to
fatigue failure than the more ductile submarine steels with which we have had
many years of experience.
   It has been argued that if a submarine is to go deep we must use HY–80 steel.
It has been reported that the *Thresher* would have been [classified matter de-
leted] heavier, [classified matter deleted] longer, and [classified matter de-
leted] slower, if she had been built of high-tensile steel, HTS instead of HY–80,
but perhaps a [classified matter deleted] submarine hull made of material in
which we have a high degree of confidence would provide a more acceptable ship
than one in which we must, on a regular basis, bring the ship back, inspect
welds, where accessible, and repair the cracks we find. What about the areas
of the hull that are completely inaccessible due to the installation of equipment,
tankage, cableways, etc.? What sort of situation is developing in these areas
of the hull as the years go by? What about the cracks we cannot see? I am
not implying that greater depth is not necessary, or that we should not work at
it, but it seems to me that until we know more about HY–80, and why it cracks,
and until we can definitely determine whether it is suitable for its intended application, we cannot have full confidence in the reliability of this material.
   The cracking susceptibility of welds in HY–80, make it especially important
that submarine structures using this material be welded in accordance with approved welding procedures, the welds radiographed in accordance with Bureau
requirements, and accepted only if they fully meet Bureau specifications.
   In 1959 the nuclear power superintendent—

that is my representative—

of the Mare Island Naval Shipyard discovered, and, with my assistance, brought
out a condition of unsatisfactory hull welding [classified matter deleted]. The
ensuing review uncovered inadequate radiography and quality control practices
at Mare Island. It also raised the basic issue of the acceptability of HY–80
as a hull material, including the question of fatigue effects. I insisted on complete inspections of that part of [classified matter deleted] hull that surrounded
the reactor plant. This inspection involved partial dismantling of the reactor
plant, since many of the hull welds would otherwise have been inaccessible. It
was found necessary to replace all the reactor compartment frame-to-hull welding. Faulty butt welds in the hull in this compartment also required repair.
In the rest of the ship the welding was only sampled, and only those defects
found by the sampling were repaired. I consider that when sampling techniques
are used to ascertain if flaws exist, the findings of such flaws should be followed
by extensive additional inspections.
   One of the symptoms that led to the findings of cracks in the HY–80 frame-to-
hull welds in the reactor compartment [classified matter deleted] occurred
during air tests on the canning plates over the shielding lead covering these
welds. The air, in some cases, was leaking out through cracks in the HY–80
welds under the lead. When he learned of this situation at Mare Island, the
nuclear power superintendent at Portsmouth looked for and found similar symptoms in the conduct of canning plate air tests in the *Thresher* reactor
compartment.

The *Thresher* was being built there at that time.

Representative MORRIS. The submarine was being built at Mare Island at the same time as the *Thresher* was being built?

Admiral RICKOVER. Yes, sir. [Continuing:]

> He reported this to the production officer of the yard. Recognizing the potential seriousness, the nuclear power superintendent asked that he be given written affirmation of the reactor compartment hull integrity. This was given him by the shipbuilding superintendent.
>
> The Bureau of Ships, faced with this situation at Mare Island, sent a representative to Portsmouth to review the adequacy of their HY–80 welding radiography. He reported that there were many deficiencies in the *Thresher* hull radiographs. His report indicated that the quality of the radiography was such as to raise the question of whether there existed an adequate basis for determining integrity of the *Thresher*'s hull. I do not know what action was subsequently taken.[2]

Representative MORRIS. That was in 1959 according to your statement?

Admiral RICKOVER. It was about that time.

Representative MORRIS. On page 33 you state in 1959——

Admiral RICKOVER. Yes, it was before the *Thresher* went to sea.

Mr. LEIGHTON. Admiral, by the time you got up to that point you had gotten into 1960, however——

Admiral RICKOVER. This condition obtained before the ship went to sea.

Mr. LEIGHTON. That is correct.

Admiral RICKOVER (continuing):

> Another example: Recent inspections of two nuclear submarines built at Ingalls at Pascagoula, Miss., revealed that in each ship a significant amount of weld metal had been omitted in the circumference of the pressure hull at a highly stressed transition joint.
>
> Now, I will get into [classified matter deleted] submarine design. [Classified matter deleted.] I am doing everything possible to overcome the types of problems I have discussed. This was not prompted by the loss of *Thresher;* but was begun some time ago in response to lessons learned in building, testing, and operating our nuclear submarines; specifically, [classified matter deleted]. I have taken the following actions:
>
> [Classified matter deleted.] Only welded joints will be used in salt water system, regardless of pipe size.

SPECIFICATIONS FOR REACTOR COMPARTMENT

You see I set the specifications for this plant myself.

Representative HOLIFIELD. You are talking about the nuclear portion——

Admiral RICKOVER. I am talking about the [classified matter deleted] plant.

Representative HOLIFIELD. Not the hull and auxiliary pipes.

Admiral RICKOVER. I am not responsible for the hull. If there is some question raised about the part of the hull that surrounds the reactor plant, I may have my people check into it unofficially and informally. But legally I do not have authority on the hull area. I just do a kibitzing proposition.

I am talking now about the [classified matter deleted] plant. Therefore I specified all piping will be welded—no silver brazing.

Representative HOLIFIELD. Whether it goes into your compartment or not?

---

[2] The trip report of the BuShips representative is app. 15, p. 183.

Admiral RICKOVER. I am only talking about the machinery part of the ship—the reactor part [classified matter deleted]. They will all have the same specifications.

Representative HOLIFIELD. Does this include the blowout tanks?

Admiral RICKOVER. No.

Representative HOLIFIELD. It does not.

Admiral RICKOVER. No, sir.

Representative HOLIFIELD. Does it include the pipes in and out of your blowout tanks?

Admiral RICKOVER. No. It does not include the ship's other systems. It includes [classified matter deleted] the reactor part, [classified matter deleted] the whole business will be built and inspected and handled in accordance with my specifications.

Representative BATES. How much of the ship does that represent?

Admiral RICKOVER. A small part of the ship in length.

Mr. CONWAY. You have responsibility for the first of a kind, but not the follow-on.

Admiral RICKOVER. That is correct, sir. I always retain the reactor plant, but they may change the machinery plant on the next ship. I can't control that.

What I am getting at in this testimony is when I started out I did not realize all of these conditions existed. Gradually I had to assume more and more responsibility for various parts of the machinery plant in order to make sure there was no difficulty with the reactor. That is why I am in things as extensively as I am.

This decision to use welding instead of silver brazing was made before the *Thresher*, mind you. This has nothing to do with the *Thresher*. What I am saying now has nothing to do with any lessons learned from the *Thresher*.

Mr. CONWAY. When the *Thresher* was under shakedown availability at the shipyard prior to the last cruise, did you or did you not change the piping in the reactor compartment?

Admiral RICKOVER. Yes; we did.

Mr. CONWAY. Did you pull out all silver brazings?

Admiral RICKOVER. In my part of the ship I pulled out all silver brazed parts in salt water systems and had them changed to welding. When she went to sea and when she was lost she had all welded salt water pipes in the part of the ship for which I was responsible.

Mr. CONWAY. Admiral, doesn't some of that piping extend out into other sections so that you have parts of a pipe——

Admiral RICKOVER. The parts I was responsible for had welding, but the same pipe could continue elsewhere and be silver brazed.

Representative BATES. What is the authority for first of a kind?

Admiral RICKOVER. Since the propulsion plant is intimately tied to the reactor plant in a new design arrangement, it has been worked out with the Bureau of Ships and with the shipyards that I am technically responsible to the Bureau for the whole propulsion plant of a new type. I had that technical responsibility for the *Enterprise*, the *Bainbridge*, and the *Long Beach*. It was the same for the *Nautilus* and the *Skipjack* but not the *Thresher*.

Representative BATES. Why didn't you have that responsibility for the *Thresher*?

Admiral RICKOVER. Because it was a follow-on ship. At a certain time it is turned over to the Bureau and they take charge.

Representative BATES. Wasn't *Thresher* the first of a class?

Admiral RICKOVER. The *Thresher* was essentially a *Skipjack*-type submarine except that all the equipment was mounted on resilient mounting [classified matter deleted]. She was different in that respect to the *Thresher*.

Representative BATES. Didn't somebody use the expression that the *Tinosa* was of the *Thresher* class?

Admiral BROCKETT. The *Thresher* reactor plant was the same as in the *Skipjack*.

Admiral RICKOVER. The propulsion plant was changed by the Bureau to introduce resilient mounting. [Classified matter deleted.]

Representative BATES. I am trying to decide to what class *Thresher* belonged?

Admiral RICKOVER. From the reactor standpoint she belongs to the *Skipjack* class.

Representative BATES. How would she be classified in "Jane's Fighting Ships"?

Admiral RICKOVER. From the standpoint that "Jane's Fighting Ships" doesn't know the kind of machinery she has outside of the reactor part, she would be a different ship.

Representative BATES. It is mixed up.

Admiral RICKOVER. I will explain it to you later on, sir.

Now I will continue with the submarine design.

All such welds will be made and inspected to established reactor plant welding specifications. I have also extended welding to nearly all of the other [classified matter deleted] plant systems. [Classified matter deleted.]

Further, all machinery and equipment under my cognizance, which is exposed to sea pressure, is being designed and built to the same standards used for the reactor plant. [Classified matter deleted.]

(6) Every pipe in the entire [classified matter deleted] plant is mocked up.

That means we build a full-scale wooden ship and every pipe is laid out in that wooden mockup.

Every weld and every system has identification to insure that the number of welds is minimized, and that all are readily accessible, and easily weldable.

(7) The shipbuilders and the equipment manufacturers are being required to institute comprehensive quality control to insure that all systems and components are designed, built and installed to the same standards [classified matter deleted].

(9) In some cases, equipment manufacturers have proposed the use of HY–80 in the design of machinery, because this material had previously been accepted by the Bureau of Ships. I have not accepted HY–80 material in any machinery or structure for which I am responsible.

What I have said represents but a partial list of the steps which I am taking to assure that the plant [classified matter deleted] will be of high integrity. Based on the operating experiences we have had to date, we must do no less. [Classified matter deleted.]

Now I will conclude. I believe the loss of the *Thresher* should not be viewed solely as the result of failure of a specific braze, weld, system, or component, but rather should be considered a consequence of the philosophy of design, construction, and inspection, that has been permitted in our naval shipbuilding programs. I think it is important that we reevaluate our present practices where, in the desire to make advancements, we may have foresaken the fundamentals of good engineering.

Acceptance of a structural hull material which is prone to cracking, and which frequently must be inspected and repaired, as the price of being able to go deeper, is questionable.

SAFETY AS IT RELATES TO DEPTH OF OPERATION

Representative HOLIFIELD. May I stop you there for just a minute. A layman like myself needs an explanation. What is the difference involved in the safety of a submarine going deeper? Is it from that standpoint of being able to escape the effects of depth charges? Can depth charges go deep? What do you gain by that extra depth.

Admiral RICKOVER. You gain several things. For example, there are layers of——

Representative HOLIFIELD. Thermal currents——

Admiral RICKOVER. Temperatures. If you get down low enough you may get under a layer which protects you from being detected. The deeper you go the more room you have to maneuver in a vertical way to escape depth charges and other things. You would be harder to detect. There are a good many military reasons for going deeper.

But again I touch on this subject. I recommend that the operators should not consider they are getting this for nothing. They are paying a price in much greater danger. I doubt if there has been an evaluation of what they are paying to get this. I recommend that we go back and really find out how much we are paying.

Senator BENNETT. That is balanced against the additional risk.

Admiral RICKOVER. This is one of the recommendations I made. I don't say that you should not do this. I think you should do it with your eyes open. That is all.

Senator BENNETT. You know you can maneuver to a certain depth without appreciable danger. As you go below that [classified matter deleted] you have less responsiveness in your equipment and more danger from pressure.

BRAZING AND WELDING DIFFERENCES

Admiral RICKOVER. Oh, yes. Also as a submarine submerges it compresses which makes it smaller and puts intense stress on material. Everything inside the hull gets compressed too, because a lot of it is secured to foundations and these all compress.

Take the silver-brazed joints compared to the welded joints. The weld becomes part of the parent metal. It is one thing.

Senator BENNETT. Providing it is homogeneous as in a weld——

Admiral RICKOVER. But it doesn't become homogeneous with a silver braze and not even with a weld if the weld isn't properly made. But it is possible to thoroughly inspect a weld and make sure it is all right. You can do that with a weld. You cannot do that with a silver braze. We have no way of determining absolutely that a silver braze is all right.

Senator BENNETT. Do you not have different expansion and contraction in silver and in the pipe?

Admiral RICKOVER. I will try to explain it in a simple way. You have two pieces of metal which you are trying to join together. You have a foreign material which is holding it together. Therefore, if you get stress or shock, this thing could break loose. This is an easy and rough way of saying it. This is the reason I do not believe in silver brazing.

Testing it by whatever means you have today might tell you it is all right. However, ultrasonic is not a sure proof way. It may show it is all right today. Tomorrow or even an hour from now something can happen with some vibration or shock which will break that joint loose. You can't do that with a weld. For instance, studies made by the Portsmouth Naval Shipyard show that a weld is relatively as good as—what is that exact figure? [Question directed to Admiral Rickover's staff.]

Mr. LEIGHTON. It is hard to put in numbers, but several times.

Admiral RICKOVER. Several times better. So that gets back to the question: Why do you do it?

Representative HOLIFIELD. You trade for convenience and ease.

Admiral RICKOVER. It was thought to be cheaper. I don't think it is really cheaper. When you get through and have a good silver-brazed joint, you still have the possibility of it going bad. I think you are a lot better off with a welded joint. I know I personally would rather go on a submarine with welded joints than I would with silver-brazed joints.

INVESTIGATION OF PROPERTIES OF HY–80

Senator BENNETT. May I ask a question? Are metallurgists in the steel industry trying to substitute or develop information on a replacement for HY–80? Are you working from that angle?

Admiral RICKOVER. The Bureau is conducting a very extensive program to find out all about HY–80 and how you can weld it properly. The only way you get a greater strength with a thinner section is to make it tougher. When you make it tougher it loses some of its resilience. That is your difficulty. It can crack easier. It is more brittle.

Representative HOLIFIELD. In other words HY–80 was actually given to the Navy as a superior product over the other.

Admiral RICKOVER. That is right.

Representative HOLIFIELD. But an element of judgment now comes in. Did you trade enough to get that additional toughness in ductile steel?

Admiral RICKOVER. That is right.

In my opinion—and I will come to this in a moment—I would rather have a [classified matter deleted] ship with carbon steel which we know how to weld and which doesn't crack. It has no susceptibility for cracking. If I were a submarine captain, I would rather have that and feel I could go down [classified matter deleted] any time without worrying about the hull than have to worry about welds in parts of the ship that can never be inspected. You don't know what is happening in those welds.

On one submarine, in order to investigate we had to rip out parts of the ship. We did find cracks. You can claim the cracks won't break. How do you know? Cracks that were found in two submarines from Pascagoula were in transition joints. That is where the hull stops being a nicely rounded contour and comes down and gets smaller. It is a point of great stress. They found a considerable amount of weld material had been left out. Such a ship could go to sea and under severe conditions the hull might crack. You would never find out what had happened. That is the sort of thing I am talking about.

If you are at war and you have to take chances that is one thing, but I don't think you take so many chances in peacetime. If your equipment doesn't stand up in peacetime, how will it stand up under the adverse conditions of wartime with depth charges and so on?

I believe a thorough evaluation by the operators is needed as to what depth they require balancing this against the increased risk they have to put these ships to. I can't say what they should have. If the operators say they must have deeper depth, then we have to give it to them. But we must recognize at this state of the art it is not as safe. It is again a case of judgment. You can't lay down rules. It is a case of judgment depending on the exigencies of the situation.

Representative BATES. What are you doing about these welds that you can't see and can't reach?

Admiral RICKOVER. You can bring the ships in regularly and inspect the other parts. You can inspect those. You hope that nothing has happened.

Mr. PANOFF. One of the recommendations made by the design group reviewing this is to leave some of the ones that were cracked unrepaired and use this as a gage to postulate what might be the case with those that you can't see.

Admiral RICKOVER. I would want this to be some other fellow's ship and not mine.

Representative BATES. That is what I was going to say. That might be all right for a test in the yard. I don't like to think of our men going to sea under those circumstances. Whose recommendation was that?

Mr. PANOFF. The recommendation was to have one older HY–80 boat or nuclear type and have some control by watching this one very carefully so as to guess what the others might be doing.

Representative BATES. Whose recommendation?

Mr. PANOFF. I think the Design Board——

Admiral BROCKETT. This was a Board chaired by Adm. Andy McKee, who is probably the best submarine design man in the country.

Representative BATES. Is he going to make these trips?

Admiral BROCKETT. He would.

I might add this about the characteristics of HY–80. The cracks do occur, but the propagation of them is very slow. It is not a catastrophic kind of propagation like you get in normal brittle material. This is a rather involved subject.

Representative BATES. If you were going to take this down [classified matter deleted] and you don't know how much of a crack you have, what is going to happen?

Admiral BROCKETT. A little bit of water comes in—just a spray. You have eight-tenths scale samples of this under that kind of pressure in a tank at Portsmouth. This is what happens when the crack goes all the way through.

Admiral RICKOVER. May I proceed, sir?

Representative BATES. Yes.

HIGH-PRESSURE HYDRAULIC SYSTEMS

Admiral RICKOVER (continuing):

The use of high-pressure hydraulic systems with their small clearances and delicate valves susceptible to malfunction by small particles of foreign matter, is another area which needs review.

The complexity and the gadgetry resulting from automatic depth control, automatic depth-seeking equipment, and automatic steering should make us reevaluate whether these features are really necessary. The fact that ship's control systems are so designed that the ship's safety depends upon the reliability of a single rubber or plastic "O" ring—

gasket—

or that the ballast tank blowing system depends on a single remotely operated valve that needs electric power should be reevaluated.

DEBALLASTING SYSTEM

Representative HOLIFIELD. We had quite a discussion about the increased pressure of the air tanks. As I remember it was some high pressure but because of reduction valves a lower pressure is used which is what had been used on previous ships which did not go to such extreme depths. I never did get clear in my layman's mind what was the advantage of increasing your air pressure and then cutting the use of it back down with these reduction valves which could not help but be a source of trouble and which would not give you the additional pressure at lower depth to expel that water from the ballast tanks.

Admiral RICKOVER. I think Admiral Brockett probably should answer that question. However, I believe the reason is you would have to build everything capable of withstanding that high pressure. That would also make the ship heavier.

Do you want to answer? [Question directed to Admiral Brockett.]

Admiral BROCKETT. The fundamental reason is that we use lower pressure air for blow and going to high pressure gives you more pounds of air per cubic foot——

Representative HOLIFIELD. Gives you a longer blow?

Admiral BROCKETT. Gives you more air.

Representative HOLIFIELD. And, therefore, a longer time to blow.

Admiral BROCKETT. Yes, sir; but what we are looking for is so many cubic feet of air in the ballast tank at the existing pressure. When you have [classified material deleted] higher storage pressure that means by Boyle's law that you have volume cutback [classified material deleted] to put the same amount of air into the ballast tanks and bring up the pressure.

Representative HOLIFIELD. You don't gain pressure but you gain in time of exertion of pressure——

Admiral BROCKETT. You gain——

Representative BATES. Can you store more air?

Admiral BROCKETT. Basically you can store more air in the same space.

Admiral RICKOVER. The real situation is the Navy from the time of the 400-foot submarine [classified material deleted] did not basically change the blowing requirements as they went deeper.

Representative HOLIFIELD. That doesn't seem right to me.

Admiral RICKOVER. This isn't right. They have recognized it. Again I will answer your question shortly. I have covered that too. [Continuing:]

SPECIFICATIONS AND QUALITY CONTROL

The lack of adequate specifications and quality control can result in questionable workmanship in brazed piping in salt water systems. These are an integral part of the ship's hull boundary and should be considered as such.

It is, therefore, most important that we reappraise our approach in the design and building of submarines. In doing this it would be well to remember the words of Admiral Carney, then the Chief of Naval Operations, who wrote in July of 1955, and I will quote:

"It is realized that in the ships laid down in the last few years, and being delivered at this time, it was the desire of the Bureau to incorporate a number of advances and techniques and materials. Undoubtedly, some of these have contributed to the efficiency of the ship, but unfortunately, other items have proved faulty and have resulted in long delays in the delivery of the ships to the fleet, and in costly alterations or replacements.

"The Chief of Naval Operations has supported the Bureau of Ships in the construction of ships for experimental and development purposes. Examples are U.S.S. *Timmerman*, U.S.S. *Albacore*, experimental PT boats, and the Miami hydrofoil boat. Each of these has made its contribution to the improvement of future designs.

"However, a large number of ships which are enumerated in the 1956 shipbuilding and conversion program are for service in the fleet and are not to be considered as being built for experimental purposes. Neither the ships nor the appurtenances thereto.

"The Chief of Naval Operations welcomes and encourages progress in the design of ships and their component parts, and in the use of new and improved materials, all of which should lead to improvements in efficiency and effectiveness. It is mandatory, however, that the traditional naval characteristics of ruggedness and reliability not be sacrificed or in any way impaired in future construction."

Now, I will come to my recommendation.

RECOMMENDATIONS

These are my recommendations. I am speaking just for myself now.

DEPTH LIMITATIONS

As a first step, I would start with the following:

(1) For submarines that are operating, I recommend:

(*a*) Limit, for the time being, the normal operating depths [classified matter deleted] unless the operation of the ship requires otherwise. In this case the depth should be left to the discretion of the commanding officer. Limiting the depth [classified matter deleted] would enhance safety as follows:

(1) Reduce stresses on the hull and salt water piping systems.

(2) Reduce the amount of flooding for a given size of leak.

(3) Give the ship proper buoyancy margin when blowing ballast tanks. The buoyancy attainable from blowing these tanks decreases with the depth.

BRAZING ELIMINATION

(*b*) It is my opinion from the many failures that we have had in silver brazed joints that they should be eliminated in sea water and high pressure systems wherever possible. I do not consider such joints to have the integrity required of salt water systems in deep diving submarines.

(*c*) I would check, as soon as practicable, one operating submarine from each building yard for integrity of the hull, the salt water systems, the hydraulic and high pressure air systems.

(*d*) In addition, I would institute a program to check all operating ships as they are made available. Here I would give priority to ships from yards where the workmanship is found to require it.

(2) For ships in design or early construction stages, the following should be considered:

(*a*) Modify the designs to specify welded salt water systems, high pressure air and hydraulic systems. If this cannot be done in the space or time available, then I would limit a submarine having brazed joints in its salt water system [classified matter deleted] or else make the changes necessary to accommodate welded systems.

COMPLIANCE WITH SPECIFICATIONS

(*b*) The question of whether applicable specifications are being complied with by the yard should be looked into. It is possible that the specifications have been waived from time to time. In the future waivers to specifications should be granted only by the Bureau of Ships.

(*c*) Standards comparable to those I have instituted for the reactor plants in welding, radiography, nondestructive testing, and quality control should be used for all systems and structures involving ship's safety, and training programs for welders and radiography personnel instituted to accomplish this. These personnel must meet prescribed standards with respect to competence and qualifications.

(3) The operating forces should be requested to reassess the need for deep operating depth. Account should be taken by them of the increased danger as the depth is increased. It is possible that insufficient consideration to increased hazards and reduced margins under casualty conditions has been given when decisions were made to increase the operating depth of our submarines.

This, sir, completes my formal testimony.

However, there were a few questions asked by the court which I think are worthy of your attention.

Q. Admiral Rickover, you have discussed the design of ships. Would you discuss in a little more detail how you think they should be designed and what precautions should be taken with certain systems before they are put into ships?
A. * * *.
In the case of the design of the reactor plant, we get an idea; we work it up with competent scientific and engineering design people; it is then checked by the people in my own office; we then start building the developmental piece of equipment. We constantly reanalyze it as it is being built. We make mockups of it. We then actually try it out ashore before we place it in the ship. All of our plants are thoroughly mocked up. I mentioned earlier, that in the case of these new submarines, even the piping, even the type of weld on each pipe is indicated. We make sure by inspections conducted by my own people that it is accessible and that it can be properly welded. We found previously that many welds were difficult to get at, and in some instances, as a consequence, were not completely made. This is a very brief and general answer, and it could be elaborated upon to a great extent.

* * * * * *

Also we adopted the system on all new ships of having the officers and crew report to the ship quite a few months before she was placed into commission, so that they could act as inspectors. They could act as inspectors for the testing of the various systems in the ship which they would take to sea. This was done for two reasons: (1) it would be absolutely impossible, in my opinion, to get a yard to have the kind of people who could do the testing which we required. Furthermore, it was highly desirable to give this training with the plant to the very people who would have to operate this ship at sea.
I would add one thing: I instituted what we call a "fast cruise" or a "dry run." People refer to this in different ways. This was a case where, just prior to the ship's being declared ready to go to sea, we lock up the ship, and the crew runs it for approximately 4 days. During this time, any "bugs" which might develop—and we run the plant up to full power—are brought out and corrected. If they are not corrected, we don't go to sea.

You understand, this is done alongside the dock but we act as though the ship were at sea.

PRESIDENT. We would appreciate any help you can give us in this direction. The court appreciates your analysis and your background information. It appreciates also the suggestions which you have made, many of which have occurred to us already, and we do hope that this session together has increased your ability to help the court further in the reactor area. If there is anything further, Admiral Rickover, that you would like to say before you leave the stand, we would entertain any suggestions you may have.

DEBALLASTING CAPACITY

The WITNESS. I do have some further observations. As the court probably knows, I have been out on all first trials of all nuclear-powered ships except two, when I was in the hospital, and some things have occurred to me. I will try to relate them to the Thresher as closely as possible. Prior to the Thresher's trials in April 1961, in connection with some casualty studies I had run with a new reactor plant design, I became aware that the blow capacity of Thresher was small. I pointed this out to the officer in charge of the Bureau of Ships Submarine Type Desk at that time. During the Thresher's trials I also pointed this out to the navy yard, to the Bureau of Ships, the Board of Inspection and Survey, and Commander of Submarine Forces Atlantic Fleet representatives who were on board. I think this is a point which should go in the record.
Another incident in connection with the Thresher was about 2 weeks before the Thresher's first sea trials. As I was to be in charge of these trials, I asked my people to look into the measurements and tests and proposed method of conducting this first dive. [Classified matter deleted.] I found little thought had been given to the details of how this dive was to be conducted. Outside of measurements to be obtained by the usual model basin hull instruments, little else was to be done.
I arrived at Portsmouth the evening before the trials. I met with the following: The Deputy Chief of the Bureau of Ships, the head of the Bureau of

Ships Submarine Type Desk, the shipyard commander, the shipyard planning officer, the shipyard design superintendent, the commanding officer of *Thresher*, and others. I requested them, on a crash basis, to detail in writing the whole sequence to insure safety during the dive. Of course all this was done during the night. The plan, as finally evolved, which I approved, provided for a slow, deliberate descent at given stages; at each stage there was to be a cycling of all sea valves, flapper valves, and other items affected by pressures. At each valve station a man was present to observe and to act, if necessary. I did this to assure that, as the ship went deeper, our damage control devices were instantly operable. I also did this because of my concern at the lack of blowing margin. Also I considered all this would be necessary since this was the first time one of our submarines was to go to so great a depth, and particularly because of the large number of new development items, including sea valves and rubber piping.

The lack of planning for this dive was indicative to me of what I considered the causal way in which the Navy was going to those great depths. An indication of this casualness can be obtained by reading the minutes of the meeting held by the Ship's Characteristics Board and the Bureau of Ships in early 1959, at which the *Thresher*'s depth was discussed.

I did the best I could to bring the HY-80 situation to the highest level in the Navy. I took the matter up with the Chief of the Bureau of Ships and the Chief of Naval Operations early in 1959. Later that year, when cracks were discovered in the submarine at Mare Island, I again took it up with the Chief of Naval Operations. Submarine captains recommended to COMSUBLANT that more extensive use of welding be made instead of sil-braze. In one case a captain recommended full welding of all sea water lines on deeper submarines. Despite this, the endorsement that came out of COMSUBLANT merely recommended that an economic assessment of this be made. Now insofar as deeper submarines, I did not object to having one ship do this and try it out. I did object to predicating a large number of ships until the *Thresher* design had been fully proved at sea. I went to the Chief of Naval Operations, who appointed the President of the Board of Inspection and Survey to conduct a study. He recommended to the Chief of Naval Operations that the Navy proceed as planned.

CONCLUSIONS

Now, Mr. Chairman, I come to my conclusions and these conclusions represent the quintessence of much that I have learned in my naval career, so I will read them rather slowly.

From the testimony I have presented, you might, well ask, What, in my opinion, should be done to bring about improvements which could serve to reduce the risk of additional accidents such as the *Thresher*?

I consider that the most important step to be taken by the Navy is to eliminate transient technical management. No industrial organization that operates on a profit and loss basis would ever dream of continually shifting its top people. An industrial organization so operated would soon go out of business. Changing this concept of transient technical management in the Navy will be difficult. I doubt the Navy, if left to itself, will do this in a timely manner.

The system whereby each ensign is set on a course to become Chief of Naval Operations, or if he's an engineering duty officer to become Chief of the Bureau of Ships, is not in consonance with the present technical milieu. I know of no large industrial organization which has programs to train every college graduate it hires to become president of the company.

In my opinion, unless, to paraphrase Lord Acton's famous epigram, there is a change so that the individual exists for the Navy and not the Navy for the individual, we will not eliminate the basic difficulties. I know the counterargument—if we can't provide this career pattern with a promise to get to the top, we will not keep good people in the Navy. Why then is it reasonable to expect good civilians to want to work for the Navy if they are denied the ability to get to the top in their fields, provided they have the requisite talents? I have long advocated that the best man should get the job whether he is an officer or a civilian.

Another factor I believe to be responsible for many of the Navy's technical difficulties is the lack of individual responsibility. Of course, the present transient management concept generally precludes assignment of individual responsibility. It is significant to me how few of the senior people in the responsible management positions at the time of *Thresher's* loss had anything to do with her basic design. It is rare for an officer both to start and finish a job. For example, during the 5 to 6 years encompassed in the design, construction, and evaluation of the *Thresher*, some of the key job changes were approximately as follows: The Portsmouth Naval Shipyard, which was assigned the detail design responsibility for the *Thresher*, had three shipyard commanders, three production officers, five planning officers, and three design superintendents. The Bureau of Ships during this period had two Chiefs of Bureau, six or so heads of the Design Division, and three heads of the submarine type desk. Some of the individual Bureau technical codes concerned with the *Thresher* had about four to six changes of management during this same period. Of course, these figures do not include the numerous changes in the subordinate ranks which were made during this period. How can you have individual responsibility on this basis?

Much of the effort of the court was directed to finding out who was responsible for the design of the *Thresher;* who made the fundamental technical decisions; who authorized deviations from plans; who authorized deviations from the specifications. The inadequate ballast tank blowing system is a case in point: Who is responsible? With the present Navy system, this is an almost impossible question to answer. The nearest you can come is to say that "The Navy is responsible." In other words all you can do is to point to a collectivity. In my own area, for example, when the adequacy of a scram procedure is questioned—"It is Rickover's procedure." And this is as it should be.

In this connection I believe you will be interested in the following testimony I gave this committee on June 15, 1961:

Senator JACKSON. * * * One of the problems concerning the committee is the pinpointing of responsibility in the event of nuclear accidents. We had the one at Arco, the SL-1. How can the Joint Committee ascertain what individual or individuals are responsible for a specific project?

Admiral RICKOVER. * * * Responsibility is a unique concept: it can only reside and inhere in a single individual. You may share it with others, but your portion is not diminished. You may delegate it, but it is still with you. You may disclaim it, but you cannot divest yourself of it. Even if you do not recognize it or admit its presence, you cannot escape it. If responsibility is rightfully yours, no evasion, or ignorance, or passing the blame can shift the burden to someone else. Unless you can point your finger at the man who is responsible when something goes wrong, then you have never had anyone really responsible * * *.

Representative BATES. Did you say that "off the cuff"?

Admiral RICKOVER. Most of it, yes.

Representative BATES. That is pretty well said.

Senator ANDERSON. I think you did say it all "off the cuff."

Admiral RICKOVER. I don't remember whether I did or not. I think you were there, sir.

I think that last sentence:

Unless you can point your finger at the man who is responsible when something goes wrong, then you have never had anyone really responsible—

expresses the real dilemma and it is not going to be changed by the military services. Of that I can assure you. It will only be changed by Congress.

Congress after all does share this responsibility. You have a concurrent responsibility. Your responsibility doesn't end once you have appropriated the money.

Representative MORRIS. I am glad you brought that out, Admiral.

Representative HOLIFIELD. I believe this is true.

Representative MORRIS. Not only with respect to the military but with the civilian agencies also. With civilian agencies you may waste money, but with the military you may waste the country's life.

Commissioner RAMEY. The AEC has some responsibility too.

Admiral RICKOVER. Yes. I was talking here of the relation of Congress to the Military Establishment. I was not implying that the Atomic Energy Commission does not have responsibility.

Representative HOLIFIELD. Of course a procedure of specialization has grown up in these giant corporations like Standard Oil, for instance. A corporation like that wouldn't think of having a man from the production department take over the advertising department or the sales department. You do have these large organizations with responsibility placed in specialized compartments.

However, with the military, it seems to me, to a great extent you have to make every member of the Armed Forces a generalist rather than a specialist.

Admiral RICKOVER. Mr. Chairman, this is a subject on which I hope the Armed Services Committee of the House or Senate might call on me to testify. Essentially it gets down to personnel. It gets down to the kind of people you bring into the organization, how you educate and train them and what ideas you inculcate in them.

Whenever something goes wrong, do you say: "Read another book on leadership"? We have a long document which lists the leadership books you should read. That is the easy way to solve problems. "Read another book on leadership. Find out how to persuade a man to work hard and to keep him happy while he is working hard." You not only have to get him to work hard, but get him to feel happy about working hard.

Sometimes I feel all we do is talk about leadership and principles and define them by rules of conduct. What are those rules? You are not supposed to have a soup spot on your blouse. Abraham Lincoln had a lot of soup spots. You are not supposed to drink. Ulysses S. Grant drank.

Representative HOLIFIELD. Let's not take this too far. [Laughter.]

Admiral RICKOVER. I was only talking about military people.

You are not supposed to run around with women. Napoleon ran around with women.

Such rules are not the basic essentials of leadership. There is more to it than that. I think perhaps we lose sight of this with our nice easy rules and the idea that all we have to do is to follow rules and we are great leaders. I have never been a great leader, but then I have never read the rules.

Representative HOLIFIELD. You had better continue.

Admiral RICKOVER. The present-day technical complexity is beyond the point where you can count on "the system" to do the job well. So, while steps are being taken to correct obvious deficiencies as exemplified by the *Thresher*, what about all the other parts of our ships and their complicated equipment for which there is no real individual responsibility?

On the other hand, if you eliminate transient technical management and assign individual responsibility, other benefits logically follow. Only then can the necessary detailed technical control, the establishment and enforcement of proper standards, and the selection and training of personnel be done at the level commensurate with the degree of technical excellence required by modern-day weaponry. I don't mean to imply that this can be done overnight. I think it will take many years, perhaps a generation, to bring this about. Corrective action will have to be taken at every level, from the standards set for entry into the Navy for enlisted men and midshipmen through their education and training at service schools, the Naval Academy, and subsequent schools. The same applies to the civilian personnel of the Navy. Unless the civilian management of the Navy, assisted by the Congress brings about the change, it will not happen. Unless there is permanence of technical management, there can be no effective upgrading of the Navy's in-house technical capability to keep it abreast of the demands of the times.

My views sum up as follows:

(*a*) There is insufficient information to pin down what really happened to the *Thresher*. I do not know. We therefore have to look at everything that may have contributed to her loss.

(*b*) I do know there were weaknesses in her design, fabrication, and inspection that must be corrected. These are symptomatic of the basic problems facing the Navy today in the conduct of its technical work.

(*c*) Significant upgrading must be effected in our bureaus and shipyards in design, fabrication, and inspection.

(*d*) This upgrading cannot be done until there is permanence of technical management and assignment of individual responsibility.

(*e*) There must be a change in the philosophy that the Navy exists for its people and that the career of its people takes precedence. Promotion should be on the basis of results and contributions to the Navy, not on the multiplicity of jobs a man has had.

(*f*) Outdated concepts of the officer-civilian relationship should be abandoned—the best man should get the job.

Mr. Chairman, this concludes my prepared testimony.

Representative HOLIFIELD. Thank you, Admiral Rickover, for your testimony. It has been a long day for many of us. I am sure there are a lot of questions that come about as a result of your testimony. However, I think if there is no objection on the part of the members of the committee we will review your testimony and ask you to come back at a later date. I don't want to preclude anyone from asking any questions they may want now. We have another 17 minutes before 5 o'clock.

Representative BATES. I would like to make a suggestion. I feel the main emphasis of Admiral Rickover's statement has to do with people, with their training and the permanence of their assignments. This has been a matter that has been considered for many years in the service. I don't know how this could be implemented but I would appreciate it if the next time you came before the committee you would sort of spell this out and tell us how it could be worked out from a military point of view. Take as an example, an ensign who has been assigned to a certain spot.

Admiral RICKOVER. I will be glad to, sir. You realize this is a very complex problem in a large organization. I will try.

Representative BATES. Give us a little more detail.

Admiral RICKOVER. I will try, sir.

Representative BATES. We know what the general concept is, but how it would actually work is a something I have a problem wrestling with.

Representative HOLIFIELD. Mr. Morris?

Representative MORRIS. No questions.

Representative HOLIFIELD. Senator Anderson.

Senator ANDERSON. I am very happy you were here today. You have given us this fine statement. I think this is the sort of comment we have been trying to get. It is going to take some time for us to really look at this and perhaps after we look at this we should ask him to come back again.

Representative HOLIFIELD. We have some questions which were prepared by our staff. I am going to give these questions to you and ask that you give us a written reply. Some of them you may have answered in the course of your testimony. If so, you can note that fact. [Classified reply received.]

Are there any comments you other gentlemen who are here today wish to make?

Mr. Secretary, do you have anything you would like to say?

Secretary BELIEU. Not today, sir. I greatly appreciate the opportunity of being here and I hope to return, if I may.

Representative HOLIFIELD. Mr. Ramey.

Commissioner RAMEY. I do not have a statement. We also appreciate the opportunity of having Commission representatives here. If you have any questions for us at the next session, we would be glad to participate.

Representative HOLIFIELD. Thank you.

The committee will stand adjourned.

(Whereupon at 4:45 p.m., Tuesday, July 23, 1963, the meeting was adjourned.)

LOSS OF THE U.S.S. "THRESHER"

WEDNESDAY, JULY 1, 1964

CONGRESS OF THE UNITED STATES,
JOINT COMMITTEE ON ATOMIC ENERGY,
Washington, D.C.

The Joint Committee on Atomic Energy met, pursuant to call, at 1 p.m., in the committee room, the Capitol, Hon. Chet Holifield (vice chairman) presiding.

Present were: Senators John O. Pastore and George D. Aiken; Representative Chet Holifield (presiding), Thomas G. Morris, Craig Hosmer, and William H. Bates.

Committee staff present: John T. Conway, executive director; Edward J. Bauser, assistant director, James B. Graham, technical adviser; George F. Murphy, Jr., professional staff member; and Maj. Jack Rosen, staff consultant.

Representatives of the Department of Navy:

Hon. Kenneth E. BeLieu, Assistant Secretary of Navy (Installations and Logistics) ; Vice Adm. L. P. Ramage, Deputy Chief of Naval Operations (Fleet Operations and Readiness) ; Rear Adm. C. A. Curtze, Deputy Chief, Bureau of Ships; Rear Adm. E. P. Wilkinson, Director, Submarine Warfare, Office of Chief of Naval Operations; Capt. D. H. Kern, Head of Submarine Branch, Bureau of Ships; and Capt. Spencer E. Robbins, Director of Congressional Investigations (Office of Legislative Affairs).

Representatives of the Atomic Energy Commission:

John G. Palfrey, Commissioner, and Gerald F. Tape, Commissioner; Vice Adm. Hyman G. Rickover, Manager, Naval Reactors Branch, Division of Reactor Development; Robert Panoff, Assistant Manager for Submarine Projects, Naval Reactors Branch, Division of Reactor Development; Comdr. William Wegner, Deputy Manager, Naval Reactors Branch, Division of Reactor Development; and Robert D. O'Neill, Office of Congressional Relations.

Representative HOLIFIELD. The committee will be in order.

Today we resume hearings on the tragic loss of *Thresher*. Earlier hearings were held in executive session on June 26, June 27, and July 23, 1963.

At the termination of our hearings last year, the Joint Committee made known its intention of releasing all unclassified portions of the hearings. This committee, from its inception, has always strongly supported proper security of classified information. At the same time, however, it believes that the American public is entitled to all information, the publication of which will not be detrimental to the security of the country.

Up to a few months ago, the Navy Department had taken the position that all of the earlier hearings were classified and nothing could be made public.[1] Although we did not agree with the Navy that everything discussed at our hearings was classified and continued to argue the point, I would like to note for the record that pending resolution of this disagreement no information from our hearings was released by this committee despite the fact that numerous stories and public statements have been made by others, including Navy sources.   (See app. 8, p. 159.)

In the past few months with the excellent cooperation of Secretary BeLieu, Adm. William Brockett, and Admiral Wilkinson—I understand you were made admiral today.   On behalf of the committee I wish to extend our congratulations—specific points have been identified in the earlier hearings which are classified and must remain so.   Secretary BeLieu, Admiral Brockett, and Admiral Wilkinson have been very cooperative and helpful to this committee in our desire to present as complete a public record as is possible in this case.

With the deletion of the classified material, we are now ready to release the record of our earlier hearings in order that the public can be adequately informed of the circumstances surrounding the loss of *Thresher*. The public will also be made aware of the changes which are required in our nuclear submarine program and have before them a record of the progress that has been made as a result of the lessons learned from the loss of *Thresher*.

Before releasing last year's hearings, the chairman thought that it would be only fair that the Navy Department have an opportunity to testify as to the corrective actions that have been taken since last year and that this be made part of the record to be released.   A key report, and one which the committee very much appreciated receiving, was a memorandum furnished to the committee by Secretary Nitze on February 5, 1964, commenting on progress made in a number of the significant areas discussed during the earlier hearings.   (See app. 9, p. 166.)

Today we resume our hearings with the purpose of learning what improvements have been brought about in the field of development, design, fabrication, test, and operation of nuclear submarines.

We are also interested in learning what changes have been made with respect to one of the personnel problems identified; namely that of transient technical management in the Navy's submarine program.

The importance of nuclear submarines to the Nation's security is so great that I believe no stone should be left unturned to keep our submarine program second to none.

We are very pleased to have with us this afternoon, Admiral Rickover, without whose efforts we probably would not be in this preeminent position concerning nuclear submarines, Admiral Curtze, Deputy Chief of the Bureau of Ships; Admiral Ramage, Deputy Chief of Naval Operations, Admiral Wilkinson, Director of Submarine Warfare; and their principal assistants.   I understand Mr. Ken BeLieu, who is at the moment the Acting Secretary of the Navy, will be here shortly.   He has been unavoidably detained for a short period.

Unfortunately Admiral Brockett, Chief of the Bureau of Ships, is unable to be with us this afternoon because of a previous commitment. He is now on the west coast with Secretary Nitze.

---

[1] See app. 8, pp. 159 to 166 for exchange of correspondence on this point.

Our first witness will be Admiral Ramage, Deputy Chief of Naval Operations for Fleet Operations and Readiness.

Admiral Rickover, would you come up to the witness table also? We may have some questions for you during our discussion.

Admiral RICKOVER. Thank you.

Representative HOLIFIELD. Admiral Ramage, you may proceed.

Admiral RAMAGE. Mr. Chairman and members of the committee, I am Vice Admiral Ramage, Deputy Chief of Naval Operations for Fleet Operations and Readiness.

IMPROVEMENTS IN SUBMARINE SAFETY

I will review certain actions taken to improve submarine safety since the loss of *Thresher*. These actions include the following: changes in our operating procedures, the formation of a submarine safety center, the first steps in implementing the deep submergence system review group's recommendations, the distribution of the *Thresher* court of inquiry to the fleet commanders for dissemination, together with additional emphasis on submarine training requirements.

Admiral Curtze will describe the material aspects of the submarine safety program.

DEPTH RESTRICTION AND SUBSAFE PACKAGE

First, I will discuss the operational actions taken by the Navy since the loss of *Thresher*. The operating depth of all submarines with a deep design test depth [classified matter deleted] has been restricted. [Classified matter deleted.] This interim restriction applies to all SSN's, all SSBN's, and the 10 deep-hulled post-World War II diesel submarines, and will remain in effect until all subsafe measures have been accomplished and certified by the Bureau of Ships in the case of each submarine. [Classified matter deleted.] Until all plans and material for the complete subsafe package are available, the submarines now in overhaul and in the late stages of contruction are modified item by item. The subsafe package will be completed on these ships during their next overhaul. The builders' sea trials and the post overhaul trials have been changed to reflect the lessons learned from the loss of *Thresher*. Some of the new requirements include the following: Test dives are made in depth of water limited to 1½ times the test dive depth [classified matter deleted], a submarine rescue vessel is in attendance and tape records all communications, the main ballast tank blow capability is also tested dockside and during a shallow dive prior to the deep dive. In addition all new construction submarines are authorized to make three controlled dives [classified matter deleted]—one for a system integrity check, one to test the emergency main ballast tank blow at this depth, and one after postshakedown availability to test the same two items again. These dives [classified matter deleted] feet are done to demonstrate that the ship is safe to this depth in the event of a depth excursion below the [classified matter deleted] operational limit. Prior to each submarine sea trial, the Bureau of Ships conducts an audit of the ship and the building records, and certifies the ship to be materially ready for the trials. Various other procedural changes have been made to improve the safety of submarine operations. As an example, the deep submergence procedures have been revised, including new instructions; restrictions have been placed on speed at various depths, and all submarines will maintain positive buoyancy when feasible. The engineering plant procedures have been modified. [Classified matter deleted.] Our nuclear submariners have all been trained in these procedures.

SUBMARINE SAFETY CENTER

On February 18, 1964, the Secretary of the Navy established the Submarine Safety Center at Groton, Conn. This activity is under the military command of the Chief of Naval Operations. Its mission is to devote full-time attention to all aspects of submarine safety in order to advise and assist the Chief of Naval Operations, fleet, and the submarine force commanders in promoting and monitoring safety of all submarines. This group will be of great value in improving submarine operational procedures. Some of the projects which have been started include a subsafe manual, subsafe lesson fliers, casualty information collection, a submarine damage control book, and a study concerned with habitability and submarine safety. In April, the Deep Submergence System Review Group, under Rear Adm. E. C. Stephan, submitted its recommendations to the Secretary of the Navy. Recently, the Chief of Naval Operations formed the Deep Submergence Steering Group—composed of OPNAV and fleet representatives, to specify CNO requirements in this particular area. Management control for implementation of the CNO requirements has been assigned to the Director of Special Projects. We are giving primary attention to extending current means and facilities for rescuing personnel. At present our [classified matter deleted] submarines could be disabled in water too shallow to collapse the hull and still be beyond our rescue capability.

SUBMARINE SAFETY TRAINING

Another important area where actions have been taken to improve submarine safety is that of training. The fleet commanders have been directed to give wide dissemination of the *Thresher* court of inquiry findings within the submarine forces. The Chief of Naval Operations has directed modification of submarine trainers to provide flooding and plane casualty simulation. The Chief of Naval Personnel and the director, special projects are now implementing these changes at our various submarine training bases. The first days at sea are potentially the most hazardous for a new submarine or one completing a long overhaul. Accordingly CNO has instituted more rigid inspections and trials required of these submarines. Prior to sea trials the fleet commanders determine that the officers and crew are prepared for safe operation of this ship. This is done in two steps. Prior to dock trials such items as the ship's operating procedures, casualty bills, and team training requirements are reviewed for adequacy. After dock trials and before sea trials, an uninterrupted period is provided in the shipyard for crew operational training on board the ship.

In summary, the officers and men of the submarine force have learned many valuable lessons from the tragic loss of *Thresher*. We have made significant improvements and are continuing to devote maximum attention to all these problem areas.

Representative HOLIFIELD. Thank you, Admiral.

The Chair will just say it is indeed sad that we had to have the tragic loss of 129 lives in order to put in the safeguards which have been put in since that time.

I understand Admiral Curtze is to make the next statement. Is that right?

Admiral CURTZE. Yes, sir.

Representative HOLIFIELD. Unfortunately the members are under pressure of time today. They are reading the foreign aid amendments on the floor. This is not your fault.

Admiral CURTZE. I think I can do this in half an hour, sir.

Representative HOLIFIELD. Will you proceed? I do not mean to indicate this is not important to us but we are just caught in a bad situation this afternoon.

Admiral CURTZE. I understand, sir.

[Classified matter deleted.]

MATERIAL ASPECTS OF SUBMARINE SAFETY

Admiral CURTZE. Mr. Chairman, we welcome this opportunity to review the progress of the Bureau of Ships' submarine safety program for you. We have had an opportunity to work closely with members of your staff concerning certain specific details of the submarine safety program although my intent today is to touch briefly on all aspects of the program and to review in general its current status.

Over the past year the subject of submarine safety has been under a searchlight of attention as a direct result of the loss of *Thresher*. During this period there has been a tendency, even within the Navy family, to associate the genesis of our submarine safety effort to the loss of *Thresher*. It is important that we place the Navy's current effort in this field in proper perspective. Therefore I must emphasize that submarine safety has been a continuing program in the Bureau of Ships; it has been a matter given to closest scrutiny by all engineering personnel within the Bureau's organization who are associated with the design, construction, and maintenance of submarines. The genesis of this effort was not *Thresher*'s loss but stemmed from our very first attempts to design and construct combatant submarines.

In considering submarine safety it is important that we recognize that the U.S. Navy's submarine design and construction program has been rapidly gaining momentum since the close of World War II, both with respect to performance and numbers and types of submarines constructed. Throughout this period of development and expansion three basic thrusts have permeated our submarine design effort:

First, offensive capability has been emphasized and this has produced:

(1) A [classified matter deleted] increase in submerged speed.

(2) Unlimited submerged endurance.

(3) A [classified matter deleted] increase in depth of submergence.

(4) Marked improvements in sonar search capability.

(5) Major strides in weapon launching capabilities such as wire guided torpedoes, Subroc missiles, Polaris missiles.

Secondly, producing a submarine with a hard-core defensive capability has generated marked improvements in quieting of propulsion machinery, and in the ability of a submarine to resist underwater explosive attack.

Third, the provision of an adequate level of safety has been superimposed on the first two great objectives, giving due consideration to the greater risks involved in higher speeds, greater depths, and sophisticated weapons. Throughout the evolution of improved offensive and defensive capabilities, certain basic and fundamental safety features were retained. For example:

(1) For rescue and salvage, today's submarine designs still require messenger buoys, free ascent escape hatches, emergency underwater voice communication equipment, compartmentation for escape, and air habitability to sustain life (oxygen supply, carbon dioxide absorbents).

(2) Flooding recovery capability has been provided through air blowing of main ballast tanks to gain buoyancy, and sea valve closure features to stop flooding.

(3) Pressure boundary integrity has not been sacrificed. The factor of safety built into submarine hull structure to resist sea pressure has not been reduced; [classified matter deleted]. Hull openings and penetrations have been kept to a minimum.

The provision of safety features may not, on hindsight, have kept pace with other advances made in the area of military capabilities, but the level of safety did not remain static. Some significant effort was expended to improve the safety of our modern submarines, and improvements were achieved and injected into our submarine construction program. For example:

(1) The decision to go deeper [classified matter deleted] had considerable impact on our approach to submarine design. In 1958, Project Pressure was set up to look at every possible component, seals, flexible joints, and hull penetrations to determine the new parameters for safe design. It is pertinent to note that a similar project named Glaucus is now underway to bridge the gap between our current knowledge of deep-diving-submarine requirements and those required by the test vehicle, *Dolphin* (AGSS–555), which is to be capable of operating at [classified matter deleted] depth. The improvements developed as a result of these projects have been injected directly as specific design features and indirectly via quality assurance, inspection, controls, tests, and new fabrication techniques used in the process of construction.

Chairman PASTORE. May I ask a question? I wasn't here at the beginning so you may have already covered it. Has the decision been made to go below [classified matter deleted]? Are we going below [classified matter deleted]?

Admiral CURTZE. Not yet.

(2) A system for emergency use of stored high-pressure air for breathing has been developed and installed in all nuclear-powered submarines. This was introduced to provide a means of sustaining life during a fire or toxic gas casualty where the submarine would not surface due to enemy action or operations under the ice.

(3) Remote hydraulic closure of sea-water valves has provided our submarines with a significant improvement in their ability to isolate quickly sea-water systems in case of damage at points distant from the source of flooding.

Summarizing, submarine safety over the years since World War II has not been slighted or degraded. It has been a continuing and important part of the Bureau of Ships submarine design programs. However, on hindsight, following *Thresher*'s loss, we must in all honesty say, as Rear Admiral Brockett, Chief of the Bureau of Ships, has already said, with respect to submarine design, we moved too fast and too far in areas of offensive and defensive capabilities. Submarine safety did not keep pace.

The loss of *Thresher* has now raised many questions as to whether the safety features provided, and the quality of construction in our high performance nuclear submarines, are adequate. The Bureau of Ships, in consonance with the thinking of the entire Navy family, considers it mandatory at this juncture that all aspects of our approach to submarine design, construction, maintenance, and operation be reviewed and, where weaknesses are found, that corrective action be initiated at the earliest. It is pertinent to note that pending completion of these reviews the maximum operating depths of all deep diving submarines has been restricted, by the operational commanders [classified material deleted].

SUBMARINE SAFETY STEERING TASK GROUP

Submarine safety program: Anticipating the need for an extensive and continuing engineering program to undertake the necessary investigative actions, reviews and studies aimed at determining potential areas of weakness in our submarine design concepts, components, construction practices and quality assurance programs and further, to provide a mechanism for review and implementation of the technical recommendations of the *Thresher* court of inquiry and Design Appraisal Board, the Chief of the Bureau of Ships on June 3, 1963, directed the establishment within the Bureau of a submarine safety program. In establishing this program he directed that cognizance be taken of the urgency of the immediate problem of providing sufficient safety features to permit the removal of depth restrictions now imposed on our operating submarines, and further directed a searching examination of all aspects of our current and future submarine development, design, and construction programs to insure provision of adequate safety features.

For the purposes of administering this program, establishing program scope, providing technical direction and insuring adequate funding and technical support, the Chief of the Bureau of Ships established a Submarine Safety Steering Task Group. I am chairman and my committee is composed of leading men from all branches of BuShips that are interested in this. They are listed here:

Deputy Chief of the Bureau of Ships, Rear Adm. C. A. Curtze, U.S. Navy, chairman.
Director, Ship Design Division, vice chairman, Capt. N. Sonenshein, U.S. Navy.
Head, Submarine Branch, Capt. D. H. Kern, U.S. Navy.
Director, Applied Research Division, Capt. M. L. Pittman, Jr., U.S. Navy.
Head, Machinery Design Branch, Capt. W. R. Riblett, U.S. Navy.
Director, Hull Division, Capt. D. L. Creed, U.S. Navy.
Director, Machinery Division, Capt. D. G. Phillips, U.S. Navy.
Director, Assurance Systems Engineering Division, Comdr. R. J. Leuschner, U.S. Navy.
Project Officer, Deep Diving Submarines, Submarine Branch—Recorder, Comdr. J. E. Rasmussen, U.S. Navy.

The Submarine Safety Steering Task Group has developed and promulgated an instruction for the conduct of the submarine safety program (BuShips Instruction 5100.18 of July 8, 1963). This instruction establishes certain specific safety tasks and assigns responsibilities for prosecution of these tasks to cognizant technical codes within the Bureau of Ships. The Submarine Safety Steering Task Group reviewed the technical recommendations of the *Thresher* court of inquiry and the Design Appraisal Board against its own initial problem definition. No thought or recommendation of any group passed unconsidered. The task group monitors and continually reviews the progress of action on these tasks to insure proper technical direction and early completion. The program consists of 16 tasks and 91 subtasks covering all aspects of submarine design, fabrication, testing and maintenance affecting safety. Many aspects of the program have been completed and appropriate administrative action taken.

Representative HOLIFIELD. Before you leave that subject, will you furnish us the names of the people that you have in these different posts and also give us some idea of the continuity of service in these respective posts? One of the problems we found in the Portsmouth Shipyard was the changing of shipyard commanders during the course of construction of one submarine so there was a lack of continuity in knowledge of the background of happenings and the problems that pertain to each one of these submarines. Have you done anything at all along the line of assigning one person to a specific submarine and keeping him there until it is finished?

(The information requested appears in app. 12, p. 174.)

ADMIRAL CURTZE. May I have permission to address that in greater detail later?

Representative HOLIFIELD. Yes.

Admiral CURTZE. I will be glad to provide the names.

Addressing myself to the composition of the Board, I have only lost one member—and this was by retirement yesterday—since the Board's inception.

I have listed the submarine safety program tasks here and I can read them if you wish.

Representative HOLIFIELD. I think we will accept those for the record.

(Submarine safety program tasks were listed as follows:)

Task No.	Brief description
1	Review design of sea-water systems subjected to submergence pressure.
2	Investigate hazardous piping systems with respect to adequacy of materials, fabrication methods, and test procedures.
3	Review design of machinery components in hazardous sea-water systems.
4	Mandatory use of class plans and components in vital systems.
5	Review design of high-pressure air systems, including MBT blow systems.
6	Insure proper readiness requirements for submarine builders and insure sea trials.
7	Investigate electrical systems—to provide protection from sea water.
8	Review adequacy of submarine pressure structure penetrations.
9	Consolidation of information for damage control sections of ships information book.
10	Review the reliability of ship control systems.
11	Investigate habitability features to insure that safety is not degraded.
12	Investigating the feasibility and cost of constructing submarine test tank capability of testing full size submarines.
13 14	Review safety aspects of submarine shock tests against manned submarines.
	Revised and expanded quality assurance programs.
15	Investigate possibility of modifying submarine diving trainers to permit training in flooding recovery action.
16	Investigate submarine location, salvage, and rescue features.

ADEQUACY OF HY–80 STEEL

Admiral CURTZE. In reviewing the record of previous hearings of June and July, I noted a great deal of interest in hull structure. I would like to address myself to that in greater detail.

A review of testimony before this committee in June 1963 indicated an interest in the adequacy of HY–80 steel for hull construction in view of the early problems experienced with this material in submarine construction. I'd like to outline the Bureau of Ships investigative and development work which provides the background for our confidence in this material.

In establishing the submarine safety program it was considered that the previously established submarine structural program should continue to function as a separate entity. This particular program was initiated on November 6, 1959, by the Chief, Bureau of Ships, who directed that a comprehensive review be conducted of the problems encountered in employing HY–80 steel in submarine construction.

This type of steel had been specified for the shell of U.S.S. *Albacore* (AGSS–569) in 1950 and was used without particular difficulty. After further developmental effort, during which weldability, workability, cost and availability, as well as chemical and physical properties, were thoroughly reviewed, it was approved for use in September 1955 for the submarine building program.

The superior yield strength of this steel at 80,000 pounds per square inch compared with previously used high-tensile steels at 44,000 pounds per square inch made its use in large diameter pressure hulls; that is, over 20 feet, most attractive. Further, its superior nil ductility transition (NDT) temperature, which ranged from minus 135° to minus

150°, insured against brittle fracture in low ambient air and ocean temperatures (a problem with mild steels with NDT range 0° F. to plus 40° F. which are temperatures we do encounter). Further, tests made at Dahlgren Proving Grounds in 1950 had demonstrated a fracture toughness that was as good as any steel previously tested, giving ballistic properties at least 95 percent as effective as the average quality of special treatment steel (STS), commonly used as armor plate.

Despite the fact that during construction of the experimental submarine *Albacore*, HY–80 had proved to be weldable, problems in welding this steel began to manifest themselves as various submarine building yards began to use HY–80 in the greater thicknesses needed for larger diameter, deeper depth submarines than had been employed in *Albacore*. Further, nonuniformities developed among the various yards in carrying out critical HY–80 welding techniques. As a consequence, the Chief, Bureau of Ships. ordered a complete review into the use of this material for submarine hulls.

A detailed engineering review was completed and reported in a comprehensive summary entitled "A Review of HY–80 in Submarine Construction," dated January 5, 1960. This report was prepared by a "blue ribbon" committee of the Bureau's Ship Design Division military and civilian experts in ships structures and submarine design. To assure appropriate breadth of view, this group consulted extensively with experts in the academic, scientific, and industrial worlds. Professor Freudenthal of Columbia University and Professor Munsie of the University of Illinois made available their highly specialized knowledge in structures, especially with regard to fatigue. Representatives of Babcock & Wilcox Co., Air Reduction Co., Electric Boat Division, Newport News Shipbuilding & Dry Dock Co., as well as those of the Naval Research Laboratory (then called the Material Laboratory) and welding engineers from all naval shipyards involved in submarine construction contributed to the analysis.

The principal conclusions and recommendations that were developed by this review were that use of HY–80 steel should be continued for high-performance military submarines of present characteristics; that a surveillance program be established for submarines constructed of this material; that certain improvements be made in the design and fabrication techniques; and that a continuing program of research and investigation into fatigue strength aspects be initiated.

This committee also recommended the establishment of a continuing submarine structural program to encompass the foregoing recommendations as well as to develop procedures and methods for applying newly developed materials (including HY–80) to the construction of submarine hulls. This was done by the Bureau of Ships Instruction 4760.19 of February 18, 1960. This program is still in full force and effect. An Advisory Panel was formed to help assure establishment of a sound and comprehensive long-range program. This Panel was composed of some of the principal advisers who had been consulted during the conduct of the review which led to the writing of "A Review of HY–80 in Submarine Construction," as well as other academic, scientific, and industrial experts of similar stature.

WELDING DIFFICULTIES OF HY–80

During the course of this program, the initial difficulties encountered in welding HY–80 steel have been largely overcome. The problem of fatigue of highly stressed details has also been extensively studied. In more recent submarines, welding problems have been largely overcome, and, starting with U.S.S. *Thresher*, the causes of fatigue cracking were understood and could be adequately controlled.

Representative HOLIFIELD. Let me stop you right there for a minute. I don't understand your statement that "starting with U.S.S. *Thresher*, the causes of fatigue cracking were understood and could be adequately controlled." What does that mean? As I remember, the testimony showed that fine cracking in the welding was known both before and after the *Thresher* incident. Isn't that true? How do you control it? You have said "the causes were understood and could be adequately controlled." Are you sure they were controlled?

Admiral CURTZE. Our radiographic techniques weren't quite up to the art of welding at the time, in my opinion, and we were unable to give the same attention to detail to welds that existed in the *Thresher* as we are since able to do. Insofar as the state of the art was concerned at the time, we were in control.

MISSING WELDING INSPECTION RECORDS

Representative HOLIFIELD. You don't know because you do not have all the records. You could not find some of the records.

Admiral CURTZE. That is right, sir. I am addressing myself merely to our knowledge of techniques at the time, sir.

Representative HOLIFIELD. Now or then?

Admiral CURTZE. Then, sir.

Representative HOLIFIELD. The point remains that you do not know what was the situation with either brazing or welding in the *Thresher*.

Admiral CURTZE. Unfortunately not in the detail we would like, sir. We would if we had it to do over again.

Representative HOLIFIELD. Is that because the techniques at the time were not known for the ascertainment of defects or because your records are lost?

Admiral CURTZE. Our records aren't complete. In accordance with your suggestion at a prior hearing we have gone into a tremendous amount of detail on the *Tinosa*, to which I will address myself later.

However, we found in the *Tinosa* that of the 22,000 hull radiographs that are actually required to do the job probably only about 1 percent of these are missing. When we radiographed these we found in those areas in which radiographs had been made and repairs made that the level of excellence of these welds was appreciably better than the remaining ones. So we feel we can only extrapolate what we found in *Tinosa* because *Thresher* was built at a comparable period of art and time that *Thresher* was similarly configured.

Representative HOLIFIELD. Your remarks are addressed at this time to welding and not to brazing?

Admiral CURTZE. That is right, only hull welding. We feel in our new boats we are in control of this. That is my point, sir.

Representative BATES. Has simultaneous welding presented any problem recently?

Admiral CURTZE. Do you mean both sides of the frame concurrently, twin arc welding? I think it has presented some problems merely in preparation of the joints so that you don't burn through from one side, but I don't think there is any real problem.

Representative BATES. Some welders advised me at one time that this was a problem. As far as you know it does not present any problem.

Admiral CURTZE. The last time I was in Portsmouth I watched them twin arcing strength frames on *Dolphin*, AGSS–555 [classified matter deleted.] They were beautifully jigged and rolled under the welder's covered arc. It was the most beautiful weld I have ever seen. There was no problem at all.

Representative BATES. So they are continuing to do that?

Admiral CURTZE. Yes, sir.

Representative BATES. As far as you know there has been no problem.

Admiral CURTZE. Right.

Admiral RICKOVER. If you have adequate radiographic procedures it doesn't make any difference because the radiograph will show whether you have a fault in your welding and you can correct it.

Admiral CURTZE. That is right.

Representative BATES. The welders to whom I talked said this was a new experience and they did not feel satisfied with it. However, that was 4 or 5 years ago.

Admiral CURTZE. I watched this a month or two ago with completely submerged arcs; doing everything downhand under control and it was a beautiful job.

Captain KERN. Admiral Curtze, in that area there have been new NDT techniques developed to inspect twin arc welding by ultrasonics and we have controls now on the twin arc welding techniques that we did not have at that time.

Admiral CURTZE. May I proceed, sir?

Representative HOLIFIELD. Go ahead.

Admiral CURTZE (reading): Further, it has been possible to backfit improvements to minimize the problem of fatigue cracking in earlier HY–80 submarines whose design details contributed to stress concentrations that became significant under cyclic loading.

The later submarines incorporated improved structural details which lower the stress to which the connections are subjected, thereby further decreasing probability of fatigue cracking problems. Although fatigue is not peculiar to HY–80 but is a problem in any highly stressed steel under cyclic loading, special care must be exercised in its use. The surveillance program is being carried out as was recommended.

Thus, the submarine structural program has been and promises to continue to be a highly productive and effective effort. Continuous and active review of all aspects of the use of HY–80 steel in submarine structures assures the integrity of the submarine hull.

The *Thresher* design appraisal board, Admiral McKee's board, made an independent examination of the use of HY–80 structure in submarines, and concluded in its report of July 15, 1963, that "HY–80 clearly is the best steel for military submarine hull construction and the only satisfactory material available today." This conclusion was based on the facts that HY–80 steel is the only proven material in common usage among submarine builders which will give the structural strength, toughness, resistance to brittle fracture, workability, weldability, and fatigue resistance with an adequate strength-to-weight ratio to achieve the vertical sea room required by modern high-performance submarines.

I am convinced that we have the best material currently available. We have the ability to weld it. We are increasing our efforts to train our people in the use of radiography as a welding inspection tool. Control of auditing of weld inspection at Bureau and shipyard levels has been tightened. The loss of radiographs as happened in *Tinosa* will not happen again—and I will address myself to this in the next paragraph.

"TINOSA" RADIOGRAPHS

The shipyard commander at Portsmouth ordered an investigation into the loss of radiographs for *Tinosa*. See app. 7, p. 155.) The findings reveal a shipyard team which resembled a football team whose general blocking, tackling, and ball handling, in other words, the fundamentals around which a winning team is built, were just not up to the competition. Further, the team members wondered why they did not win. For example, "lost" radiographs were termed "lost" because the chalk marks locating the key points in an overlapping series of photographs were rubbed off or painted out or a picture given to a welder to show him where repairs were required would be stuffed in his pocket after the repair was made and not returned to complete the record. The last measure of attention to detail just was not there.

Inasmuch as every yard has had growing pains in this area and the general quality control problem is now generally recognized for what it is, a personal, individual problem; and organizations exist and are at work to keep everyone's nose constantly rubbed into the problem whether they like it or are self-styled, self-starters, self-perpetuators, or not.

SUBMARINE SAFETY CERTIFICATION CRITERION

As noted above, shortly following loss of *Thresher* depth restrictions [classified matter deleted] were imposed by operational commanders on all submarines with deep design test depths. [Classified matter deleted.] As already has been stated one of the primary efforts of the submarine safety program was to define the efforts necessary to remove these restrictions to permit Bureau of Ships certification of the material condition of these submarines for unrestricted operation to design test depth. It consists of the following categories of design, construction, installation, and testing:

1. Critical piping systems and hull boundary integrity

(*a*) The first portion of this criterion consists of the work necessary to provide an assured level of integrity in the hull boundary and critical piping systems. These are the sea water, high-pressure air, hydraulics, and oxygen. Primary emphasis is placed on sea water systems since sea connections penetrate the hull envelope and, together with the piping systems they serve, appreciably extend the sea water excluding portions of the hull subjected to full submergence pressure. A review of the findings of the court and Board makes it evident that these systems should be given the same painstaking fabrication and inspection treatment as is given to the hull structure. We are attacking these problems along two basic lines: (1) the fewer such systems, the lower the risk; (2) the higher the integrity of the remaining systems, the smaller the risk. This criterion provides integrity whereas improvements discussed later address themselves to reduction in the extent sea water piping aboard. The following areas are ones of particular concern where increased nondestructive testing, improved materials, or redesigned components must be provided.

Speaking of joints, in view of past failures in silver brazed piping joints, certain joints depending upon size and location must be proved by ultrasonic inspection if sil-brazed or be welded and radiographed. Specifically:

(1) All joints in sea-connected systems between the hull and backup valves for all submarines, and inboard down to one-half inch in sea water, that are open below 200 feet for all [classified matter deleted] submarines. All joints in these areas [classified matter deleted] and above in all sea water systems must be welded.

(2) High pressure air system piping necessary to the integrity of the new emergency main ballast tank blow system.

(3) Hydraulic piping whose failure could cause loss of all means of stern plane control, must be ultrasonically inspected if sil-brazed or in lieu of that welded.

(4) All oxygen system piping must be welded.

(b) *Flexible connections.*—The history of failures in flexible hoses installed in submarines for silencing requires replacement of certain sizes with a more reliable design of flexible connection and in those smaller sizes where hoses are permitted, installation of hoses of a more reliable type. The size of replacement required is dependent upon design test depth of the submarine. In addition revised instructions on the design, installation, and replacement for both hose and the new design flexible connections were issued in December 1963.

(c) *Castings.*—Improved radiography techniques and standards have been developed and invoked to an increasing degree in recent classes of submarines. Application of this radiography has resulted in rejection of large numbers of castings due to radiographic defects. Consequently, it is necessary to examine castings in vital areas such as outboard or backup valves in sea-connected systems and large sizes inboard and exposed to sea pressure to insure an adequate level of integrity.

(d) *Aluminum bronze.*—The determination that aluminum bronze of certain chemistry and in certain locations was subject to intergranular corrosion in contact with sea water requires the elimination of these unsatisfactory materials from the hull boundary and certain sea water systems. Individual ship surveys have indicated that in certain locations where components are galvanically protected by surrounding ship structure this material is acceptable in service.

(e) *Fasteners.*—In certain cases shipyards material control systems have been inadequate to insure that proper fasteners such as bolts and studs were of proper material. Consequently, a survey of all fasteners in the hull boundary is being conducted to assure that materials installed are acceptable. More stringent material control procedures have improved the overall material control.

(f) *Design review.*—To insure that all aspects of design affecting the hull boundary and sea water systems are acceptable for the service intended throughout the life of the submarine, a design review is being conducted for deep depth.

Representative HOLIFIELD. May I ask if all of these items you are listing here are in effect at this time or are they planned to be put into effect?

Admiral CURTZE. They are in effect at this time, sir. I have included in this paper a schedule for completion of these tasks for all submarines in existence that require this kind of attack.

Representative HOLIFIELD. Is it possible to make these revisions retroactively where you have to go between the inner hull and outer hull with connections?

Admiral CURTZE. We are doing so at great expense, sir. We don't think we will be able to finish all of this until [classified matter deleted] but we are doing so.

Representative HOLIFIELD. Does that mean the submarines which are not changed will be restricted [classified matter deleted] until they are changed?

Admiral CURTZE. That is right, sir.

Representative HOLIFIELD. Even though it takes until [classified matter deleted].

Admiral CURTZE. That is right, sir.

Representative BATES. Admiral, have you completed all of these changes on any submarine?

Admiral CURTZE. No, sir.

Representative BATES. None of these submarines is going below [classified matter deleted].

Admiral CURTZE. Not yet, sir.

Representative BATES. As soon as you complete these changes they will start to go to maximum test depth?

Admiral CURTZE. Yes, sir. Of course, all of these requirements are being ground into the specifications for the submarines that are being contracted for. They will be delivered so fitted. There are certain submarines just barely started in our overall program into which these are being backfitted, and these submarines will be delivered with this capability.

Representative BATES. Is *Tinosa* the first one that will be completed?

Admiral CURTZE. She won't be the first one to be certified; no, sir.

[Classified matter deleted.]

Admiral CURTZE. The *Tinosa*, we hope, will be going to sea in August of this year. She has not been completely taken apart and put together in all of these areas.

Admiral RICKOVER. We do test all current submarines to [classified matter deleted] on their trials even though we don't operate below [classified matter deleted]. They are tested at [classified matter deleted].

Admiral RAMAGE. May I point out that we make three dives [classified matter deleted].

Admiral CURTZE. I will cover that in detail in just a few seconds.

WELDING VERSUS BRAZING

Representative HOLIFIELD. May I go back to item 1(a), "Joints," for just a minute.

You state,

All joints in sea-connected systems between the hull and backup valves for all submarines, and inboard down to one-half inch in sea water open below 200 feet for all [classified matter deleted] submarines. All joints in these areas [classified matter deleted] inches and above in all sea-water systems must be welded.

In your answer did you intend to convey that is going to be done to all existing submarines?

Admiral CURTZE. We are doing the welding only on the SS(N)–671, which is the one we have just contracted for. This is for half inch and above in all critical systems. This will not be done on the other boats.

Representative HOLIFIELD. Then this is not retroactive as my question would have implied a minute ago.

Admiral CURTZE. [Classified matter deleted] inches and larger, sir, but half an inch to [classified matter deleted] inches——

Admiral RICKOVER. The SS(N)–671 submarine will have a [classified matter deleted]. The Bureau is about to award the contract. That is the first one and the only one that will have these things that you have mentioned. The others and the new ones that have been awarded this year do not have it.

Representative HOLIFIELD. This interests me. If this is a requirement on future submarines, why shouldn't it be a requirement for existing ones? Is it because the expense is too great?

Admiral CURTZE. We don't think with our present knowledge of silver-brazed joints, Mr. Chairman, that we are in as bad a position as we thought we were a year ago. We have trained our people. We have trained people in the use of this ultrasonic testing technique. Our specifications have been raised to reject any joint less than 60 percent full bond throughout the periphery of the joint where something less than 40 percent is all that is required to develop the strength of the pipe as a pipe, not as a joint. We think by this careful quality control and training that we need not backfit all of these submarines with welded joints and fittings.

Representative HOLIFIELD. Are you requiring it on the SS(N)–671?

Admiral CURTZE. Yes, sir; we agree with Admiral Rickover that this is the way to go.

Representative HOLIFIELD. This seems inconsistent to me. I could understand it if you were to say, "This job is just too big and we cannot go back to it, but there is going to be a permanent requirement that the depth will be [classified matter deleted]." I could understand that flexibility, but I can't understand your saying that this is something we are going to do in the future for safety purposes, but we are not going to make it retroactive.

Admiral CURTZE. Mr. Chairman, it is possible to configure the design of a new boat to permit this. It requires different spaces between the piping. As Admiral Rickover has pointed out, he mocks up everything to permit this to happen.

In the meantime we are developing automatic pipe-welding machines which will operate in these constricted spaces. This is being done at Mare Island. Admiral Brockett and I feel strongly that wherever possible we should go to 100-percent welding and the SS(N)–671 is the first ship in which we are actually trying that.

We don't really know what all of the problems will be. The problem of getting the boat back down to deep submergence in as short a time as possible is a tremendous one. If you go to welded joints throughout, we automatically generate a radiographic bottleneck to insure the integrity of the joints.

Right now we have a silver-brazing capability. Admiral Brockett and I are not convinced in our own minds yet that with silver braze, inspected with the techniques we have available to us and the people trained at the level they now are, that we don't have a secure system.

One other thing we are looking at is the configuration of the piping in new boats. The reason for this is that when the hull of a submarine compresses, the piping system within them with fixed-end connections alters. At least those secured to bulkheads or pumps or the hull of the ship are wracked when the ship compresses. We have to go through the piping systems of the submarine and make an entirely new layout in *671* so that compression of the boat doesn't bring about sheer failures and wracking failures in the body of the pipe, not in the joint.

We feel that we are on sound ground for these reasons, Mr. Chairman.

Representative HOLIFIELD. Then is *671* to be the only one or will all of the submarines after *671* be given this new treatment?

Admiral CURTZE. I can just give you my opinion on that, sir, and I think Admiral Brockett shares it. We wish to try for all critical systems to be welded from *671* on out, sir.

Representative HOLIFIELD. All right, proceed.

2. *Flooding control and recovery*

Admiral CURTZE. In addition to the above minimum level of integrity in the hull boundary and critical piping systems, an improved flooding control and recovery capability will be installed.

(*a*) An emergency main ballast tank blow system in addition to the normal main ballast tank blow system must be provided with a capability of recovering from a [classified matter deleted] hole flooding continuously. This system basically short circuits air from the air storage banks into the ballast tanks and has a minimum of components and piping which could fail or restrict the flow of air.

(*b*) *Sea water valve control.*—Centralized remote hydraulic control will be provided for hull and backup valves in sea-connected systems open to the sea below 200 feet to control flooding in case of failure of piping or components inside the ship. Both hull and backup valves [classified matter deleted] and larger will be so controlled for all submarines and hull valves down to 1 inch in [classified matter deleted] submarines. Provision will be made to provide flexibility to permit retention of main propulsion power while shutting down the maximum number of other valves from a minimum number of levers.

Representative HOLIFIELD. Will this be done retroactively wherever it is possible?

Admiral CURTZE. Yes, sir. As a matter of fact the main ballast tank emergency blow system is in a lot of operating systems right now. This is one thing we went at immediately, to provide immediate capability for surfacing under any normal casualty condition.

(*c*) *Access to and operation of vital equipment.*—Each ship is being studied to determine the adequacy of access to and operation of vital equipment to insure that the tight machinery arrangement, silencing efforts, and habitability improvements do not encroach on essential access during emergency.

Representative BATES. What happened on icing? What have you done with respect to icing?

Admiral CURTZE. I will talk to that later, sir, but I don't mind discussing it now. (Also see pp. 32, 35, 37, and 112.)

Representative BATES. All right, as long as you are going to cover it.

3. Ship control

Admiral CURTZE. High-speed, highly maneuverable submarines on occasion have experienced malfunctions of diving planes causing loss of depth control which could have resulted in serious consequences due to large trim angles and exceeding test depth. The diving plane system is being reviewed and steps taken to insure that maximum integrity exists in these systems.

All work outlined above must be documented to permit the Bureau of Ships to audit and certify that the required level of integrity and system improvements have been accomplished.

The above certification criterion to permit unrestricted operation at design test depth will be conducted on all [classified matter deleted] design test depth submarines. Submarines of lesser depth will not be given this full submarine safety treatment in view of their lesser operating depths and years of successful operation including wartime. However, some specific submarine safety improvement modifications may be accomplished on these boats.

In addition to the above certification requirements, submarine safety improvements not required for certification but which provide significant improvements in safety will be accomplished in certain ships on a case basis depending upon their status of construction, operating depth, and feasibility from an arrangement and cost viewpoint. There are in general:

[Classified matter deleted.]

Admiral CURTZE. There is a tremendous improvement in the piping that is being really first realized in the 671.

Representative HOLIFIELD. This is possible because of new design. Is that it?

Admiral CURTZE. Yes, sir; but we are finding—and I will address that later too—we are finding it possible to backfit some of this thinking; however, not as a mandatory, as an improvement item.

2. Use of improved fittings where these penetrate the hull.

3. Protection of electrical equipment from damage due to sea water system failures.

4. Restricted size in sea water valve openings under certain operating conditions.

5. Reduction in the number of hull penetrations.

Next is our overall plan of accomplishment, addressed to when these boats will come into being.

PLAN OF ACCOMPLISHMENT

The accomplishment of the above certification and submarine safety improvements will be carried out along the following lines:

New construction

Polaris submarines now under construction of the SSBN–616 class.—
On a not-to-delay ship delivery basis although certain portions must be
complete prior to deployment. Depth restrictions will not be removed
until complete certification requirements are fulfilled.

*Polaris submarines in the fiscal year 1963 and subsequent year build-
ing programs SSBN–640 class.*—All certification items will be accomplished prior to delivery which will permit lifting of current depth
restrictions.

Thresher-type attack submarines of the SSN–593 class prior to
SSN–612 will be treated in the same way as SSBN–616 class.

SSN–612 to SSN–615 and SSN–621 will be delivered certified for
test depth operations.

SSN–637 class will be delivered certified for test depth operations.

Addressing myself to submarines in operation—the old boats:

SS and SSN's starting overhaul in fiscal year 1964 will be certified
where practicable based on availability of designs and material procurement. They are at the bottom of the list naturally.

SS and SSN fiscal years 1965 and subsequent will be certified for
test depth operation during their overhaul.

SSBN's not certified during construction will be certified for test
depth during first overhaul commencing with SSBN–598.

This program will be brought to fruition [classified matter deleted]
in total.

The following paragraphs address themselves to our plans for
funding.

COST OF MODIFYING SUBMARINES

Representative HOLIFIELD. Could we take up this individual ship
cost for just a minute? I don't think you have read that.

Admiral CURTZE. No, sir; I will take that up and I will skip the rest.

Individual ship costs for submarine safety certification and improvements are dependent on the size, depth, complexity of the ship
and the amount of work accomplished during current construction.

Representative costs are as follows: SSN–585, $4,152,000; SSBN–
609, $8,366,000; SSBN–626, $8,289,000.

For the SS's—and I am trusting my memory—about $200,000 and
for the later World War II boats—what would be the most expensive?

Captain KERN. $2 million.

Admiral CURTZE. The paragraphs that come after this address themselves to this in greater detail.   I think we could just make that part of
the record rather than taking time to read it now.

Representative BATES. At one time it was estimated you would need
$50 million to bring about the necessary repairs, welding, etc.   Does
that figure mean anything to you?

Admiral CURTZE. It doesn't ring a bell to me, sir.

Representative BATES. I heard it from several sources.

Admiral CURTZE. A number like that must have been for some kind
of a program.

Representative BATES. It was $50 million to be taken out of the cur-
rent fiscal year's funds.

Admiral RAMAGE. I think it was for the whole package in that particular year.   It covered several submarines.

Representative BATES. Right.

Admiral RAMAGE. This is an individual breakdown by individual boats.

Admiral CURTZE. The first problem, sir, was to address ourselves to those boats that would come in for overhaul during the fiscal year and our first requirement for money was to cover that. I don't remember the number, but I know we required a large sum of money to get cracking on this.

Representative BATES. These figures were included in the $50 million.

Admiral CURTZE. If you will turn to the next page, you will see by fiscal year the total amount of money we are actually spending on submarine safety improvements on the ships under overhaul and checking out some other submarines that are coming into overhaul for planning purposes would be: $34 M for fiscal year 1964, $50 M for fiscal year 1965, and $46 M for fiscal year 1966.

Representative BATES. Fiscal year 1964 estimates for repairs and so on was 34——

Admiral CURTZE. Yes, sir——

Admiral RAMAGE. 34 and 65 is 50——

Admiral CURTZE. You can see the breakdown by fiscal year of the amount of money available.

(Portion of statement not read but to be included in this record follows:)

Funding plans

1. All operating submarines prior to SSN-594 and SSBN-616 will receive certification during first or second overhauls and will be funded with O. & M.N. SSN-594 and subsequent SSN's will be funded under SCN either during construction, PSA or first overhaul. SSBN's 616 class will be funded under SCN for items accomplished prior to deployment and under O. & M.N. for remaining work accomplished during first overhaul. SSBN-640 and subsequent SSBN's will be funded under SCN.

The total requirements of the submarine safety program for O. & M.N., R.D.T. & E., and OPN have been determined and are outlined below. Fiscal year 1964 funds have been reprogramed within current appropriations. Funds for subsequent years will be incorporated in annual budget requests. Changes in the overhaul schedule and adjustments in unit costs may occasion some future changes in these total figures:

[In millions of dollars]

	Fiscal year 1964	Fiscal year 1965
O. & M.N.	25	45
R.D.T. & E.	6	4
OPN	3	1
Total	34	50

The total funding requirements for SCN funding have been determined and are as follows:

[In millions]

Fiscal year 1958	$22. 4
Fiscal year 1959	36. 1
Fiscal year 1960	26. 5
Fiscal year 1961	29. 9
Fiscal year 1962	41. 3
Fiscal year 1963	28. 8

It has been determined that the above submarine safety effort can be funded with currently available SCN funds.

Length of overhauls

The impact of overhaul length of SS, SSN, SSBN, and A-3 retrofit has been evaluated and is outlined below:
[Classified material deleted.]
I think of interest on the next page are the plans for implementation calling [classified matter deleted].

Implementation

The above certification and improvement work has been implemented by change orders in all new construction submarines and by letter on all applicable submarines undergoing overhaul during fiscal years 1964 and 1965. Current plans call for completion of certification according to the following time schedule:
[Classified material deleted.]

General improvements

In addition to the above certification and improvement items developed for and being applied to individual submarines many general improvements and developments of interest are being accomplished under the submarine safety program.

Flooding recovery capability

Flooding recovery capability studies have been completed in all post-World War II classes of submarines, and reports of these studies have been provided to forces afloat. In addition the recovery capabilities for most classes of submarines with the improved emergency main ballast tank blow system required for certification have been conducted and issued. These studies and others will be incorporated in a new damage control manual for which prototypes are being prepared. Indications to date are that, with a few exceptions, an increase or redistribution of high-pressure air storage is not required in existing submarines. The flooding recovery studies conducted to date indicate that the use of stored high-pressure air provides adequate recovery capability in current operating and new construction submarines.
[Classified matter deleted.]
These emergency main ballast tank blow systems have a minimum of piping, joints, and components installed to minimize the potential of failure or freezeup. New blow valves have been developed which provide the desired high air flow rates and permit positive remote control over the valve and local manual overrides. All plans and components for this system are reviewed and approved by the Bureau of Ships. Tests of this blow system in submarines where installed have been conducted on the surface and down to depths [classified matter deleted] to demonstrate its reliability and greatly increased recovery potential of this system over the normal main ballast tank blow system provided in earlier submarines.

DEBALLASTING SYSTEM TESTS

Representative BATES. Mr. Chairman, may I ask a question?
On these tests, do you blow as you would in time of emergency?
Admiral CURTZE. Yes; blow first on the surface and then to satisfy ourselves that this freezing up is no longer a problem; that by removing the restrictions in the line, by having the direct bottle through control valve back into a tank arrangement—we could blow unrestrictedly; we have done so, starting on the surface and going ultimately to the [classified matter deleted] level. We have actually blown up from that level.
Admiral RICKOVER. We do that on all trials. The lever for doing that is right where the captain stands. Even though there isn't any emergency, on trials they test it, anyway.
Representative HOLIFIELD. This was not done before. You only had your dockside blowout. Actually this doesn't go to the depth where the *Thresher* apparently got into trouble. [Classified matter deleted.]
Admiral RICKOVER. There wasn't enough blowing capability until these modifications were made.

Representative HOLIFIELD. I know, but even with additional air and additional capacity you have still tested. [Classified matter deleted.] Isn't that correct?

Admiral CURTZE. It is our intention. For example, if we were to certify a ship tomorrow, we couldn't go to [classified matter deleted] on the first dive. We would take it incrementally and blow up from the incremental steps until we had the final blow.

[Classified matter deleted.]

FREEZING DEBALLASTING AIR LINES

Representative BATES. Did you ever blow at all—even at dockside—to the maximum degree before this happened to the *Thresher?* [1]

Admiral CURTZE. I don't know. I don't think so.

Representative BATES. Did you on *Tinosa?*

Admiral CURTZE. Yes, sir, and we found all of the troubles: Freeze and jamming of screens, which have since all been removed.

Representative HOSMER. Do you have a substitute for the strainer or do you just do without it?

Admiral CURTZE. A clean system.

Captain KERN. There is no strainer in the emergency blow system now, sir.

Representative BATES. There wasn't supposed to be in the other one either.

Captain KERN. Do you mean the original system?

Representative BATES. Yes.

Captain KERN. It depends on the ship and the particular system design. There were some requirements for strainers.

Representative BATES. Let's say the *Thresher* and be specific.

Captain KERN. In *Thresher* there were certain locations that were not supposed to have strainers.

Representative BATES. And you were supposed to take them out.

Admiral CURTZE. If my memory is correct, I think they were designed in and we had written orders to take them out and it hadn't been done yet. Is that right?

Captain KERN. Yes. There was more than one strainer though. Certain strainers remained. Others came out.

Representative BATES. My question related to the ones that were supposed to be taken out. Were they taken out?

Admiral CURTZE. In other ships.

Representative BATES. No, in *Thresher*. (Also see pp. 32, 35, 37, and 108.)

Captain KERN. We don't believe they were.

SEA WATER SYSTEMS

Admiral CURTZE. All sea-connected systems on all post-World War II classes of submarines are being studied with the objective of reducing the number of hull penetrations and the extent of piping subjected to submergence pressure. Work is being done by the Bureau with assistance from naval shipyards and design activities with completion anticipated in September 1964. Efforts are being limited to corrective measures which can be accomplished without enlarging the hull. Depending on the class, changes are expected to vary from a

---

[1] Subsequent to the loss of *Thresher*, dockside tests were conducted of an identical high-pressure air system aboard the *Tinosa*, sister ship to *Thresher*. The *Tinosa* was nearing completion at the Portsmouth Naval Shipyard. The purpose of the high-pressure air system is to provide air in order to displace water from the ship's ballast tanks thereby increasing buoyancy. During the tests, ice formed on the screen-type wire strainers in the air piping system cutting off air flow to the ballast tanks. Also see pages 32, 35, 37 and 108.

partial secondary low-pressure cooling system to minor modifications to existing systems.

In order to make the task of ruptured system isolation easier and more immediately responsive to personnel action, we are designing, developing, and testing sea water hull or backup valves that will provide intermediate valve positions that better match valve opening with actual sea water flow requirements for operation of the submarine or components served at less than full power or full load.

Valves with intermediate positions have been designed by the Electric Boat Division, General Dynamics Corp., and will be used in future construction programs if it makes operational engineering and safety sense to do so. We are not sure it does yet. Studies are underway to highlight problems which would result from using the currently installed hull and backup valves in throttled positions to reduce flow rate. If developments indicate this is desirable, procedures will be given to the fleet.

There are 3,000 joints in the sea water systems in *Thresher* and over 5,000 joints in other critical systems. A reduction in these joints will give an immediate return in increased security of the system. We are redesigning the piping systems in new construction submarines with joint elimination as one of the primary objectives. Those joints remaining must still be either welded or brazed. Freedom of choice between all welded or a mix of welded and silver brazed joints in existing submarines is limited by the space problems inherent in any major revamp of piping layouts to provide the accessibility required to use present welding techniques.

We are requiring more welded joints in new construction and our latest design will require all critical piping systems to be welded. It is worthy to note that all previous tests have shown that a properly made silver brazed joint is equal to a properly made welded joint. The problem is to insure a joint properly made. Additional tests have been conducted which reconfirm the strength of silver brazed joints under all service conditions. New techniques in welding may simplify the use of additional welded joints.

A single document has been developed and published covering all aspects of silver brazing of submarine critical piping system joints. This document includes brazer qualification, workmanship, quality control, inspection requirements, acceptance standards, ultrasonic inspection procedures, and recordkeeping. Field experience and tests to date indicate a high degree of reliability is provided in silver brazed joints using these instructions and inspection techniques.

MATERIALS, FABRICATION METHODS, AND TEST PROCEDURES FOR CRITICAL PIPING SYSTEM

Those piping and end connections which cannot be eliminated must be the equal of the hull. Material fabrication methods, destructive and nondestructive test standards, specifications, training, and programs for continuing surveillance were reviewed. Mil Standard 438-B for piping systems was "updated." This, backed by required inspection, will insure materials specified in hazardous piping systems are compatible with the medium they confine, their shipboard environment, and are exclusive; that is, may not be substituted for without qualifying tests and Bureau of Ships approval.

We are reviewing ship specifications, Mil Standards, NAVSHIPS Publications, BUSHIPS Technical Manual, and quality control requirements to be sure these documents accurately describe the required fabrication processes and are consistent with one another. Most of these actions have been completed and necessary corrective action has been taken.

A complete review of manual welding procedures including training and equipment has been completed. Automatic in-place pipe welding is being developed at high priority at Mare Island Naval Shipyard. Silver brazing procedures have been improved and are currently under revision at all yards. Increasing use is being made of induction brazing. This had already been adapted to our piping problems by Mare Island Naval Shipyard.

A program is now being developed to completely review the area of fatigue as it applies to sea water systems.

Test techniques have been reviewed for all categories of nondestructive tests. Radiography and ultrasonic testing are currently the most useful and practicable. The remainder of the techniques are generally special purpose and no major program is underway at this time. However, new techniques will be kept under continuing examination to attempt to cut down the cost and time necessary to conduct the nondestructive tests now required.

Most importantly we are reviewing our existing training programs in shipbuilding and fleet activities to determine adequacy to meet the new requirements of silver brazing and welding of hazardous piping systems.

Training facilities have been established at the Electric Boat Division, General Dynamics Corp., for fleet units in the area of sil-brazed fitting inspection by ultrasonics. Training programs for radiographers and radiographic readers have been developed under the Portsmouth welding project and have been submitted to all interested activities. Radiographic training programs indicate additional needs for training facilities. This will be studied. We not only have to guarantee initial safety but life-of-the-boat safety. We do have programs for continuing hull surveillance; we are developing similar programs for sea water systems in conjunction with the submarine type commanders. The equipment needed for pipe surveillance exists. Standards for pipe replacement have already been issued.

Machinery components

Machinery components in hazardous sea water systems must also equal the hull. The adequacy of components to resist cyclic stresses must be assured by developing accurate stress level design criteria.

The accuracy of stress level data for materials subject to fatigue loadings is under study. More accurate tests have been authorized to obtain fatigue data on cast copper-nickel, valve bronze and monel-monel and monel-steel weldments.

Full-scale fatigue tests are underway at Southwest Research Institute on main condenser heads which will further verify the adequacy of the fatigue stress data. Full-scale fatigue tests are planned on components further to check the adequacy of stress level data as well as the adequacy of the design configuration of the selected components.

A program of strain gaging main circulating piping and condenser inlet-outlet waterboxes during ships' trial dives is underway. Adequacy of piping and condensers was demonstrated for SSN-594 and

SSBN–608 in this way. This program is being expanded to cover a prototype ship for each main circulating system configuration, and broadened to include strain gaging of circulating pumps and valves for these systems.

Existing specifications for hydrostatic tests of pump casings and heat exchangers are being hardened to insure that these components will not fail under cyclic pressure surfaces. The specifications are being revised to require:

(*a*) Rigorous stress analysis, where analysis is possible.

(*b*) Require stress gaging and cyclic fatigue testing, where analysis is not possible.

Representative heat exchanger waterbox heads are to be cyclic pressure tested under a current contract. Procurement requests are being developed to obtain similar tests of samples of each different pump design on submarines. In order to limit the problem we are taking a new look at standard components, sole source procurement and our procurement regulations. Relief in these areas may be required. We are reviewing existing material specifications for pump casings, heat exchanger heads and nozzles, bolting and tubing with regard to eliminating materials which although technically satisfactory, have poor acceptability records due to complexity of fabrication and inspection techniques.

Existing material specifications are being reviewed. Certain classes of aluminum bronze (low nickel) are being eliminated as allowable materials. Defective K-monel bolting has been found on submarines; nondestructive test procedures for identifying bolts have been developed and promulgated.

A program for an improved method for stress design of the main circulating water systems on submarines has been initiated. Problem areas include methods of computing hull deformations and machinery movements resulting from submergence effects and relating these to the cyclic strength criteria. This project is assigned to the Marine Engineering Laboratory for accomplishment, with the assistance of outside consultants.

Modifications to applicable equipment specifications are underway to specify inspection techniques and quality control procedures of these systems.

Every equipment already procured under inadequate inspection techniques is being examined for correctness of materials and radiographed or dye-penetrant-tested to determine soundness of welds and castings. Where possible equipments now connected to and cooled by sea water will be connected to fresh water cooling systems to further reduce the areas subjected to submergence pressure, and thus reduce the risk. This is a very fruitful area.

Protection of electrical systems from sea water

Although insuring integrity of the piping systems is the primary way to protect the electrical systems, we are looking at vital electrical components such as switchboards, group controls, rotating machines and controls, battery, separately mounted circuit breakers, emergency lighting and other items for adequacy of protection against SW jets, sprays, mists, and flooding.

Newport News Shipbuilding & Drydock Co. is preparing a proposal for enclosures for such components as switchboards and group controls. Emergency lighting is presently sufficiently protected. Action to upgrade the degree of enclosure of electrical rotating equipment is not contemplated.

An instruction has been prepared outlining means of sealing the bottom of switchboards from entrance of water, steam, and so forth.

Ship control systems

We are determining the boundaries of safe and hazardous operating conditions for each class of submarine and will promulgate this into the fleet on a progressive basis as specific parameters are determined.

We are looking at the old and investigating the possibilities of new and different concepts of ship control systems. These will include, but not be limited to:

(*a*) Investigation of rate control, position control, degree of automation, the reliance on electrical order signals and means for limiting plane angles at high speeds.

(*b*) Inclusion of new or modified sensor, instrumentation, and alarm systems to present the conning officer with immediate information as to ship safety.

(*c*) New methods to provide emergency pullout capability, and

(*d*) Simulator studies to determine the maneuverability versus safety trade-offs for various modes of control and control system designs.

We are concurrently examining the effects of machinery and operating equipment of very large angles which may occur during and after an emergency pullout and the stability and safety aspects of the submarine after recovery from a casualty.

Representative BATES. How do you provide for greater pullout capability and at the same time limit the angle in planes? Is that consistent?

Admiral CURTZE. No, it isn't really.

I think one of the boards made mention of this and said that there should be some mechanical arrangement to prevent the use of tremendous angles at high speed because you might get into trouble. We have approached it on the basis that if a mechanical stop wasn't the prudent thing to do, we might be able to change the valving so instead of having full angle with full movement of control, you would change the ratio so that full movement of control would ultimately result in one 5°.

Representative BATES. If you are going down at these tremendous speeds, isn't that the very time you need greater angle?

Admiral CURTZE. I think Admiral Ramage would be better able to talk to the operational difficulties of this.

Admiral RAMAGE. Essentially what we have in mind is to try to limit the amount of plane at high speeds because you don't need very much plane angle to control. Then, of course, we don't want catastrophic failure of that plane. To go to hard rise or hard dive at those speeds sometime you might lose control of the plane and put yourself in a hazardous condition.

So this is essentially another reason for trying to eliminate full throw at high speeds. Any one of these will then inject another possibility of casualty. You might need that plane so you have to have means of overriding any possible safety feature you put in there. This is being studied. I don't think we have an adequate answer.

Admiral CURTZE. Whatever we apply, of course, can only be applied if the operating people think this is the proper way to go and it makes sense to do it.

Admiral RAMAGE. I think one of the primary things we are trying to inculcate into people now is when they are going deep to be sure they have a positive trim. In other words, they don't go down heavy so that when they get down there they will be in a positive buoyancy so if anything happens at least you can start up and have that much advantage to begin with.

Representative HOLIFIELD. Proceed.

QUALITY ASSURANCE

Admiral CURTZE. No matter what we do on paper, without quality assurance and the means of achieving it, the program would fall on its face. Pressure and vigilance must be eternal, performance can never be taken for granted, the assumption must be made that no one will always perform to the required standards. Our success depends on using our materials and techniques to the limits of their inherent capabilities. The standards of lesser days and materials aren't good enough.

Quality assurance in naval and commercial shipyards has been improved by the requirement to have written procedures in each shipyard. And these requirements are part and parcel of shipbuilding specifications and contract. To permit more positive product control the Bureau of Ships in writing definitive specifications requiring compliance has issued instructions to the effect that departure from these specification requirements will be approved only by the Bureau of Ships. To insure the adequacy of the application of the quality assurance program in shipyards a system of audits has been established consisting of functional audits covering seven major areas of quality control. These are material identification, nondestructive testing, HY–80 steel fabrication, pipe welding, sil-brazing, inspection system, waivers and rip-out control. Each of the 12 shipyards involved in submarine construction or repair is required to conduct an internal audit of which 54 have been conducted to date. These are followed by a Bureau of Ships audit of which 30 have been conducted to date. To assure the adequacy of all quality assurance measures on individual new construction submarines, audits are conducted by the Bureau of Ships prior to sea trials. As of this date 21 such ship audits have been conducted.

Another important feature is the nondeviation plans.

On later classes of submarines certain critical areas such as sea water systems have been made nondeviation whereby all details of the system are developed by the design activity and approved by the Bureau of Ships. Any deviation from the basic design by fellow shipyards must be approved by the Bureau of Ships and made the subject of a contract change order. I might add that every one of these requests for deviation has to be accompanied by a complete rundown of engineering logic behind the request.

The above brief outline of the submarine safety program has attempted to convey to the committee the broad aspects of the program with its many investigative areas concerning submarine safety, the specific and detailed efforts applicable to individual submarines to permit their unrestricted operation down to their design test depth, and to touch briefly on some of the highlights of general improvements effected in the recent past. Most of this information and many specific details have been provided already to the committee through its staff and executive director. Additional details are available in documentary form which I would be pleased to make available to the committee or its staff for future study. The details of the submarine safety program tasks and subtasks and their status can be provided, the detailed requirements of the submarine safety certification criterion have been published and are available upon request, the ship-by-ship plan for accomplishment has been developed, is being implemented, and can be available as an up-to-date summary at any time. Detailed information concerning current estimates of submarine safety costs by individual ship hull numbers has been prepared and approved within the Defense Department. These costs, as outlined above, will be the subject of continual review and revision as more experience is gained in implementation of this program.

PERMANENCY OF PERSONNEL

The question of permanency of personnel, I think, is probably one of the most important ones.

During the earlier hearings great interest was shown in the permanency of assignment or tenure of our submarine engineering duty officers. Such aspects as continuity of responsibility, knowledge, and authority were cited as important, as indeed they are. I think it would be helpful for your committee if I explored this in some detail.

Within the engineering duty group there are 167 officers, about 17 percent of the total group, that form a hard core possessing the capability of submarine design, building, and repair. In addition, to meet the increasing demand we have for the past 2 years ordered additional officers to Navy yards and supervisors of shipbuilding offices to obtain training in the field of submarines. Also, we have officers in training at the submarine school and serving in submarines afloat who become engineering duty officers upon qualifying in submarines. The great majority of these officers are continuously assigned to duties involving the many submarine-type requirements from development of equipment to the actual construction or design of the final product. The present tour length of these officers is made as long as possible, 3 to 4 years. Succeeding assignments are made to take advantage of the increased technical and management abilities developed. This is one of the recommendations of the Pride Board, of which Admiral Brockett was a member. I feel that specialization is the order of the day; that specialization with increasing responsibility is not harmful to an officer's career.

In general, it is my policy to have engineering duty officers remain in one activity as long as they are effectively utilized, appropriately ranked, and available when considering the overall responsibilities of the Bureau of Ships. In general, the optimum tour length is about 4 years. More often than not, rotation within the engineering duty group is triggered by purely mechanical influences such as input, promotion, area tours—by that I mean tours outside the continental limits—and retirements. Rotation for professional development is not a prime consideration.

In general the following summary applies:

(a) It is my policy that a minimum of 4 years is the appropriate tour length in all ED flag billets. This cannot be realized in all cases because of the 7-year rank limitation, qualification of flag officers for a particular job, and the use of this talent for new high-priority programs.

(b) For captains, commanders, and lieutenant commanders a minimum of 4 years is also an appropriate tour length. However, many billets such as fleet staff, Boards of Inspection and Survey, and oversea assignments are limited to 2 and 3 years because of location and the need for cycling more officers through these jobs to gain up-to-date knowledge of the needs of the fleet for input into new designs and changes of existing ships. Many captains and commanders have remained much longer than 4 years with a particular project or ship-type problem where their specialized talents are required. Examples include Project Caesar, NTDS, Bullseye, special projects, nuclear power, SSN program, and other ship-type programs. In some cases these officers are rotated in 2 to 4 years from one geographical location to another but remain in the same project.

It may be of interest to you to compare Mare Island and Portsmouth insofar as officer longevity is concerned. Speaking to shipyard commanders you probably are already aware that Admiral Palmer is retiring this year. He has a very active case of glaucoma and finds it very difficult to carry on with the medication that is required. Captain Hushing, who is now the supervisor of shipbuilding at Groton, is going up to relieve him. He has a tremendous depth of continuity with respect to the nuclear submarine building program. He will carry this up to Portsmouth and bring his "can do" personality to Portsmouth along with the information he has available.

Admiral Fahy is at Mare Island. Admiral Brockett intends to just leave him there. He is tremendously competent and has brought Mare Island back into the competitive picture again. We think this is a good thing.

Speaking for the overall tenure of the other officers, and I know I am right plus or minus one or two people, of the 21 officers, for example, available in Mare Island, I believe before rotation 8 of them have been there longer than 3 years. 16 for longer than 3½ years, and some 15 better than 4 years.

Strangely enough the same situation obtains at Portsmouth at the moment, I think, out of 22 officers total. The shipyard commander, of course, is retiring. The only man that is leaving Portsmouth this year is one captain who is retiring shortly. Of the remaining officers, I believe, before rotation 18 out of 20 will have been there more than 3 years and perhaps 15 more than 4 years.

Inasmuch as one of my duties in the Bureau of Ships is the administration of personnel, in the assignment of personnel I make it a policy to call the shipyard commander or the officer who has these people working for him to determine when it would be most convenient in the normal tour length of 4 years to have this man relieved. It is my desire throughout this area never to cause a man to be relieved in the middle of an important project such as happened at Portsmouth in the case of the *Thresher*.

Representative HOLIFIELD. This is a very complete statement, Admiral.

I consider this latter part very important. This is something I have been waiting several years to hear. I am not saying you haven't been doing anything. However, the acknowledgement of the principle that specialization is the order of the day and that specialization with increased responsibility is not harmful to an officer's career, particularly in these highly technical and long leadtime fields, I think is a very important policy statement.

I hope it can be carried out within the bounds of reason. I know it will be interrupted by sickness, death, and possibly other personal reasons. But wherever possible that policy should be carried out with an adequate understudy who has the continuity of experience and knowledge to take over for the top man who has to be replaced during the leadtime on a certain major project.

It would seem to me that would plug one hole leading to a lack of continuity of knowledge and experience with a major project since it is the kind of knowledge and experience which cannot be acquired from a book. It can only be acquired gradually during the course of a project.

The Chair would like to note for the record that Secretary BeLieu came in shortly after this statement was started. Mr. Secretary, we are happy to have you here.

Do you have anything you would like to add to the admiral's statement?

Secretary BeLIEU. I would like to express my appreciation for the opportunity to be here. I apologize for being a little tardy. I had to go to the White House first.

I have no prepared statement. However, I came for two reasons. One is to express my appreciation to the committee for its help during the past months and especially to your fine and talented staff who have been strong arms on which to lean. They have helped us in this program.

Also I wish to express not only my own personal deep and abiding interest in this but that of Secretary Nitze. We both feel that while we have perhaps not achieved all of the things we would have liked certainly there has been a tremendous improvement over the last year. The cooperation that I personally have received from the Chief of the Bureau of Ships, Admiral Brockett, and his deputy, who has just finished reading his statement, Admiral Curtze and, of course, the constant positive support you always get from Admiral Rickover has made the work in this area very pleasant and fruitful in the last few months.

I would like to emphasize what has been said, Mr. Chairman, on the tenure of personnel. This is a positive program. We intend to follow it to the best of our ability. This is not my basic responsibility. My basic responsibility does not lie in the personnel field or the administration of such, but in our daily conversations we have emphasized and reemphasized that this is an age of specialization and that we need to keep people on these jobs longer. We intend to do that. I think it will pay off a great deal in the long run.

I personally have given Admiral Brockett instructions if higher authority outside of my office or outside of his seems to need for good reason to take talented people away from him, he shall not do this until he has come to me. This is one way of control.

Basically when you read this statement you see that we are endeavoring to understand more precisely what we need to do and then to follow up with precise and clear instructions and finally to supervise constantly so that these things are done. I think if these three fundamentals are followed, the program will be all right.

Representative HOLIFIELD. As we move into this highly technological age we not only need to have competent men who can use evaluated judgment on these highly complicated items we have to procure and use, but we need individual continuity with specific projects in certain circumstances in order to obtain efficiency in administration.

In my experience not only with this committee but with the Subcommittee on Military Operations of the House Committee on Government Operations in investigating the contract procurement mistakes that have been made or the defects in our procurement procedures that one of the primary defects we have found has been too rapid rotation of the responsible people and the rotation of people who have acquired a peculiar competence in a field. It has been the practice to put such people into something completely different and then bring in a person, perhaps with field experience or something like that into a technical procurement job, whereby you have a consequent loss of efficiency in the operation of the procurement contract.

Secretary BELIEU. There is no question but what that happens, sir.

Representative HOLIFIELD. Of course we are told this is necessary, because these men must have these rotations in order to have their record show up for promotions. This may have been all right in the early days, but I think now rules and regulations in recognition of excellent service within a specialized field ought to be developed to the point where rotation would be certainly secondary in importance and yet there would be no penalty against the individual involved.

Secretary BELIEU. I strongly subscribe to that principle.

Representative HOLIFIELD. I am glad to have that statement. I hope it is being applied throughout the Navy and other agencies of the Defense Department.

I hope the committee will bear with me while I go through as quickly as possible certain pickup questions from our previous hearings for the record since we may be needed on the floor.

In our earlier hearings it was stated that no action has yet been taken with reference to the commanding officer, U.S.S. *Skylark* and commanding officer Portsmouth Naval Shipyard. Is this still the case?

Admiral RAMAGE. No disciplinary action has been taken. Is that what you were referring to?

Representative HOLIFIELD. Yes.

Admiral RAMAGE. No, sir. The commanding officer, *Skylark*, has since been transferred to the command of a submarine—an advancement in his career.

Representative HOLIFIELD. And the commanding officer of the Portsmouth Naval Shipyard——

Admiral RAMAGE. He is retiring.

REASSESSMENT OF NEED FOR DEEP OPERATING DEPTH

Representative HOLIFIELD. Admiral Rickover testified that the operating forces should be requested to reassess the need for deep operating depth, in view of the fact that insufficient consideration might have been given to the increased hazards and reduced margins under casualty conditions at the time the decision was made to go [classified matter deleted].

Has the need for this operating depth been reevaluated?

Admiral RAMAGE. It is constantly under review, Mr. Chairman. I think we feel that we don't necessarily have to operate at [classified matter deleted] all the time but we do need the capability to go to those depths under certain operating conditions, certain tactical situations and in case we lost control that we would have an opportunity to recover safely. If you build a ship to go to, say [classified matter deleted] and you get into trouble for some reason or another and are forced deeper, you are lost.

It is the same thing as a high-speed jet aircraft. If you fly that aircraft at [classified matter deleted] off the ground and you get off bubble about 1°, you are underground before you know it. It is the same thing with these high-speed submarines. If you lose control for a minute with that amount of weight you have a tremendous amount of momentum and you have to have room to recover. If you build ships to go to [classified matter deleted] you are going to lose them all the time. I think [classified matter deleted] is primarily a safety factor here.

Admiral RICKOVER. May I say something?

Representative HOLIFIELD. Yes.

Admiral RICKOVER. I would like to tell you how that magic number [classified matter deleted] first came about. Several years ago the Bureau of Ships was asked, "How deep can you go without a major increase in the cost of submarines?" They made a quick calculation and came up with [classified matter deleted]. They said if you were to go beyond that the cost went up quite rapidly. That is the origin of that magic number [classified matter deleted].

There has been no real evaluation made yet. I don't believe Admiral Ramage knows this, but I do know it because I was involved in it at the time. I don't say that we should go to [classified matter deleted] or shouldn't go to [classified matter deleted]. I don't know. But an evaluation should be made by the operating people taking into account the increased danger involved. It was originally just on the basis of cost.

Sure you can intuitively say—as Admiral Ramage said in the comparison he made—you would like to go deeper. It is good to have a machine that can perform better. However, I claim we have to be realistic and we should find out how important this is first because right now we are incurring considerable expense in building these ships [classified matter deleted].

Admiral RAMAGE. I agree with Admiral Rickover that there is nothing particularly magic in [classified matter deleted] but——

Admiral RICKOVER. That is where many of the problems in construction come in because we are designing to [classified matter deleted]. Therefore, if we don't really need it, we could save money and increase safety.

Representative HOLIFIELD. I can understand the desire of an engineer to see if he can go, for instance, to this [classified matter deleted] depth.

Admiral RICKOVER. Yes.

Representative HOLIFIELD. It seems to me commonsense would indicate that very good tactical reasons should exist before you take on the additional burdens of the expense involved, the design and quality of the fittings, and all that sort of thing that goes into the hazards of operating at that depth. Has there really been a study from the tactical standpoint which says this will give us a certain amount of additional safety, maneuverability, freedom from detection, and sets forth just what the tactical advantages are and then compares these with the disadvantages in design, operation, and so forth?

Admiral RAMAGE. I can state the historical point of view. I know Admiral Rickover was there at the time this decision was made.

Admiral Burke had a board of inspection and survey make a study of this area. Various people came in and testified. We had a meeting in 1960——

Admiral RICKOVER. That was only an HY–80 meeting——

Admiral RAMAGE. At any rate the question before the house at that time was whether we should continue to design ships for [classified matter deleted]. At that time Admiral Burke asked me whether I thought we needed [classified matter deleted]. I said from the actual operational point of view I thought [classified matter deleted] was adequate, but for safety reasons we did need the additional depth in order to recover from any operational casualty. About right then and there he said, "All right, we will go to [classified matter deleted]." That is where the decision was made.

Secretary BeLIEU. I think there is another point we must not lose sight of. The raison d'être of the Navy, of course, is to fight successfully at sea. I don't think we will ever come to a finite answer to all tactics, but we are increasing our emphasis on the undersea warfare aspects of the Navy. There are many studies going on right now dealing in strategy and tactics. I don't know that anyone could prove today whether [classified matter deleted] or [classified matter deleted] would be the best depth at which to operate under any given combat condition.

Representative HOSMER. Whichever it is, it won't be that for very long.

Secretary BeLIEU. As we get more information about what a potential enemy might do, we might want to go to [classified matter deleted] or even [classified matter deleted] even as the B–17 went to 30,000 feet in World War II and now we can go much higher——

Admiral RICKOVER. I wish we could take the same attitude toward nuclear power in surface ships.

Representative HOLIFIELD. The committee would have the same wish on that.

Secretary BeLIEU. In any event there hasn't been a specific study made on this. Such study and thought as have been given to it have been given in a secondary way rather than having a primary study on this important point. As Admiral Ramage mentioned, it is continually under review. As we find different environmental conditions we can get better sonar ranges and better protection from the enemy detection and their sonars. This will be something we have to look at all the time. I don't think we can just review the need for [classified matter deleted] and revise it upward necessarily. I think we are doing our level best to improve the submarine to operate at this depth now.

Admiral WILKINSON. May I say for the record that to my knowledge there have been three studies in this area conducted since the time you mentioned. One is with the Electric Boat Division of General Dynamics Corp., and another with General Electric Tempo of Santa Barbara. They both relate to tactical things only and not to the cost of going deep or the problems of construction.

The general conclusion on both these studies is that there may be some tactical value in going down to [classified matter deleted] with respect to sonars, and what not, but they don't know for sure—and this is not really significant to this problem.

There has been one other study in the Office of Chief of Naval Operations that relates to the problems we are talking about. The general conclusion there is that we need the safety Admiral Ramage has been discussing but that, in general, the depth to which we would go is what the state of the art will allow us. Therefore, there is not a tactical justification for [classified matter deleted] feet or any other depth. But there have been three formal studies that I know of related to this problem.

Representative HOLIFIELD. That is quite responsive, I think, to the intent of my question at least.

REEVALUATION OF PRESENT ENGINEERING PRACTICES

Admiral Rickover in his testimony recommended that the Navy reevaluate its present practices where, in the desire to make advancements, the fundamentals of good engineering may have been forsaken, for example:

In the acceptance of a structural hull material which is prone to cracking and which frequently must be inspected and repaired as the price of being able to go deeper; and

In the use of high pressure hydraulic systems with their small clearances and delicate valves susceptible to malfunction by small particles of foreign matter.

I understand from your testimony today this has been under very careful study.

Admiral CURTZE. Yes, sir.

Representative HOLIFIELD. Then that the complexity and gadgetry resulting from automatic depth control, automatic depth seeking, and automatic steering should force the Navy to reevaluate the necessity for these systems.

Can you tell us what action has been taken in those two areas?

HY–80 STEEL

Admiral RICKOVER. May I say, sir, with respect to the first one you mentioned, which is known as the HY–80 problem and to which Admiral Curtze addressed himself at length, that I personally do not agree with using it until we learn more about it. I would rather take the lesser depth because cracks do develop in HY–80 material. The Bureau of Ships has been studying this for several years.

Recently there was a meeting among Admiral Brockett, Admiral Curtze, myself, and my people where they presented the result of these tests. However, if you take those tests on a statistical basis such as we use in the nuclear laboratories you can only give 10-percent credit to them because there have been only one or two tests and that is not enough to make a good judgment.

We do know there are cracks in this material—cracks that you can't easily see and that are covered up by various foundations. We have had this happen. One case where cracks developed in the HY–80 was [classified matter deleted] at Mare Island. You just don't know what you have.

I think it is basically unsound in engineering to use a material that has a propensity for cracking—that is from an engineering philosophical standpoint. If we could design for a lesser depth, we could use steel which is not susceptible to cracking. Obviously HY–80 has some advantages. As Admiral Curtze has said it is a much tougher material; it has higher yield strength.

Still I worry when cracks develop in a material and I can't readily inspect it all to determine whether I have cracks. That is my problem. I am not setting myself up as an expert on these things. I am merely talking as an engineer. I wouldn't use this in my equipment. In fact I wouldn't use this in the foundation of nuclear equipment because I am worried about cracks.

Representative HOLIFIELD. Are those cracks still showing up?

Admiral RICKOVER. Yes, sir. Maybe it is all right and nothing will happen. I certainly don't want to pose as any expert. You have other people who have spent many years in this field. I am just giving you my personal reaction as an engineer. I may be completely wrong on this.

HIGH PRESSURE AIR SYSTEMS

You also mentioned the area of high pressure air systems. We still use these systems. We have taken greater pains in their construction and in assembling them. But I still do not believe in using anything at a higher pressure or higher temperature in submarines unless we have to do so. If you have to do it, you do.

I would look into these things and see if I couldn't get them down to a lower pressure. Obviously lower pressure is safer. There is not as much chance of anything going wrong.

The third point you mentioned was the elimination of automatic devices. There is considerable feeling among the operating people in the Navy that many of these things should be eliminated. No attempt at elimination has been made. I think it would be wise to do so They are expensive. They take up space, add weight, and in many cases you need special people to operate them. You would save people. A reason given for the installation of this expensive and complex equipment is that it would reduce the number of men needed to operate the ship. Actually we have been able to reduce the number of untrained seamen, but we have had to increase the complement with highly skilled men to repair the complicated equipment. So there has been no saving of manpower. In fact, it has caused problems in skilled manpower.

There is a question in the minds of many people whether these equipments are necessary and whether they should not be removed. I think it should have a really thoroughgoing study. It is really more of an operational problem than one for the Bureau of Ships. If the operator doesn't want a thing, get rid of it. There is no substitute for simplicity—complication makes for unreliability.

Those are the three points.

Admiral CURTZE. I would like to repeat that I think as of this date HY–80 steel is the finest hull-building material we have for deep submergence submarines. I recognize that that steel is susceptible, as all steels are, to fatigue cracking. However, one of the things that makes it such a good steel is its toughness and once these cracks, which are almost bound to occur in time in any structure, do occur, they do not propagate with the same rate which is a higher degree of safety and we have assurance against a catastrophic failure of any particular joint much greater than we would of the alternate steel which could be used for submarines of lesser depth, namely the HTS steels.

I submit this steel is the best material. Even as late as today I have in my lap a piece cut out of [classified matter deleted] HTS steel, which indicates [classified matter deleted] is now suspect. It is full of cracks. So all I am saying is that HY–80 has so many advantages beyond the others that with the controls we now have at our disposal, with the hull surveillance systems and the programs we have in effect, we can keep it under control.

Representative HOLIFIELD. This gets into a field of expertness in which there is some controversy involved. Certainly the committee is not competent to make a judgment on this matter.

Admiral RICKOVER. Mr. Chairman, I will never talk about HY–80 again. I gave you my personal opinion. I just would not do it.

The cracking on [classified matter deleted] is in a frame which was of defective material when it was installed.

Why has it been necessary for the Bureau to spend millions of dollars investigating HY–80 over the last few years but none on other steel which is supposed to be just as bad? There is an anomaly there.

Admiral CURTZE. We haven't spent millions, but we have spent money to prove the one is tougher than the other.

Admiral RICKOVER. You know the other is fine. Nobody questions it. Everybody questions HY–80. But if the other is just as bad, you are using it in lots of places in the Navy.

Admiral CURTZE. You and I just have to disagree on that one.

Representative HOLIFIELD. Do you have any questions, Mr. Hosmer.

Representative HOSMER. No, Mr. Chairman. I merely wanted to note with pleasure the presence of the new shoulder board here today on Admiral Wilkinson.

Representative BATES. On page 17 of your statement you indicated you were requiring more welding and just below that you discussed silver brazing procedures. Are you using more silver brazing or less?

Admiral CURTZE. We are using less, sir.

We are trying to eliminate joints and in the new designs in these critical systems we are going to 100-percent welding.

Representative HOLIFIELD. Mr. Morris.

COMPLIANCE WITH SPECIFICATIONS

Representative MORRIS. Mr. Chairman, I believe in the other hearing there was some testimony with respect to a difference in the hull
propulsion part of the boat and the other part of the hull. Is there
still this difference?

Admiral RICKOVER. It is not a question of difference of material in
the hull, sir. The piping that was involved in the nuclear part was all
welded. Is that what you are referring to, sir? The same line of
piping that went into the nonnuclear part would be silver brazed.

Representative MORRIS. I think the word "standards" was used. As
I recall it, the testimony was that the standards in the propulsion part
were higher than in the rest.

Admiral RICKOVER. I have not relaxed or revised my standards.
Admiral Curtze's prepared statement on the correction of *Thresher*
deficiencies is some 23 pages long. This discussion of corrections is
not based on any known reasons for the loss of the ship for the simple
reason we do not know what caused the loss. It results from the
Navy's investigation into weakneses which have been found to exist at
the time of the *Thresher's* loss. I think one of the questions that
should result from this testimony—and I am not talking about the
present administration of the Bureau of Ships—is why it has been
necessary to have a 23-page discussion of items that are now being corrected as a result of the loss of *Thresher*. Unless we find the answer
to that question, we cannot be sure that we have taken all steps necessary to prevent another accident. While we may never know the
specific failure which was the cause of the *Thresher's* loss, we should
be able to reach a better understanding of the conditions which make
such failures possible, and then do everything we can to prevent their
recurrence.

In my opinion the *Thresher* is a warning made at great sacrifice of
life, that we must change our way of doing business to meet the requirements of modern technology. Our management concepts must
be changed if we are to keep pace with technology requirements of
our high-performance ships. We must correct the conditions that
permitted the inadequate design, poor fabrication methods and incomplete inspection to exist, if we are not to have another *Thresher*.

I have made a few notes. First there is written procedures for construction of ships. I have always had written procedures for the
nuclear part. They are now going to written procedures for the rest
of the ship.

They are now having audits. I have always had audits. The Bureau
is now going to have the yard keep records. We have always kept our
records. We have all our radiographs. At the beginning we required
them to be kept for 3 years. Now we require they be kept for 7 years.
The Bureau is now requiring that these records be kept.

Next is nondeviation. Right now the shipyards are permitted to
have deviations on nonnuclear items in a submarine. But not on the
nuclear items. We have never permitted any deviation, for nuclear
items; but the yards still are fighting it. It is only recently the Bureau
has stated that the yards cannot deviate from specifications without
their permission. We have always required this for the nuclear plant.
In fact, if anyone wants to change from our nuclear specifications, he

has to write an official letter, which we call a "degradation of specifications." That is an expression I have instituted. If a manufacturer wants to change anything, he must write an official letter requesting a degradation of specifications."

Representative MORRIS. Suppose he wants to upgrade the specifications.

Admiral RICKOVER. That has never occurred.

The Bureau is doing a great deal. The most significant thing, I believe, is adding more blow capacity to the ships. But they are now doing many other things. However, we have been doing these things all of the time.

Representative MORRIS. Wouldn't it be a more simplified procedure if you were to put those together.

Admiral RICKOVER. You believe in a certain religion so you think it would be a good idea for all the others because you know it is the best one. You can't legislate it.

We have used these procedures all the time. The Bureau of Ships has known about these procedures, but they thought they weren't necessary. The specifications on welding are the ones that have been in existence since the inception of the nuclear program but they weren't complied with in other parts of the ship. Sure it was a good idea. However, I think the way it ought to be done is if the Bureau or anyone else in the Navy thinks I am doing a pretty good stunt, they ought to copy it. If they think it is wrong, they shouldn't. We should have one set of standards for the entire ship. I thoroughly agree.

Representative HOLIFIELD. Admiral Rickover, I understand that before the *Thresher* incident at least there was quite a bit of pressure to get you to reduce some of your rather strict requirements in the selection of operators and the training of those operators. What is the status of that situation?

Admiral RICKOVER. The attempts toward "degradation of specifications" on personnel—I will use that simple expression—still go on. However, I have had fine cooperation from Vice Admiral Semmes, who is Chief of Naval Personnel. He has stopped a lot of the attempts at degradation. We have the cooperation of Admiral Ramage and Admiral Wilkinson and from the very top staff.

Our real problem is in the submarine staffs where nearly all of the people are nonnuclear people some of whom have a deep resentment against the nuclear navy because it has put them out of business. They are constantly trying to get the personnel degraded. It takes a lot of fighting to keep it going. In accordance with the request this committee previously made of me, I will advise you if the problem starts getting to the point where I need help.

Their argument is that the plants are running so well our high standards of selection and training aren't necessary. However, we have 45 submarines in operation now. By the end of this year we will have 51 in operation in all parts of the world. Because of the vast increase in the number of nuclear ships, and the correspondingly decreased attention we can therefore give to an individual ship it is all the more important to maintain rigid selection and training. We have to pay very close attention to any little thing that happens and a lot of little things do happen. It is because of the fact that we do have these trained people that not a single naval nuclear operation has ever aborted and, at this committee knows, they have all been safe. (See app. 13, p. 175.)

We do have this constant attempt to lower the selection and training required. My remedy for that would be to eliminate some of the unnecessary staffs and to take quite a number of people off the remaining staffs and send them somewhere in the rest of the Navy where they can be of some use. I think our trouble comes from having too many people around who are inimical to this program.

Representative HOLIFIELD. The committee would hope that a degradation of standards in the selection of operators and a degradation in their training would not occur. I can foresee a lot of trouble if we look upon this as a conventional submarine even though we hope in time it will become so. However, I would hope that there would be no deterioration in the specialized training that is necessary to understand the nuclear side of this and to appreciate the problems involved.

Mr. Secretary, as we prepare this record for printing, there are certain things we may need.

First we would like to have the status of the Navy's review of the reports submitted by the Naval Court of Inquiry and what responses have been made to the recommendations.[1] Also if you will assign some member of your staff or some other proper person to confer with Captain Bauser and others of our staff, we would appreciate it.

We would like to have your cooperation also in the review of the transcripts and in the identification of specific items which are classified as against those that are not classified so that such material can be deleted from the published record.

Secretary BELIEU. I will assign Captain Robbins right now for liaison with your staff and anyone else whom your staff thinks is necessary.

I would like to add one personal comment to the subject Admiral Rickover was discussing. This is something we understand and it has been discussed at the highest level—with the Secretary.

I don't know of any living viable organization that doesn't have a constant chitting book which pulls back and forth between the various compartments. It is our intention to keep this program going and to keep these procedures and standards. I know Admiral Rickover has complete freedom night and day in my office and the Secretary's office as well. So the committee does not need to fear there is any lack of attention to this area.

We would be most delighted to cooperate with you in any way. It is always a pleasure to do business with this committee, sir.

PERSONNEL AND ROTATION OF DUTY ASSIGNMENT

Representative HOSMER. Is it still rather difficult to get officers into the Polaris fleet because of the feeling that from a career standpoint they may be in one spot too long? Is there any of that feeling?

Admiral RICKOVER. Not at all, sir. The morale in both Polaris and other nuclear submarines is certainly as high as in any ship in the Navy.

Secretary BELIEU. I think this is evidenced as far as enlisted personnel is concerned by the fact that reenlistment is at an alltime high in the Polaris program.

---

[1] Action on recommendations incomplete as of December 1964.

Representative HOSMER. Off the record.

(Off the record discussion.)

Representative HOSMER. At one time there was a feeling it was a blind alley from a career standpoint.

Admiral RICKOVER. That was because the number of ships was growing so rapidly that in order to keep them going the people saw they could never get shore duty. That situation has started to change. With the larger number of officers being put into the program we expect in a short time that all of the normal rotation of duty, going to school and all of that will be possible. That is being worked out. We are taking some 400 young officers a year into the program now.

Admiral RAMAGE. I think a point to bear in mind is that we have never challenged the level of standard of quality of people going in. It was a question of getting them in sufficient numbers as the program was expanding and particularly where you can get sufficient numbers once you get the program rolling to feed them in from the bottom in direct input. We needed some level of competence and experience in people who had been to sea in submarines to be commanding officers and No. 2 and so on. We just can't take an ensign and put him in command of a ship of this type even though he has been trained. He has to have some additional experience of years and the benefit of other associations in the program. The big problem was to fill this gap of experienced officers. This has been done largely. At least as far as we can see now, the program is growing and all of these ships will be manned. Now it is just a question of how long these people stay with the program.

Representative HOSMER. As an officer in and of your submarine program does he have an opportunity to develop other phases of his career when the time comes? Is he at a disadvantage with a selection board?

Admiral RAMAGE. Up to this point we have been plowing him right back in because of the numbers that were being built and the rate of construction. But we anticipate from this point on that we can—and of course we have been breaking some of them off. There is Wilkinson, and we have some others.

Representative HOSMER. You will have to build some surface ships. You bust him out and make him an admiral, but there isn't any place for him so he has to get out of the program.

Admiral RICKOVER. We have trained or have under training, some 1,500 officers and 10,000 men. This has been a terrific program. When we put, for example, 15 Polaris submarines in commission in 1 year with their 30 crews, that is over 3,000 people we have to make ready. It is a great strain to maintain the quality. However, we are getting mostly young people. We take no enlisted man into training who has had over 4 years in the Navy and very few officers who have had over 2 or 3 years of commissioned service. This means we are going to get a lot of use out of them. So in a short time we are going to be able to have officers rotate to shore duty such as postgraduate school.

Representative HOLIFIELD. This committee is aware of this and is very proud of the record that has been made in the whole field of nuclear submarine activity. We want to continue to support it because we are deeply committed to the importance there is in this project.

Admiral RICKOVER. I am committed to have no radioactive accident.

Representative HOLIFIELD. I think that is important.

Admiral Rickover. I am committed to this committee.

Representative Holifield. I have said much the same thing in regard to our civilian reactors. If we err at all, we must err on the side of safety because the repercussions would be too great. It would be a tremendous tragedy if we had a nuclear accident within the confines of one of these ships.

Because of the urgency of the legislation on the floor, I must bring this meeting to a close at this time.

Thank you, gentlemen, for coming and testifying.

(Whereupon at 3 : 30 p.m., the meeting was adjourned.)

APPENDIXES

APPENDIX 1

NAVY MEMORANDUM CONCERNING SUBMARINE SALT WATER PIPING SYSTEMS

(RECEIVED SEPT. 13, 1961—1618)

FM Depcomsublant.
To: BuShips.
Info: CNO.
CINCLANTFLT.
COMSUBLANT.
COMSUBPAC.
Bt.

SUBMARINE SALT WATER PIPING SYSTEMS

A. CNO letter serial 1356P43 of August 25:

1. Recent instances of flooding in submarines because of defective sea water piping or flexible hoses are cause for grave concern.

2. Critical review of design principles and fabrication techniques and publishing of corrective measures resulted from *Barbel* flooding incident. Although recognizing that nature of problem was such that immediate and complete solution was not possible Tycom must emphasize that in spite of corrective measures LANTFLT salt water piping incidents continue to occur with alarming regularity. For example subsequent to *Barbel* incident:

A. *Skate* shock tests—silver-braze joint failures occurred on each shot. Cause attributed to faulty design.

B. *Thresher* first builders trials—¼-inch salt water vent line joint failed, cause attributed to use of steel vice monel pipe.

C. *Thresher* second builders trials—One-inch ID trim system priming line failed due lack silver-braze insert ring.

D. *Ethan Allen* builders trials—Threaded plug blew out of trim line priming line strainer. Electrical switchboards were sprayed, reactor scrammed, minor fires ensued. Cause attributed to use of improper strainer incorporating plug with tapered pipe threads.

E. *Snook* first builders trials—Three grease lines passing through the after engine room bulkhead carried away, cause attributed to faulty workmanship on flared fittings. 1¼-inch nipple in HPAC cooling water discharge pulled out of pipe boss at test depth. Cause attributed to use of stainless vice monel pipe, subsequent inspection during trial revealed leaking silver-braze joint in 5-inch line.

3. Recently following incidents have occurred because of flexible hose failures:

A. In LANTFLT, *Argonaut* flooded after engineroom and grounded two main generators when retaining ring on aeroquip flex hose fitting failed.

B. In PACFLT, *Caiman* flooded forward engineroom when 4-inch flex hose burst near test depth.

4. We have been fortunate thus far in that casualties have been handled promptly and correctly and that, except in case of *Ethan Allen*, electrical apparatus has not been involved. Continued dependence upon such tenuous and fortunate circumstances, particularly when considering additional hazards imposed under wartime conditions, is obviously unacceptable. COMSUBLANT appreciates efforts expended and results already achieved by BuShips in improving situation. However, it is considered that urgency of problem and inherent danger of disaster must be brought more forcibly to attention of all concerned and that corrective preventive action must be pursued even more aggressively than has been done. To this end, it is requested that BuShips take the following action on a top priority basis:

A. Impress on all building yards the serious consequences of laxity in design and fabrication of submarine piping systems. As exemplified in *Ethan Allen*, a seemingly minor departure from the rules can produce complex casualties which imperil the lives of submarines and/or render the ship unable to perform her mission.

B. Expedite action to eliminate improperly designed connections from all operating submarines.

C. Expedite replacement of steel retaining rings on flex hoses with monel and review flex hose failures to determine what further corrective action may be required to provide reliable installations.

D. Expedite development of reliable nondestructive test method for silver-braze fittings. This is urgently needed to enable operating forces to locate and repair defects.

E. In new design, reduce wherever possible potential hazard of salt water spray damage to electrical equipment by physical separation, shielding of salt water lines, provision of watertight closures for electrical equipment, or other appropriate means.

APPENDIX 2

NAVY MEMORANDUM CONCERNING SILVER-BRAZED PIPING IN U.S.S. "THRESHER"

DEPARTMENT OF THE NAVY,
BUREAU OF SHIPS,
Washington, D.C., August 28, 1962.

In reply refer to: C-SS(N) 593C1/9020—Serial 525-0232.
From: Chief, Bureau of Ships.
To: Commander, Portsmouth Naval Shipyard.
Subject: U.S.S. *Thresher* silver-brazed piping (U).
Reference: (a) Navshipyd Ptsmh conf ltr ser 0114–62 of May 9, 1962
      (b) Buships ltr ser 648X–160 of February 13, 1962
      (c) Buships ltr ser 525–1325 of May 29, 1962
      (d) Datmobas Report C–1399 of March 1962 (*Skipjack*)
      (e) Datmobas Report C–1445 of July 1962 (*Thresher*).
Enclosure: (1) U/T results *Thresher* hydraulic piping (prechock test available).

1. Reference (a) suggests that measures taken in *Thresher* (SS(N)593) to insure the integrity of silver-brazed piping are adequate and that no additional measures should be required. In particular the suggestion is that the intent of reference (b) has been met and that no more testing should be required during *Thresher*'s PSA. Reference (c) was written prior to *Thresher*'s shock tests and requires the shipyard to visually inspect salt water piping for visible defects and to certify materials within the salt water piping system in accordance with Navships 250–648–8.

2. It is significant that failures in silver-braze joints occurred during previous shock test series of other submarines and, that as the shock loading was increased, the number of silver-brazed piping failures increased. These failures were for the most part due to substandard bond, insufficient pipe support, or use of threaded fittings. To illustrate this point the following data have been extracted from references (d) and (e) (classified matter deleted):

3. In the documented silver-braze failures in *Thresher*, the majority occurred in pipe joints less than 1 inch i.p.s. which were of the insert type but no solder insert ring had been used. The result was no bond achieved in the joint but very slight bond appeared in the vicinity of the face fed fillet.

4. Another factor (briefly alluded to in par. 2 above) which has contributed to silver-braze joint failures is inadequate support of piping and valves. Long unsupported runs of piping place undue stress upon the pipe and piping joints when subjected to shock. An example is the failure of the drain line [classified material deleted] in which a ¾ inch i.p.s. silver-braze joint supported the valves and piping associated with a vertical run of pipe about 10 feet long.

5. In an effort to demonstrate the validity of ultrasonic testing of silver-brazed joints the Electric Boat Division was directed to conduct an inspection of certain joints in *Thresher* prior to the shock test series. The results of this inspection are contained in enclosure (1). Preliminary review by the Bureau of the joints which failed during shock test indicates that none of the failures occurred in joints which had been certified as satisfactory in the pretest ultrasonic inspection. It is requested that Portsmouth Naval Shipyard make a detailed review of enclosure (1) for the purpose of verification. If the detailed review confirms this finding the Bureau considers that the ultrasonic techniques employed by Electric Boat Division provide a mechanism for quality control

during fabrication of silver-brazed joints in new construction work and for purging operational ships of defective joints.

6. The significance of gross failures of silver-brazed joints in vital submarine systems is such that the Bureau considers it a matter of urgency that an inspection program be developed for these systems that will ultimately permit the certification of all piping joints in submarines as meeting minimum Bureau acceptance standards for the type of joint involved. It is recognized that the number of joints involved is large; that, in completed ships, many are inaccessible and that any program developed to certify all joints could be unacceptably costly both in dollars and time required. The importance of this matter to the submarine forces is such, however, that we must commence at the earliest possible date to attack the problem in a planned, step-by-step approach which will ultimately lead to the certification of all vital piping system joints. To this end Portsmouth Naval Shipyard is directed to initiate the following actions during *Thresher's* PSA.

a. Employ a minimum of at least one ultrasonic test team throughout the entire assigned PSA to examine, insofar as possible, the maximum number of silver-braze joints.

b. The inspection team(s) should examine accessible silver-brazed joints in the following order of priority:

(1) Sea water systems (non-nuclear) between hull valve and backup valve (visually examine to ascertain all "short bosses" and threaded fittings have been eliminated). See casualty 6–29 reference (e).

(2) Hydraulic high pressure piping:

    (a) Vital hydraulic system.

    (b) Main hydraulic system.

    (c) External hydraulic system.

(3) Compressed gas systems (if installed in accordance with Mil. Std. 438B. If not the fittings shall be removed and replaced with authorized fittings.)

(4) Salt water systems inboard of backup valves.

c. A complete checkoff record shall be maintained of each joint inspected. This record shall be retained by the shipyard for future planning action and a copy of the record of inspection shall be furnished to *Thresher* for retention as a part of the ship's machinery record.

d. All joints which do not indicate by U/T an average of 40 percent bond with a minimum of 25 percent bond on either land shall be considered defective. Defective joints shall be repaired or replaced on a "not-to-delay" ship basis. Defective joints which cannot be corrected within the assigned availability shall be delineated as part of the inspection record in order that replacement may be made during *Thresher's* next availability. Joints in vital systems exhibiting gross defects which cannot be repaired without extending *Thresher's* PSA completion date shall be referred to the Bureau for a decision as to whether or not the repair will be deferred.

e. The inspection team shall visually inspect each joint prior to ultrasonically testing it to establish acceptability in accordance with the visual criteria contained in NavShips 250–648–8.

f. All applicable piping shall be inspected to insure that adequate support is provided and that the type of joints used are proper for the service and size of the piping (see Mil. Std. 438B). All discrepancies shall be rectified or duly noted on the inspection report if insufficient time prohibits action during this availability.

g. The joints previously U/T inspected by the Electric Boat Division during the preshock test availability shall not be reinspected.

7. The intent of the Bureau is that the inspection directed by this letter shall serve as a pilot test of silver-brazed piping inspections in operating ships which were constructed without benefit of present-day quality controls. A similar pilot test is contemplated for silver-brazed piping which will be conducted by another shipbuilding activity. The results of these trial inspections will serve as the basis for a Bureau instruction which will have as its purpose a "step-by-step" program of certifying vital submarine piping systems as meeting minimum Bureau acceptance standards in ships constructed prior to the current quality control program. To this end Portsmouth Naval Shipyard is requested to forward comments, suggestions, and recommendations based upon their experience as a result of this pilot test.

8. Charges for the actions required by this letter shall be lodged against Project Order 20995 741 SCN SH 2457 Cost Cat. 2A.

                        R. L. MOORE, Jr., *Deputy Chief of Bureau.*

APPENDIX 3

(This speech reflects the views of the author and does not necessarily reflect the views of the Secretary of the Navy or the Department of the Navy.)

THE NEVER-ENDING CHALLENGE

(By Vice Adm. H. G. Rickover, USN, at the 44th annual National Metal Congress, New York, N.Y., October 29, 1962)

Progress—like freedom—is desired by nearly all men, but not all understand that both come at a cost. Whenever society advances—be it in culture and education or science and technology—there is a rise in the requirements man must meet to function successfully. The price of progress is acceptance of these more exacting standards of performance and relinquishment of familiar habits and conventions rendered obsolete because they no longer meet the new standards. To move but one rung up the ladder of civilization man must surpass himself. The simple life comes "naturally," the civilized life compels effort.

In any advancing society some elements will accept the advantages of life at a higher plateau yet ignore its obligations. This is readily seen when backward people seek to modernize their society. Sociologists call it a "culture lag." Something akin to culture lag exists even in highly developed countries such as the United States. And, because all parts of a modern society are interdependent, failure to meet rising standards in any sector becomes a brake on general progress and harms society as a whole.

I need not spell out to this audience that we have no choice but to keep in the forefront of civilization. Progress today is the sine qua non of national survival. It is the paramount national interest. Since our country is self-governing democracy, this paramount national interest is in the safekeeping of each and every one of us. If we do not look after the national interest, no one else will. That is what self-government means. In this instance, moreover, civic duty is strongly reinforced by private interest. Were the Nation to falter in its forward movement, we should all suffer dire consequences in our most private lives. The Nation's paramount interest coincides with every citizen's paramount self-interest.

It follows that the existence of a "culture lag" in any important sector of our society is the legitimate concern of every citizen. Insofar as special competencies allow us to do so, we each have a right and a duty to call attention to factors seriously impeding progress, and to suggest ways and means for overcoming these obstacles. I submit that in my own field of reactor technology we have a culture lag in that many involved with this new technology fail to recognize that to exploit the power locked in the atom we must rise to a higher technological plateau. And that consequently a more exacting standard must be met in everything pertaining to this new source of power. Failure to understand this reduces the benefit the Nation obtains from nuclear power.

Take the ways we make use of our nuclear power potential or how we operate nuclear powerplants. If this is to be done wisely persons in authority must possess an unusually high degree of general and technical knowledge and competence. Unfortunately decisions affecting this field are sometimes made by people who have little knowledge of nuclear engineering and of science. There is danger this may lead to errors highly damaging to the position of the United States or to the health and safety of the American people.

Thus, when persons who are authorized to deal with nuclear power as an instrument of national policy are technically ignorant, they may incorrectly appraise its importance. They may underrate the value to our Nation of the near monopoly we currently enjoy in reactor technology and in consequence fail to guard this asset with sufficient care. Again, when persons who are authorized to administer nuclear powerplants are technically ignorant, they may underestimate the hazards and in consequence fail to understand that nuclear powerplants cannot be operated safely except by highly competent and rigorously trained men. Reserving this task to persons so qualified may run counter to traditional personnel policies based on equalizing career opportunities. Administrators unfamiliar with nuclear science and engineering frequently resist change in established practices. They do this because they have little conception of the potential danger to large numbers of people if nuclear powerplants are handled ineptly. If they understood the dangers of radiation they would realize that safety must take precedence over their otherwise laudable desire to give everyone a chance at running a nuclear plant.

As I have said, some elements of society will accept the advantages of life at a higher plateau, yet ignore its obligations.

My remarks today concern the harmful results caused by failure of American industry to live up to the exacting standards of reactor technology. We depend on private industry to supply the materials and equipments for our nuclear powerplants. Current industrial practices are, on the whole, not geared to the standards imposed by this new technology.

While it has not been too difficult to focus management attention on the nuclear reactor itself, which represents a novel development, it has been extremely difficult to get management to give effective attention to the conventional components of these plants. Routine manufacturing and engineering practices continue to be followed, even though experience has shown these practices to be inadequate.

Successful operation of a nuclear powerplant depends on the reliability of all its parts, the reactor as well as the conventional components—the heat exchangers, pressure vessels, valves, turbogenerators, etc. Although these are all designed and manufactured by long established procedures and so should present no special difficulty, delivery and performance of these conventional items have been less reliable than of the nuclear reactors themselves. Senior people in the naval reactors group must therefore devote much of their time solving ever-recurring problems in the design, materials and workmanship of conventional components.

Compared with the complexity of nuclear engineering itself these problems individually are minor in nature, yet they occur so frequently as to require a disproportionate amount of our time. If we are to build successful nuclear powerplants at reasonable cost and in reasonable time, the whole plateau of industrial workmanship, engineering inspection, and quality control must be raised well above the present level. This is the responsibility of management. Management's technical function, after all, is to see to it that production meets the customer's requirements.

We are altogether too prone in this country to expect magical breakthroughs and shortcuts through science and engineering. We naively expect that the mere expenditure of large sums of money by Government will rapidly and automatically solve our technical problems and assure continued growth of our technology. We place too much emphasis on streamlined techniques such as computer programed management, instead of realizing that present technical problems are less a matter of generating new ideas than of carrying them out in a straightforward, methodical, and painstaking manner. Only in this way can the new scientific advances be turned to practical use. There is no substitute for constant personal supervision of production work by management. The higher we advance technically, the more important becomes the personal attention of the manager, the less can he reply on merely issuing orders.

Too often management is satisfied to sit in plush offices, far removed physically and mentally from the design and manufacturing areas, relying on paper reports for information about the status of design and production in the plant itself— the real center of the enterprise. This lack of firsthand evaluation results in poorly designed and manufactured equipment, late delivery, or both. During the past few years, hundreds of major conventional components, such as pressure vessels and steam generators, have been procured for naval nuclear propulsion plants. Less than 10 percent have been delivered on time. Thirty percent were delivered 6 months to a year or more later than promised. Even so, reinspection of these components after delivery showed that over 50 percent of them had to be further reworked in order to meet contract specification requirements.

We have tried to improve matters by sending representatives of the naval reactors group to manufacturer's plants to make on-the-spot checks of engineering and production progress. Often our men discover extremely unsatisfactory conditions of which management is unaware. The usual management reaction is to disbelieve the facts submitted to them. Corrective action is therefore often taken too late. The most prevalent inadequacy found in our audits is failure to recognize that timely production of high quality components requires almost infinite capacity for painstaking care and attention to detail by all elements of the organization, both management and nonmanagement; this is as true for a so-called conventional "old-line" product as for a new one.

Fortunately, some companies are forward looking and receptive to new ideas and try out our suggestions. For example, one company agreed to move the offices of their executive and supervisory personnel to the plant manufacturing areas. I would like to quote from a letter I received recently from that company:

"While we expected to obtain significant benefits from this move, the actual results achieved to date have been far beyond our expectations. As a result of this move, communications have been greatly improved among all levels of supervisory personnel and issues can be resolved face to face with shop personnel in an expeditious manner. We now have considerably less internal memorandums and telephone calls, and we have actually reduced the size of our secretarial staff.

"The fact that management personnel now have the opportunity to observe from their office windows most of our manufacturing areas has improved the attention being given to the work by operating personnel. Further, the close proximity between engineering and operating personnel has improved relationships and understanding of problems at all levels in the company; this has resulted in improved quality, better cost control and shorter fabrication time."

Failure of management to meet the standards required by advancing technology reduces the benefit our Nation obtains from huge investments in research and development. Of an annual total of about $16 billion, nearly $12 billion come out of the taxpayer's pocket. The size of these expenditures places a great responsibility on industry. It must get people into management who have the competence to make certain that stockholders and taxpayers receive full value for the money invested in new technology, and that the Nation's technical resources are effectively used. Yet, time and again I have found that management is reluctant to depart from outdated practices; that it is not informed of what is actually going on in the plant; that it fails to provide the informed and strong leadership necessary to bring about improvements in engineering and production. It is not well enough understood that conventional components of advanced systems must necessarily meet higher standards. Yet it should be obvious that failures that would be trivial if they occured in a conventional application will have serious consequences in a nuclear plant because here radioactivity is involved. Even in the non-nuclear parts of our plants we must have full reliability if the great endurance of nuclear power is to be realized.

Management has a responsibility not only for successful engineering and production in its own plant; it also has a responsibility for accuracy of the data it supplies. These data are often used by other organizations when they design components. I recall one case where the elevated temperature mechanical strength properties of a common material, as given by the manufacturer and used in the ASME Boiler and Pressure Vessel Code, were found on test to be 30 percent too high. Checking this we discovered that the mechanical properties data presented as being firm were based on a limited test that had been conducted 10 years previously and on but one heat of material which had been given but a single fabrication heat treatment. We often found it necessary to run our own tests to determine the true physical properties of many conventional materials under varying conditions. And this, despite the fact that these materials have been in widespread industrial use for over 30 years. This experience does not speak well of management or of the effectiveness of technical societies in seeing to it that correct technical data are available, and that salesmanship does not overshadow technical excellence.

I should like to discuss two areas that are in need of continuous and painstaking attention to detail by management, by engineers, and by workmen. These are:

First, incomplete understanding of basic manufacturing and inspection processes, and

Second, poor workmanship and poor quality control. Let me give you specific examples:

1. *Incomplete understanding of basic manufacturing and inspection processes.*—When we design components for nuclear powerplants we make every effort to utilize existing processes. At first we assumed basic processes that have been in widespread industrial use for many years would be well understood. Our experience showed this was not so. I will describe some of the types of difficulties we constantly encounter. They have to do with faulty welding, faulty radiography and defective casting; that is, with deficiencies in basic conventional processes of present-day technology.

The press frequently reports malfunctions of advanced components or systems caused by failure of a weld, improper use of a routine process, or use of defective materials. Industry apparently considers such failures to be inevitable, since not enough is being done to correct the causes. The naval reactors and Shippingport atomic power station programs have had their full share of these problems.

There are 99 carbon steel welds in one particular nuclear plant steam system. The manufacturer stated that all these welds were radiographed and met specifications. Our own reevaluation of these welds—using correct procedures and proper X-ray sensitivity—showed however that only 10 percent met ASME standards; 35 percent had defects definitely in excess of ASME standards and the remaining 55 percent had such a rough external surface that the radiographs obtained could not be interpreted with any degree of assurance. We found this condition of unsatisfactory welds and improper radiography to be quite prevalent in many segments of industry. When we insisted that manufacturers meet the standards which had been established for many years as being necessary, very high rejection rates for welds resulted. One manufacturer, over a 3-month period, had to reject 47 percent of all carbon steel welds made in his shop; his rejection rate for welds made in the field, where conditions were less favorable, was even higher. In other types of welds a manufacturer had 85 to 100 percent rejection rates. I would like to emphasize that this unsatisfactory welding situation came to light only because we demanded that manufacturers prove to us they were meeting the standards which they themselves had accepted in the contract.

While many of these unsatisfactory welds might be attributed to poor workmanship, the underlying cause was management's failure to enforce standards. As a result there has been insufficient incentive to develop new processes and materials that would consistently produce acceptable welds. The blame for allowing this condition to exist rests squarely with the technical societies responsible for establishing standards, and with purchasers of equipment who do not insist that these standards are met.

We need to know a great deal more about welding. Take the case of unexplained variation in weldability from one heat of stainless steel to another. Although stainless steel was developed 50 years ago and has been applied extensively throughout the world, I am constantly amazed how little is actually known about this material. Recently we encountered difficulty in welding stainless steel forgings for valve bodies; previously there had been no problems with these forgings. Investigating this we found that early this year the forging manufacturer had made what he considered a minor change in the composition of the material to improve its forgeability. His technical people failed to consider that this small change might cause the material to respond differently in subsequent manufacturing operations. Moreover, they did not even bother to test a sample forging of the slightly modified material to determine its acceptability. As a result, we now have more than 100 stainless steel forgings which may have to be scrapped.

Casting is another basic process that is not fully understood. We often have to order two to three times as many castings as we need, because we have so much trouble obtaining satisfactory ones. Otherwise we may not have enough acceptable castings on time. Here is an example of the kind of difficulties we encounter: Two low alloy steel castings, 2.5 feet in diameter and 8 feet in length, were ordered. The castings were of a simple cylindrical shape and conventional in design. The manufacturer promised a firm delivery date. The first two castings, however, had to be scrapped because of internal defects. The manufacturer then made three more castings; these also were unsatisfactory. Because of this experience it became necessary to switch to forgings in lieu of castings. Meanwhile delivery of the equipment has been greatly delayed. The case is typical of failure to understand technical casting problems. Had we, at the start, fully realized how little the manufacturer actually knew about producing good castings, we could have ordered backup material and prevented the long delay.

There have been casting problems with other common materials as well: For instance, we have been unable to obtain certain large valve castings. When we do receive acceptable castings, this is only after 200 to 300 weld repairs have been made on each casting. Although this sort of difficulty has existed for many years, industry has not yet developed adequate techniques for successfully producing large castings.

Radiography is another basic process of contemporary conventional technology where we are constantly troubled with problems. Extensive use of radiography for over 30 years led us to believe that this nondestructive testing technique for determining soundness of welds and castings was well understood, and that the sensitivity requirements of existing ASME and Navy specifications were being met. We found this definitely not to be so. For years many of these requirements have been consistently violated. In consequence, large numbers of radiographs were of little or no value for determining integrity of welds and castings. There are several reasons for this state of affairs, some of which have wider implications. These include:

(a) A general feeling or opinion that ASME and Navy specification requirements are a desirable goal rather than a firm requirement. This has brought about deterioration of quality under pressure of production schedules and cost reduction drives.

(b) Frequent lack of understanding as to what the specification requirements actually are and why it is important that they be met.

(c) The personal opinion of an individual in the manufacturer's organization that a particular part of the specification is not necessary. In consequence no attempt is even made to meet the requirement, but the customer is not informed of this.

(d) In some instances it was impracticable to conform to a particular specification requirement. We should have been advised that the requirement was impracticable. Instead, an individual would take it upon himself to waive the requirement without notifying his company or us.

(e) A belief that radiography is such a highly specialized technology that persons outside this field are not capable of contributing to its interpretation or improvement. Actually, the highly unsatisfactory situation in radiography was brought to light by individuals in the naval reactors program trained in other disciplines. What was needed was to look into this field with an open and skeptical mind.

Radiographic practices used by industry have deteriorated. In many companies, small deviations such as incorrect placement of the radiation source or penetrameter or improper film developing techniques produce radiographs of insufficient quality to show defects. Correction of this situation is the responsibility of industrial management. Nevertheless I have had to set up a special task force of representatives from Government, component manufacturers and shipyards to clarify the techniques necessary to meet existing radiography requirements. When material previously considered acceptable was reinspected, using these correct techniques, a high percentage—up to 90 percent—of the welds was found unacceptable.

Frequently these problems occur because inspection personnel lack the competence required to perform the highly skilled job of interpreting radiographs. We found that inspectors often were quite untrained. In fact, they were at times no better qualified to read radiographs than a layman is to interpret his own chest X-ray. We, the customer, have had to setup a special course to train personnel in the interpretation of radiographs.

Besides this unsatisfactory situation in welding, casting and radiography, practical application of nuclear power is also hampered by unresolved problems of fatigue in materials.

Present knowledge of material fatigue under thermal cycling stress is meager. In consequence, we in the reactor group have had to develop special test loops to conduct tests for determining the adequacy of conventional components. Based on results of these tests we have had to change the design of many equipments—valves, nozzles, thermal sleeves—all of which have been in use by industry for many years. Yet fatigue is not peculiar to nuclear propulsion; nor is it a new problem for industry. The Civil Aeronautics Board reports that every year several commercial airplane accidents are caused by fatigue failure of propellers, landing gear, or hydraulic pressure lines. Reporting on a recent helicopter accident caused by fatigue cracking of a main rotor blade, the CAB warned that there was urgent need for better understanding of safe fatigue life of materials and for more conservative design.

2. *Poor workmanship and poor quality control.*—Modern technology—in nuclear power, in high speed aeronautics, or in high performance computers—requires greater excellence in workmanship and in quality control than has been necessary in the past, and this even in the conventional components used in these advanced systems. This is particularly true for nuclear technology where hazards of radioactivity and difficulty of access for maintenance and repair require workmanship and quality control to be at a much higher level than in normal industrial applications. In the case of submarines, moreover, the crew lives and works between two dangerous environments—the intense sea pressure outside the hull of the ship, and the hot, high pressure primary and secondary systems of the propulsion plant. If the boundaries of either of these pressure containments should fail, serious consequences would result. The reason why I emphasize and insist on design excellence and high quality workmanship

is that our nuclear submarines have to operate submerged for long periods of time, even under the polar ice cap where it may not be possible to come to the surface.

There have been many problems in material identification and control. Recently a reactor component failed to function properly. The plant had to be shut down for several weeks in order to remove this component, determine the cause of failure, and correct it—at considerable expense. We finally traced the cause of failure to the use of the wrong material in a small pin. The material actually used was not as hard as the material specified; under adverse conditions it tended to gall. Yet this component had passed production tests and quality control inspection. The tests and inspection had obviously not been done properly. These problems are not unique to nuclear propulsion; similar incidents occur in other fields, often with serious consequences. The use of a mild steel pin instead of a special hardened steel pin in a ship's steering gear once caused collision of two surface ships during a replenishment operation at sea.

Recently we discovered that a stainless steel fitting had been welded into a nickel-copper alloy piping system. The fitting had been certified by the manufacturer as nickel-copper, and had all the required certification data including chemistry and inspection results. In fact the words "nickel-copper" were actually etched in the fitting. Yet it was the wrong material. The system was intended for sea water service; had it been placed in operation with this stainless steel fitting a serious casualty would have resulted. In checking with other customers of this manufacturer we found that they too had received fittings of the wrong material. The manufacturer simply had no effective quality control organization. As a result we now have to check every fitting ever supplied by this manufacturer. The check is only partially completed, but 12 fittings of incorrect material have already been discovered.

I feel rather strongly about this problem. On more than one occasion I have been in a deeply submerged submarine when a failure occurred in a sea-water system because a fitting was of the wrong material. But for the prompt action of the crew, the consequences would have been disastrous. In fact I might not be here today.

Not long ago we discovered a mixup in the marking and packaging of welding electrodes which also could have had very unfortunate consequences. Welding electrodes are purchased in cans, each supposedly containing electrodes of only one type. The cans and the electrodes are individually so marked. Early last year a shipyard reported that in one can several electrodes differed from the rest, even though they bore the same color code mark. During the next 3 months, while we were checking this matter in detail, we detected similar incorrect marking and packaging of electrodes in cans from nearly every major electrode manufacturer in the United States. At our instigation the welding electrode industry has now adopted an improved method of identifying each type of electrode; and has also tightened quality control. Here again industry did not fulfill its obligations. There was no reason why these corrective steps should not have been taken earlier by the manufacturers themselves since this type of electrode mixup has been going on for years. What were the technical societies doing?

The cases I have given highlight the need for industry to pay more attention to proper identification of materials from the time of melting, through the various fabrication steps and until they are finally installed. Identification must be such as will readily be understood by inspection groups, and must provide means for checking the material right through to the final stage of fabrication.

Another quality control problem is caused by failure to follow specified procedures or drawings. Here is a case in point: Material which had required a special heat treatment was delivered for a shipboard application. On examining the records, we found that the material had been processed at an incorrect temperature and had been in the furnace for an excessive length of time; also, that the furnace temperature instruments had been out of calibration. The company concerned could not have done much worse. Replacement of this material resulted in considerable delay. In another case we ordered electrical components that are used to indicate whether a valve is open or closed. After several hundred of these had been installed several failures occurred. It was discovered that a small piece of insulation, required and specified in the drawings, had been left out by the manufacturer. In order to prevent failure of the installed components, they all had to be replaced. Again there was delay and additional cost.

Similar cases of poor quality control are prevalent in areas other than nuclear propulsion; areas where safety is just as important. About 10 percent of commercial airplane accidents are traceable to poor quality control during maintenance. Take the following CAB report on one particular accident: A worn bolt was found in a control system during an overhaul and removed for replacement. But no new bolt could be found in the shop so the worn bolt was put back "finger tight," with no locking pin, apparently to stay there until a new bolt could be ordered. No note was made of this, and during the next shift the overhaul was completed and the airplane was checked out as satisfactory. On a flight next day, vibration caused the loose nut to back off, the pilot lost control and the plane crashed. In another case, a commercial airliner crashed during takeoff after a major overhaul because the aileron control cables were reversed.

These examples illustrate there is no such thing as a "detail" which does not require careful review by experienced people. In our program, we try to overcome our quality control problems by setting up special quality control evaluation teams. These teams visit our suppliers and audit the effectiveness of their quality control organizations. The teams discover many deficiencies. Some have been corrected, many have not. The same practice could profitably be applied by companies, both for internal quality control audits and for audits of their subvendors. I believe this would greatly improve the present situation.

Many quality control problems are traceable to lack of pride in workmanship. In one case a reactor component failure was caused by faulty brazing of two copper wires. We found the braze to be so poor that when the insulation was removed the two wires fell apart. This was a common type of joint, used extensively and successfully in electrical components. Obviously, little if any care had been taken to insure the joint was made properly. On rechecking all the components of this design, 10 percent were found defective and had to be replaced.

To prevent poor workmanship, quality must be considered as embracing all factors which contribute to reliable and safe operation. What is needed is an atmosphere, a subtle attitude, an uncompromising insistence on excellence, as well as a healthy pessimism in technical matters, a pessimism which offsets the normal human tendency to expect that everything will come out right and that no accident can be foreseen—and forestalled—before it happens.

I am not alone in my concern over the low quality of workmanship in conventional components. Last May, Mr. J. Lorne Gray, president of Atomic Energy of Canada, Ltd., expressed the thought succinctly to the Canadian Nuclear Association. He said:

"Those of you who feel that you always supply equipment and make installations that satisfactorily meet the performance specifications should spend some time at NPD (the 20 EMW nuclear power demonstration reactor recently gone critical) or at any nuclear plant or even at some of the modern steamplants, during the startup or running-in period. The very special equipment that has employed the newer materials to very close tolerances and advanced designs is not the major cause of our troubles; it is the poor workmanship in supply, installation and inspection of standard items."

Poor workmanship shows up glaringly in new technology such as nuclear power, missiles, satellites, but it is to be found everywhere, and everywhere it raises cost and causes delay.

In all the cases I have cited the chief responsibility for unsatisfactory delivery and performance rests with industry management. It is the management's business to establish proper quality control and to hire and train inspection and quality control personnel. Until recently many companies in our program had neither a formal quality control procedure nor a quality control organization. Companies that did have such an organization often had it set up in such a way that the man in charge reported to the production manager. The production manager was thus placed in the position of checking and reporting on his own work—a completely unacceptable state of affairs, on the face of it. Through the efforts of the naval reactors program, especially through our quality control audit teams, significant advances have been made. But we have only scratched the surface.

I assure you I am not exaggerating the situation: in fact, I have understated it. For every case I have given, I could cite a dozen more. The cost in time and money because of industry's failure to meet contractual specifications is staggering. Worse, with this time and with this money we could have developed improved nuclear powerplants and produced many more of them. It is difficult for me to understand why management does not face up to its failure and its responsibility in this respect. Since contracts are sought for, they must be profitable. Despite talk of "the dead hand of government," it is public money that has paid for all major technological advances made in the past two decades; and public agencies and officials have taken the lead in getting most development started. Surely industry has as great a stake as every citizen in helping our Nation move forward technologically. Industry can best do this by meeting the rising standards of new technologies when it supplies material and equipment.

I only wish I could tell you that the somber situation I have described no longer exists; that our efforts over the past 15 years have been successful in eliminating these problems. But I can't. As the naval reactors program grows in scope and more companies engage in manufacturing components for it, our difficulties with conventional components multiply; they get worse rather than better. I have no sweeping solution for this never ending problem, but several things can be done:

1. More effective management and engineering attention should be given to the routine and conventional aspects of our technology. Nothing must ever be taken for granted. Management must get into the details of problems, look at hardware firsthand, analyze the cause of trouble by personal investigation, and take prompt action to prevent recurrence. Management must also remember that things once corrected do not stay corrected. A credo of management ought to be that every human endeavor has a "half life."

2. Management and engineers must not conclude that their job is over once drawings have been completed and the first component successfully built and tested to these drawings. This is far from the whole story. To be satisfactory a component not only must perform its function, it must do so reliably and consistently. This requires that it be easy to manufacture, inspect, and maintain in the field—by personnel of average skills. This invariably demands simplicity of design, and usually requires redesign of the first model. I don't believe this concept of what makes a good design is well understood.

3. Industry must take responsibility for developing better understanding of many basic processes in use today. Technical societies such as yours can play an important part here. One way of reaching better understanding is by methodically investigating every problem so as to determine its cause. Customers must inform manufacturers of all deficiencies they discover in equipment. This will help manufacturers improve production performance. In the naval reactors program we make every defect or failure to meet specifications, no matter how small, the subject of a special report from the ship or shipyard. This is followed in detail until corrective action has been taken and all concerned are advised of the problem and also of its remedy.

4. Specifications and standards must be thoroughly understood, respected, and enforced by manufacturers as well as by customers. It should be of concern to us that specifications are normally written by the manufacturers and therefore usually represent the lowest standard of engineering to which all manufacturers are willing to agree. This should be changed. Specifications and standards should be set by the customer with manufacturers acting only in a consulting capacity. This is another area in which technical societies could play an important part. They ought to see to it that industry develops comprehensive specifications of high technical quality and that specification requirements are consistently and rigorously enforced. Technical societies must carefully guard against becoming "kept" organizations.

5. Quality control must be recognized as an essential tool to enable management to meet today's technological imperatives. Customers must reject deficient equipment and insist that manufacturers meet their commitments. As long as manufacturers find that defective equipment is accepted it is difficult, if not impossible, to get them to improve—to raise their plateau of engineering. One of the best ways you can help raise the level of technical excellence of American industry is by insisting, as I have, on high standards of design, workmanship, and quality control.

I hope what I have said will not be dismissed as "unconstructive criticism" or petulant grumbling about difficulties that "ought to be expected." Robert Hutchins has warned that "an uncriticized society will not endure." The point I want to make is that, at the levels of technology to which we must rise, the kind of problems we in the naval reactors group have had with conventional components of nuclear plants ought not to be "expected." They reveal human inadequacies that must be overcome if this Nation is to be competitive with its Russian challenger and with the growing power of the European Common Market.

For the first time in our history we face competition without benefit of the special advantages we enjoyed in the past: geographic isolation; enormously greater per capita wealth in land and mineral resources; the largest internal market. From now on we must excel without these advantages. Population growth and rapid exhaustion of natural resources leave us in no better position than Russia; and a united Europe will soon have as large a domestic market as we, besides possessing great resources in human competence and ingenuity. In truth, the inefficiencies we could afford in days gone by may now seriously endanger our world position.

What I have tried today is to give you an inkling of the factors that hinder progress in reactor technology and in other new engineering development projects as well. During the remainder of this 44th Annual National Metals Congress you will be hearing about new advances in many fields, particularly in metallurgy. But much of the effect of the huge sums we are spending to achieve these advances will be wasted if problems in conventional and routine areas prevent us from making full use of these advances. It is a commonplace of history that great undertakings often flounder because of negligence in some small detail, or because of some minor, obvious and easily corrected mistake.

I submit we must progress, and so we must pay the price of progress. We must accept the inexorably rising standards of technology and we must relinquish comfortable routines and practices rendered obsolete because they no longer meet the new standards.

This is our never-ending challenge.

APPENDIX 4

STATEMENT BY SENATOR JOHN O. PASTORE, CHAIRMAN, JOINT COMMITTEE ON ATOMIC ENERGY, ON THE FLOOR OF THE SENATE, APRIL 22, 1963

Mr. President, on the morning of April 9, at 8 a.m., the SS(N) 593 departed Portsmouth Naval Shipyard to undergo sea trials following extensive shipyard overhaul. This submarine, the U.S.S. *Thresher*, under command of Lt. Comdr. John W. Harvey, had aboard 112 naval personnel and 17 civilians. These men, who set sail that morning, were never again to see their families and their loved ones. The following morning, while undergoing a deep test dive, approximately 200 miles off the coast of Cape Cod, the submarine went down with all hands. I ask unanimous consent to place in the Record at this point the names of those men, civilians and military, who went down with the *Thresher*—men whose names will forever be part of the tradition and history of the U.S. Navy.[1]

The Nation mourns the loss of this submarine, the first nuclear submarine to be lost at sea. The submarine, however, can be replaced. What cannot be replaced are the lives of these 129 Americans. These men are irreplaceable.

A court of inquiry, under Vice Adm. Bernard L. Austin, has been convened, and since April 11 has been conducting an investigation to ascertain the cause of the loss. Admiral Austin, an officer experienced in the submarine service, is assisted on the court by other senior naval officers from the submarine service. They include Rear Adm. Lawrence Daspit; Capt. James B. Osborne, commanding officer of the first U.S. Polaris submarine, the U.S.S. *George Washington;* Capt. William C. Hushing; and Capt. Norman G. Nash. Capt. Saul Katz is counsel to the court.

The court has been holding hearings at New London, Conn., and Portsmouth Naval Shipyard. The hearings are in public except where classified information is involved.

The Joint Committee on Atomic Energy by law is required to make continuing studies of problems relating to the development, use, and control of atomic energy. In compliance with this responsibility, as chairman of the Joint Committee, upon notification of the loss of the *Thresher*, I sent two senior staff representatives to New London, Conn., as official observers to the court of inquiry. The two staff men—Executive Director John T. Conway and Assistant Director Edward J. Bauser—have been present during the public and closed sessions as the court of inquiry has been receiving evidence. They traveled with the court by special military plane from New London, Conn., to Portsmouth, N.H., when the court moved the site of investigation on April 12.

----

[1] See p. III for list of names.

Both of these committee staff men are particularly qualified to follow the course of the court of inquiry's investigation. Mr. Conway, a naval officer during World War II, holds a degree in engineering and in law and has been with the Joint Committee staff nearly 7 years. Mr. Bauser is a retired Navy captain with 22 years of active duty. He holds a master's degree in nuclear engineering from MIT and actively participated in the development, design, and test of nuclear submarines, including the first one, the *Nautilus*.

These two men have been in continuous contact with me and report that they are receiving the fullest cooperation from the Department of the Navy and the court of inquiry. All classified information and evidence being obtained by the court is being made available to the Joint Committee staff. Mr. Conway and Mr. Bauser advise me that in their opinion the court of inquiry is making every effort to ascertain the true cause of this terrible accident with the hope and expectation of preventing similar occurrences in the future. The members of the court, career Navy officers of the submarine service, have a bond of affinity with their lost comrades that never can be fully understood by those who have not shared the common experiences and dangers of the men in the submarine service. This bond is such that it demands every effort be made to bring forth all facts and that no stone be left unturned in discovering what the fault or faults may be.

On April 17, as chairman of the Joint Committee on Atomic Energy, I represented the committee at memorial services conducted by Francis Cardinal Spellman at the Portsmouth Naval Shipyard, at the conclusion of which His Eminence met with the families of the lost men. I cannot describe to you the full depth of the feelings shared by those who were present at these services and the other services held that day by Bishop Henry Knox Sherrill of the Episcopal Church.

Mr. President, I ask unanimous consent to place in the Record at the conclusion of my remarks the prayer by Francis Cardinal Spellman and the memorial message by Bishop Henry Knox Sherrill, together with the eulogy by Bishop Daniel Feeney. I also request unanimous consent to place in the Record at the conclusion of my remarks the remarks of Rear Adm. J. Floyd Dreith, USN, Director of the Chaplains' Division. the remarks by Comdr. Karl G. Peterson, USN, Protestant chaplain, Lt. Comdr. Keven J. Keaney, USN, Catholic chaplain, Rabbi Abraham I. Jacobson, and the Honorable Kenneth BeLieu. Assistant Secretary of the Navy, at the memorial services for the U.S.S. *Thresher* at the Portsmouth Naval Shipyard on April 15, 1963.

Many articles have been written and will be written in honor of the men of the U.S.S. *Thresher*. In a discussion with Vice Admiral Austin, president of the court of inquiry, at Portsmouth last week, he handed me a copy of an editorial of the April 13 issue of the New York Times which had been reprinted in the Portsmouth Naval Shipyard newspaper—the Portsmouth Periscope. Admiral Austin, himself a submariner, described this editorial as symbolizing the true spirit of the U.S. Navy submarine service. I ask unanimous consent to place the editorial in the Congressional Record at this point.

Mr. President, the Joint Committee on Atomic Energy at 4 p.m. today will meet in executive session at which time it will receive a report from its executive director and assistant director, Mr. Conway and Mr. Bauser, as to the investigation conducted to date by the court of inquiry. Since much of this information obtained by the court is of a classified nature the Joint Committee meeting, of necessity, will have to be in executive session. As chairman of the Joint Committee, I intend to have the committee, through its staff, continue to follow very closely the investigation of the court. The Joint Committee has a responsibility to assure that an investigation is properly and thoroughly conducted. The Joint Committee is particularly concerned that design and manufacturing standards are adequate to meet the exacting service demanded by nuclear submarines. Nuclear submarines must be operated as an integral unit. Standards of all parts must be the highest possible and carefully adhered to. I can assure the American public and the Congress that the Joint Committee will closely follow this investigation. I believe, however, the most efficient manner of obtaining the facts at this time is to permit the court of inquiry to conduct its investigation unhampered by parallel congressional investigation. I believe it is important to permit the comrades of those men lost on the *Thresher* to pursue the investigation without interference of other investigations. The Joint Committee will continue to have representatives of its staff as observers during the closed, as well as the open, session of the court. I have the assurance of the full cooperation of the court of inquiry. While the investigation may take a long time it is important that it be done thoroughly and fully in order that future tragedies may be prevented.

APPENDIX 5

CORRESPONDENCE CONCERNING JOINT COMMITTEE STAFF REPRESENTATION AT NAVAL COURT OF INQUIRY

JOINT COMMITTEE ON ATOMIC ENERGY,
CONGRESS OF THE UNITED STATES,
May 28, 1963.

Hon. FRED KORTH,
Secretary of the Navy, Washington, D.C.

DEAR MR. SECRETARY: On behalf of the Joint Committee, I want to thank you for the assistance rendered by your office in arranging for representation of the Joint Committee at the naval court of inquiry investigating the loss at sea of the U.S.S. *Thresher* on April 10, 1963. Members of the Joint Committee's professional staff have been present as observers at the open and closed hearings of the court and I understand that they have been given access to all information and evidence received by the court.

It is my understanding that as of May 23, the court of inquiry had no plans to call further witnesses or to recall previous witnesses although it was indicated that the need to do so could arise prior to the submission of a final report to the convening authority. I would like to request that in the event further witnesses are called, or additional evidence taken, that the Joint Committee be notified so that I may detail a staff member to be in attendance. In addition, I would appreciate it if a copy of the testimony taken by the court would be forwarded to the Joint Committee as soon as convenient.

The Joint Committee continues to have a strong interest in the circumstances surrounding the loss of the nuclear submarine *Thresher* and I would expect that upon completion of the court's work, a full report will be made available to the Joint Committee. I regard this as essential in order for the committee to carry out its functions and fulfill its statutory responsibilities to the Congress and the American people.

Sincerely yours,

JOHN O. PASTORE, *Chairman.*

———

DEPARTMENT OF THE NAVY,
OFFICE OF THE SECRETARY,
Washington, D.C., June 11, 1963.

Hon. JOHN O. PASTORE,
U.S. Senate,
Washington, D.C.

MY DEAR SENATOR: Thank you for your letter of May 28. I was delighted to have been of assistance in arranging for members of the Joint Committee on Atomic Energy to be present during the hearings by the naval court of inquiry investigating the *Thresher's* loss.

The court of inquiry does not plan to call any more witnesses unless the need to do so should arise. If the court should deem it necessary to question further witnesses or to receive further evidence, I shall inform you promptly.

A copy of the testimony taken by the court of inquiry will be forwarded to you upon review of the court's findings by the convening authority.

Thank you for your continued interest in this matter.

Sincerely yours,

FRED KORTH.

———

APPENDIX 6

CORRESPONDENCE CONCERNING FINDINGS OF NAVAL COURT OF INQUIRY

DEPARTMENT OF THE NAVY,
OFFICE OF THE SECRETARY,
Washington, D.C., June 20, 1963.

Hon. JOHN O. PASTORE,
Chairman, Joint Committee on Atomic Energy,
U.S. Senate, Washington, D.C.

MY DEAR MR. CHAIRMAN: Herewith is transmitted for information a copy of the record of the proceedings of the court of inquiry appointed to investigate the loss of the U.S.S. *Thresher*, together with the findings of fact, opinions and recommendations of the court and the action of the commander in chief, U.S. Atlantic Fleet, the convening authority. The record is now being routed to the interested bureaus and offices of the Department for comment prior to final action on the record.

Your attention is invited to the fact that a considerable portion of the record is classified, as are certain of the findings and recommendations and the convening authority's endorsement. The classified portions of this record contain information affecting the national security and it is of the greatest importance that it should not be released. Any unauthorized release would seriously affect our nuclear ship and Polaris programs. For this reason I am sure that you will agree with me that it is important that no information additional to that contained in the official press release should reach any unauthorized persons.

The Judge Advocate General of the Navy is preparing detailed summaries of the record which will be divided into unclassified material and classified material. As soon as these summaries are completed I will forward copies to you for the use of the committee.

Sincerely yours,

FRED KORTH.

[News release] [1]

DEPARTMENT OF DEFENSE,
OFFICE OF PUBLIC AFFAIRS,
Washington, D.C., June 20, 1963.

"THRESHER" COURT OF INQUIRY REPORTS

A flooding casualty in the engineroom is believed to be the "most probable" cause of the sinking of the nuclear submarine U.S.S. *Thresher*, lost April 10, 1963, 220 miles east of Cape Cod with 129 persons aboard.

The Navy believes it most likely that a piping system failure had occurred in one of the *Thresher*'s salt water systems, probably in the engineroom. The enormous pressure of sea water surrounding the submarine subjected her interior to a violent spray of water and progressive flooding. In all probability water affected electrical circuits and caused loss of power. *Thresher* slowed and began to sink. Within moments she had exceeded her collapse depth and totally flooded. She came to rest on the ocean floor, 8,400 feet beneath the surface.

This opinion of the court of inquiry was made public today by Secretary of the Navy Fred Korth.

The court, headed by Vice Adm. Bernard L. Austin, U.S. Navy, heard testimony from 120 witnesses, both military and civilian, during the 8 weeks it was in session at the Naval Shipyard, Portsmouth, N.H. It recorded 1,700 pages of testimony and gathered for the record some 255 charts, drawings, letters, photographs, directives, debris, and other exhibits bearing on the sinking.

The record of proceedings of the court was delivered last week to the convening authority. Adm. H. Page Smith, U.S. Navy, commander in chief, U.S. Atlantic Fleet, who transmitted it, with his comments, to the Secretary of the Navy. Copies of the bulky 12-volume record are now being studied in the Navy Department by engineers, designers, and experts in nuclear submarine operations.

The court declared that, in its opinion, "the basic design of the *Thresher*-class submarine is good, and its implementation has resulted in the development of a high-performance submarine."

The bulk of the court's recommendations stated the need for careful review of the design, construction, and inspection of vital submarine systems, such as sea water and air systems, and a review of operating procedures to improve damage control capability under casualty conditions such as flooding.

Certain actions have already been taken. For example, the Navy's Bureau of Ships is applying a newly developed inspection technique to assure the integrity of high pressure piping systems on all naval ships. Based upon ultrasonic principles, the new method is being employed initially on nuclear submarines. Personnel training and ultrasonic inspection equipment familiarization are necessary and some rescheduling of submarine construction dates and overhaul intervals will be required.

---

[1] Furnished to the Joint Committee on July 1, 1963. See p. 155.

Much of the testimony heard by the court was received in closed session and its overall report is classified "secret" to prevent disclosure of the capabilities of the Navy's nuclear submarine force. Secretary Korth has authorized the release of the following portions of the record which do not contain secret information:

Among its opinions, the court stated that "the evidence does not establish that the deaths of those embarked in *Thresher* were caused by the intent, fault, negligence, or inefficiency of any person or persons in the naval service or connected therewith."

The court also reported there was no evidence of sabotage or hostile action in connection with the loss of *Thresher*. In addition, the court found that there was no indication of increased radioactivity in the search area. Debris recovered was also found to be free of radioactive material.

The record states that it is impossible, with the information now available, to obtain a more precise determination of what actually happened.

The court did, however, offer a "reasonable rationalization of probable events" which, when pieced together with known facts, provide the following chronology of the death of the *Thresher:*

The *Thresher*, under command of Lt. Comdr. John W. Harvey, U.S. Navy, departed Portsmouth Naval Shipyard on the morning of April 9, 1963, to conduct scheduled sea trials following an overhaul period which extended from July 16, 1962, to April 11, 1963. *Thresher* was a unit of Submarine Development Group 2 and was operating under the orders of commander, Submarine Force, U.S. Atlantic Fleet (Administration) Portsmouth, for the sea trials. One hundred and twenty-nine persons were aboard *Thresher* for the purpose of executing official duties. Included in this number were 3 officers and 13 civilian employees of the Portsmouth Naval Shipyard; 1 officer from the staff of the deputy commander, Submarine Force, Atlantic Fleet; 4 civilian contractor's representatives, and 12 officers and 96 enlisted men of the ship's company.

U.S.S. *Skylark*, commanded by Lt. Comdr. Stanley Hecker, U.S. Navy, was designated to act as escort to *Thresher* during sea trials and effected a rendezvous with the submarine at 9:49 a.m. on April 9 in the vicinity of latitude 42° 56′ N, longitude 70° 26′ W. Upon completion of a scheduled shallow dive, the two ships proceeded independently during the night to a second rendezvous in the vicinity of latitude 41° 46′ N., longitude 65° 03′ W. During this transit, *Thresher* proceeded both submerged and surfaced and conducted various test evolutions, including full power propulsion.

At 7:45 a.m. on April 10, the two ships were at the rendezvous point, separated by a distance of 3,400 yards. The sea was calm with a slight swell. Wind was from the north-northeast at 7 knots. Visibility was about 10 miles. No other ships are known to have been in the vicinity.

Two minutes later, at 7 a.m., *Thresher* reported by underwater telephone that she was starting a deep dive. *Skylark* maintained her approximate position while *Thresher* reported course and depth changes as she maneuvered beneath the surface. To personnel aboard *Skylark*, the dive appeared to be progressing satisfactorily until about 9:13 a.m., when *Thresher* reported "Experiencing minor difficulties. Have positive up angle. Am attempting to blow. Will keep you informed."

Listeners aboard *Skylark* next heard sounds of compressed air rushing into the submarine's ballast tanks as *Thresher* sought to regain the surface.

Three minutes later, at about 9:16 a.m., *Skylark* heard a garbled transmission which was believed to contain the words "* * * test depth."

Upon receiving *Thresher's* message that she was experiencing minor difficulty, her escort ship *Skylark* advised *Thresher* that the area was clear. She announced her own course and requested range and bearings from the submarine. At about 9:15 a.m., *Skylark* asked *Thresher* "Are you in control?" and repeated this query. At 9:21 a.m., *Skylark* established her position by loran as latitude 42°45′ N., longitude 64°59′ W. She continued her attempts to communicate with *Thresher* by underwater telephone, sonar, and radio. Then, at 10:40 a.m., *Skylark* commenced dropping a series of hand grenades as a signal to *Thresher* that she should surface. *Skylark* then sent a message to commander, Submarine Development Group 2 reporting that she had lost contact with the submarine.

The court of inquiry concluded that the *Skylark's* message "did not convey to operational commanders the full extent of the information available." Lieutenant Commander Hecker was named a party to the investigation but, in the opinion of the court, *Skylark*'s actions "could not conceivably have contributed in any way to the loss of *Thresher*. * * *"

"The tragic loss of *Thresher* has caused the Navy to review in minute detail the design, construction, operation, and overhaul of our nuclear submarines," Secretary Korth said. "We have found nothing to cast doubt on the basic soundness of the program, but in every analysis of a major catastrophe at sea, lessons are learned. The record of proceedings of the court of inquiry headed by Vice Admiral Austin is receiving most careful and detailed scrutiny. It will undoubtedly serve to lessen the hazards inherent in operating beneath the sea."

RECEIVED FROM DEPARTMENT OF THE NAVY, JUDGE ADVOCATE GENERAL, JUNE 25, 1963,

SUMMARY OF EVENTS CONCERNING LOSS AT SEA OF U.S.S. "THRESHER"

On April 10, 1963, Adm. Robert L. Dennison, U.S. Navy, commander in chief, U.S. Atlantic Fleet, ordered a court of inquiry to inquire into the circumstances of the loss at sea of the U.S.S. *Thresher* (SS(N)–593) on April 10, 1963. The court included Vice Adm. Bernard L. Austin, U.S. Navy, president, and the additional members: Rear Adm. Lawrence R. Daspit, U.S. Navy; Capt. William C. Hushing, U.S. Navy; Capt. James B. Osborne, U.S. Navy; and Capt. Norman C. Nash, U.S. Navy. Capt. Saul Katz, U.S. Navy, was designated to serve as counsel for the court.

The court met for the first time at 8:25 p.m. on Thursday, April 11, 1963. Before the court closed on June 5, 1963, it heard 179 separate appearances of witnesses and had occasion to recall 56 witnesses. The court developed 1,718 pages of testimony and received as exhibits in evidence 255 separate offers.

Among the witnesses who testified were Vice Adm. Hyman G. Rickover, U.S. Navy, Bureau of Ships; Vice Adm. William R. Smedberg III, Chief of Naval Personnel; Vice Adm. Elton W. Grenfell, commander. Submarine Force, U.S. Atlantic Fleet; Rear Adm. Lawson P. Ramage, deputy commander, Submarine Force, U.S. Atlantic Fleet; Rear Adm. William A. Brockett, Chief, Bureau of Ships; Rear Adm. Ralph K. James, U.S. Navy, special assistant to the Secretary of the Navy; Rear Adm. Charles J. Palmer, commander, Portsmouth Naval Shipyard; and Rear Adm. Robert L. Moore, Chief, Office of Industrial Relations. Comdr. Dean L. Axene, U.S. Navy, the former commanding officer of *Thresher*, was questioned by the court very early in its proceedings and provided valuable background information.

The court considered many aspects of the circumstances surrounding *Thresher*'s loss in light of present day complexity of the modern submarine. Information was developed regarding *Thresher*'s construction, her postcommissioning operations, and her postshakedown yard availability, in addition to the operations at sea which resulted in *Thresher*'s ultimate loss. The following detailed determinations by the court of inquiry provide significant information concerning the tragic loss of the Navy's first of a new class of nuclear-powered attack submarines with her crew of 12 officers and 96 men and 21 additional passengers on official business, 17 of whom were highly qualified civilian employees.

"THRESHER" OPERATIONS AT SEA, APRIL 9 AND 10

Thresher, under the command of Lt. Comdr. J. W. Harvey, U.S. Navy, departed Portsmouth Naval Shipyard on the morning of April 9, 1963, to conduct scheduled sea trials following a postshakedown availability which extended from July 16, 1962, to April 11, 1963.

Thresher was a unit of Submarine Development Group 2, and was operating under the orders of commander, Submarine Force, U.S. Atlantic Fleet (Administration), Portsmouth, for the sea trials.

U.S.S. *Skylark* (ASR–20), under command of Lt. Comdr. Stanley Hecker, U.S. Navy, was designated to act as escort to *Thresher* during sea trials, pursuant to orders of commander, Submarine Flotilla 2. Commanding officer, *Thresher*, was officer in tactical command of the two vessels.

At about 9:49 a.m. on April 9, 1963, in the vicinity of latitude 42°56′ N., longitude 70°26′ W., *Thresher* affected a rendezvous with *Skylark*. After *Thresher* completed a scheduled shallow dive, the two ships proceeded independently during the night to a second rendezvous in the vicinity of latitude 41°46′ N., longitude 65°03′ W. During transit, *Thresher* proceeded, surfaced, and submerged and conducted various test evolutions, including full power propulsion.

At 7:45 a.m., April 10, 1963, *Skylark* was in the vicinity of latitude 41°46' N., longitude 65°03' W., and *Thresher* reported to her that *Skylark* bore 147° true, 3,400 yards from *Thresher*. Shortly thereafter *Thresher* began a deep dive which appeared to *Skylark* personnel to proceed satisfactorily until about 9:13 a.m., when *Thresher* reported to *Skylark* to the effect, "Experiencing minor difficulties. Have positive up angle. Am attempting to blow. Will keep you informed." After this last clear message, *Skylark* received two further garbled communications.

At 9 a.m. on April 10, 1963, the sea was calm, with a slight swell. Wind was from 015° true at 7 knots. Depth of water in this area is about 8,500 feet. Visibility was about 10 miles. No other ships are known to have been in the vicinity.

Thresher was lost at sea with all on board at about 9:18 a.m. on April 10, 1963, in the vicinity of latitude 41°45' N., longitude 65°00' W. There was no evidence of sabotage or enemy action in connection with the loss of *Thresher*.

"SKYLARK'S" ACTIONS DURING OPERATIONS WITH "THRESHER"

Upon receipt of *Thresher*'s 9:13 a.m. communication—"Experiencing minor difficulties * * *" etc.—*Skylark* initiated certain actions. She advised *Thresher* of *Skylark*'s course and that the area was clear, and she requested range and bearing from *Thresher*. At about 9:15 a.m., *Skylark*, in an attempt to establish communication not only by sonar and radio but also by underwater telephone, asked and repeated this query: "Are you in control?" *Skylark* established its loran position (logged at 9:21 a.m., as 41°45' N., 64°59' W.), and at 10:40 a.m. commenced dropping a series of hand grenades indicating to *Thresher* that she should surface.

At about 10:45 a.m. the commanding officer, *Skylark* directed the operations officer to initiate a message reporting the loss of contact with *Thresher*. Difficulty was encountered with transmission of the message to DBL (Radio New London), notwithstanding the fact that *Skylark* had conducted radio communication checks earlier that morning.

At 12:45 p.m. New London receipted for *Skylark*'s message which stated: "Unable to communicate with *Thresher* since 0917R. Have been calling by UQC voice and CW QHB CW every minute; explosive signals every 10 minutes with no success. Last transmission received was garbled. Indicated *Thresher* was approaching test depth. My present position 41°43' N., 64°57' W. conducting expanding search."

Therefore, *Skylark*'s message did not convey to operational commanders the full extent of the information then available, nor did any of *Skylark*'s subsequent reports include such additional information. Moreover, *Thresher*'s last messages were not disclosed to higher authority until April 12, when Lt.(j.g.) James D. Watson, navigator of *Skylark*, boarded the U.S.S. *Blandy* with the underwater telephone log which was examined by deputy commander, Submarine Force, U.S. Atlantic Feet. However, the court of inquiry formed the opinion that *Skylark*'s commanding officer's failure to promptly notify higher authority of all the information available to him pertinent to the circumstances attending the last transmission received by *Skylark* from *Thresher* on April 10, as it was his duty to do, did not contribute in any way to the loss of *Thresher* and was not materially connected therewith.

THE SEARCH FOR "THRESHER"

Deputy commander, Submarine Force, U.S. Atlantic Fleet (Rear Adm. L. P. Ramage, U.S. Navy) was en route to New London, Conn., from Key West, Fla., and arrived at Trumbull Airport, Groton, Conn., at about 6:30 p.m. Upon notification of *Thresher*'s status, he proceeded by helicopter to Newport, R.I., and embarked in the U.S.S. *Blandy* to proceed to the scene of the search.

Command of the search force passed from commanding officer, *Skylark*, to commander, Submarine Development Group 2 at about 5:30 a.m. on April 11, 1963, and was subsequently exercised, for varying and consecutive periods, by deputy commander, Submarine Force, U.S. Atlantic Fleet; commander, Submarine Development Group 2; and commander, Submarine Squadron 8.

Shortly after 9:17 a.m., April 10, when efforts to communicate with *Thresher* had been unsuccessful, *Skylark* commenced an expanding search pattern. Sonar was the principal means of underwater detection available to *Skylark*. Patrol aircraft and the U.S.S. *Recovery* (ARS–43) joined *Skylark* in the search area during the afternoon.

At about 5:30 p.m., *Recovery* sighted an oil slick about 7 miles to the southeast of *Skylark*'s 9:17 a.m. position. Samples were collected and articles of debris were recovered. These items and debris subsequently recovered were examined by laboratory personnel of the Portsmouth Naval Shipyard and were determined to be materials which could have come from *Thresher*.

Radiation measurements were taken in the search area by surface ships and submerged submarines, and the water samples and recovered debris, examined by laboratory personnel, were found to contain no radioactivity beyond normal background level.

As the search for *Thresher* continues naval units and personnel are being assisted by civilian scientists and research ships.

CONSTRUCTION OF "THRESHER"

The construction of *Thresher* commenced at the Portsmouth Naval Shipyard in 1958, and she was commissioned and delivered on August 3, 1961. *Thresher* had been designed by the Bureau of Ships, assisted by the Portsmouth Naval Shipyard in the contract design phase (1957–58) ; working plans were developed by the Portsmouth Naval Shipyard. The *Thresher* class underwent several design reviews during the building period, including a review in March 1959, by the Chief of Naval Operations.

The condition of the ship when delivered was defined by the certificates of condition furnished by the commander, Portsmouth Naval Shipyard, and the report of the Board of Inspection and Survey. In general, the ship was built in accordance with specifications and was in generally good material condition.

As part of the general construction of *Thresher*, silver-braze joints and flexible hose connections were extensively used in vital piping systems throughout the ship in accordance with usual submarine building practice and *Thresher*'s specifications. Subsequent to the investigation of a casualty involving a submarine of an earlier class, silver-braze joints in *Thresher*'s vital systems were subjected to visual examinations, mallet tests, chemical material reidentification tests, hydrostatic tests, and hydraulic pressure cycling tests, but there was no extensive retrofit of silver-braze joints in *Thresher*.

Quality assurance procedures employed at Portsmouth Naval Shipyard during *Thresher*'s construction period consisted in general of mechanic and line supervision, with some system tests being conducted by inspectors. X-ray techniques were used extensively for nondestructive testing of welds, forgings, and castings. Some ultrasonic testing was used to detect internal flaws in steel plates. To supplement these techniques, and wherever possible, hydrostatic pressures were applied to pressure vessels and piping systems. These test pressures were, in general, 150 percent of the designed working pressures. In the case of those piping systems exposed to sea pressure, this test pressure was also equal to that sea pressure expected to cause collapse of the hull. Hydrostatic pressure testing is a standard engineering technique and was the best nondestructive method of testing silver-braze piping joints available at the time of *Thresher*'s construction.

Hull production processes during *Thresher*'s building period did not include the use of all the techniques and safeguards for hull surveillance which now exist, nor was the ultrasonic method of testing silver-braze joints available.

POSTCOMMISSIONING OPERATIONS AND YARD AVAILABILITY OF "THRESHER"

Following commissioning, *Thresher* conducted operations in the eastern Atlantic area, for the purposes of shakedown, training, and evaluation. A much longer operating period was provided than is normal before a postshakedown availability due to the need to test the many new developments and equipments incorporated into *Thresher*.

From April 16, 1962, to May 21, 1962, *Thresher* received instrumentation and shock hardening at the Electric Boat Division of General Dynamics Corp., Groton, Conn., in preparation for scheduled shock tests.

During a visit to Cape Canaveral in early June, *Thresher* was struck by a tug and suffered damage to the exterior plating of one of the main ballast tanks. Upon return to the Electric Boat Division all damage was repaired, and a thorough inspection revealed no damage to the pressure hull nor any damage which affected the safety of the ship.

On July 11, 1962, *Thresher* arrived at Portsmouth, N.H., for postshakedown availability after conducting full power trials en route. Postshakedown availability commenced on July 16, 1962, with an estimate of approximately 35,000 mandays and a scheduled duration of 6 months : however, because of work added and the underestimation of the effects of new and old work, April 11, 1963, became the final completion date. The total of man-days expended was over 100,000.

During *Thresher*'s availability flexible hoses were replaced in accordance with process instructions existing in the shipyard. These instructions did not fully define specifications for allowable twist, and some flexible hoses were twisted in initial installation but were corrected. Although no formal training program existed for installing flexible hoses, an inspection program for flexible hose installations did exist and was carried out. Also, a comprehensive flexible hose listing which was used for quality assurance planning and inspection was prepared for *Thresher*.

Some valves in *Thresher*'s hydraulic, auxiliary sea water system, and other systems were installed backward during the postshakedown availability to permit testing of systems, some due to inadvertence and one due to an error in the ship's plans ; however, all were corrected and properly installed prior to departure of the ship for sea trials.

The Ship Information Book and working plans for *Thresher*'s auxiliary sea water system called for cross-connection of the system as the normal operating mode. However, installation of new check valves in the constant vent portion of this system during the postshakedown availability made possible the complete separation of the auxiliary sea water system into two loops.

Difficulties were experienced in operating the high pressure air system, and in leakage from the reducing valves. These difficulties, which began early in the life of the ship and existed throughout the postshakedown availability appeared to stem from the presence of minute particles in the system. High-pressure air and hydraulic systems require a high order of small particulate matter rejection during fabrication, installation, and repair. However, the difficulties with the high-pressure air valves, particularly leakage and venting, were reported as having been corrected prior to sea trials.

The hull repairs, access hatches, and hull stiffening work were completed in accordance with existing Bureau of Ships instructions and were checked by non-destructive tests means as being satisfactory, and the hull surveillance inspection scheduled during the postshakedown availability was completed.

The first dockside simulated cruise for purpose of crew training (fast cruise) was held March 23–26, 1963, and was terminated because of the large number of deficiencies noted. The second and last "fast cruise" was begun on March 31 and satisfactorily completed on April 1, 1963. In the second "fast cruise," during one of the drills involving a flooding casualty in the afterauxiliary sea water system, 20 minutes were required to isolate a leak. This was one of the early drills and changes had been made in the system involved during the postshakedown availability.

Thresher was at the Sound Pier for sound trials during the period April 1–4, and in drydock from April 4 to 8, 1963, to make repairs to torpedo door shutters and a main circulating water valve. During this period liberty was granted to the crew.

Testing of systems was in accordance with Portsmouth Naval Shipyard and other applicable instructions. A comprehensive test program was conducted. All work undertaken by the shipyard during *Thresher*'s postshakedown availability was reported as having been completed satisfactorily, and the commanding officer expressed his concern that the work was completed.

Portsmouth Naval Shipyard has had an extensive training program over the past 2 years, expending about $1,300,000 in the shipyard, of which the pipe shop (56) portion was about $400,000. The number of people in the quality assurance program in the Portsmouth Naval Shipyard has increased from 152 to 243, and the direct expenditures for the program from approximately $1,200,000 to approximately $2,800,000 in the past 2 years. During *Thresher*'s postshakedown availability, the total work effect performed at Portsmouth Naval Shipyard also included construction of five submarines. Other minor ship repair work and some manufacturing work also was accomplished.

Portsmouth Naval Shipyard has authority to deviate from building specifications in certain areas, and is using the specifications as goals rather than requirements in certain cases.

COMPLEXITY OF MODERN SUBMARINES AND REQUIREMENTS FOR SPECIALIZED MANPOWER

The complexity of modern submarines has increased at a rapid rate. The advent of nuclear propulsion, ballistic missiles, and greatly increased speeds and operating depths has made it essential that all information affecting their safe operation be analyzed and promptly disseminated. While there is at present no organization at any level within the Navy with the sole responsibility for submarine safety, Commander, Submarine Force, U.S. Atlantic Fleet, has a system of disseminating information which affects submarine operational safety.

During the past 4 years, while the Navy's annual shipbuilding program has increased from approximately $2.5 million to $4.5 million, the civilian personnel ceiling of the Bureau of Ships in Washington, D.C., has been reduced from 3,800 to 3,100, and the number of naval officers designated for engineering duties (ED) has declined from 1,057 to about 840. More significant, the number of naval officers serving as technical and management officers in the Portsmouth Naval Shipyard has been reduced over the past few years. This is particularly serious in the Design Division where, in 1956, five assistant design superintendents were assigned—none is so assigned today; and in the Shipbuilding Division, where the loss of 10 qualified officers (mainly ED) in 1961 and 1962 has reduced capabilities.

During recent years, the advent of the nuclear submarine has resulted in a major increase in the complexity and difficulty of submarine design, construction, and maintenance. The increase in complexity of nuclear submarines has resulted in an appreciable increase in the responsibilities imposed upon their commanding officers during the construction and postshakedown availability periods.

During *Thresher's* postshakedown availability there was a change of *Thresher's* assistant ship superintendent in November 1962, and a change of *Thresher's* ship superintendent in December 1962. Also there were changes of *Thresher's* commanding officer and executive officer in January 1963.

OPINIONS OF COURT OF INQUIRY

There is a danger that, in melding together fact and conjecture, conjecture may be stretched too far and may be accepted as fact, thus narrowing the field of search for possible causes of the casualty. The court's singling out of certain questions for study should not deter others, particularly members of the crew of similar ships, from continuing to study the many questions raised by the *Thresher's* loss.

The court concluded that a flooding casualty in the engineroom is the most probable cause of the sinking of *Thresher* and that it is most likely that a piping system failure had occurred in one of the *Thresher* salt water systems, probably in the engineroom. It was also concluded that in all probability water affected electrical circuits and caused a loss of power.

The court stated the opinion that the basic design of *Thresher* class submarines is good, and its implementation resulted in the development of a high-performance submarine. However, there are certain improvements desirable, as set forth in the recommendations, to increase the safety margin.

The basic auxiliary sea water loop system concept and design for the *Thresher* class is good, and is an improvement over the single header "Christmas tree" systems installed in other nuclear submarines. The dummy valves used as spacers and valves installed backward for test should be so marked (tagged) and should be designated in the ship's system status or "rip out" procedure.

The quality of work performed by shop 56 (pipe shop) at Portsmouth Naval Shipyard has improved since the construction of earlier class submarines, particularly in the silver-braze area and in material identification and control, workmanship, and quality assurance. In view of the many potential sources of casualties and their serious consequences in high-performance submarines, such as *Thresher*, there is a need to reemphasize and improve, where indicated, the quality assurance program in shipbuilding and repair yards. The court formed the opinion that the quality assurance program of the Portsmouth Naval Shipyard would be improved by appropriate consideration of the following:

1. Quality assurance division should report directly to the shipyard commander.

2. Quality assurance should be engineered and planned, utilizing the statistical approach and should deemphasize the "inspector" approach.

3. Quality assurance audits should be forwarded to management on a regular basis.

4. Quality assurance should record all defects, not just remaining defects (for example, brazers and inspectors reject joints and do not report defects found which are readily correctable).

5. Quality assurance ultrasonic test and welding radiographic test requirements should not depend on initiation of inspection requests by pipefitters and welders, but should be separately initiated by the job order preparing authority to facilitate cross-checking.

6. A quality assurance program should be developed for flexible hose installation and checkout.

7. The quality assurance division does not currently have power to disqualify workers observed to be violating procedures, process controls, and normal operating instructions, but must so recommend to the shop supervision involved. It might be desirable to permit quality assurance personnel to temporarily remove qualifications (brazers' cards, etc.) under such circumstances to insure that defective work is not built into submarines during the normal administrative handling time for disqualification action.

8. Welding quality is under the welding engineer and is not completely integrated with the quality assurance program in the same manner as other procedures are. It is believed desirable to integrate this effort.

9. Condition sheets (for defects discovered) should be reviewed, analyzed, and summarized by the quality assurance division for presentation to management to insure that process deficiencies are brought to management's attention.

Since high-performance submarines require full-quality assurance and a high degree of uniformity, the Bureau of Ships should require adherence to specifications.

There were many reasons for the Bureau of Ships and Portsmouth Naval Shipyard continuing the use of silver-braze joints in piping systems of submarines. These included years of shipbuilding practice and service, extensive tests, improvement in processes and nondestructive test techniques, the lack of weldable fittings, and the high welded-joint rejection in all shipyards.

The substantially contemporaneous transfer of *Thresher*'s commanding officer, executive officer, ship's superintendent, and assistant ship's superintendent in the final portion of her post-shakedown availability was not conducive to optimum completion of the work undertaken.

The evidence does not establish that the deaths of those embarked in *Thresher* were caused by the intent, fault, negligence, or inefficiency of any person or persons in the naval service or connected therewith.

The lessons learned from inquiry into the loss of *Thresher* are of such moment as to require wide dissemination within the Navy.

Certain actions have already been taken. For example, the Navy's Bureau of Ships is applying a newly developed inspection technique to assure the integrity of high-pressure piping systems on all naval ships. Based upon ultrasonic principles, the new method is being employed initially on nuclear submarines. Personnel training and ultrasonic inspection equipment familiarization are necessary and some rescheduling of submarine construction dates and overhaul intervals will be required.

RECOMMENDATIONS OF THE COURT OF INQUIRY

The bulk of the court's recommendations stated the need for careful review of the design, construction, and inspection of vital submarine systems, such as sea water and air systems, and a review of operating procedures to improve damage control capability under casualty conditions such as flooding.

The court recommended that the quality assurance program at Portsmouth Naval Shipyard be further emphasized and improved in scope along the lines indicated in the court's opinions.

Further, the Bureau of Ships should require submarine shipbuilding activities to adhere to specifications, and to obtain from it approval for all waivers where this is not practicable. The Bureau of Ships should increase its audit activity to insure adherence to specifications for submarine building, overhaul, and repair.

Early consideration should be given to the establishment of an organization, similar to that employed in naval aviation, in the interest of safe submarine operating procedures. Such an organization should be responsible for the analysis of events and developments which pertain to submarine safety and the timely dissemination of such information.

APPENDIX 7

CORRESPONDENCE CONCERNING DELAY IN SCHEDULE AND LOSS OF RADIOGRAPHS OF
U.S.S. "TINOSA"

CONGRESS OF THE UNITED STATES,
JOINT COMMITTEE ON ATOMIC ENERGY,
June 14, 1963.

Rear Adm. HORACE V. BIRD,
Chief of Legislative Affairs,
Department of the Navy, Washington, D.C.

DEAR ADMIRAL BIRD: Recent articles in the newspaper reported that the completion tests of the nuclear submarine *Tinosa* at Portsmouth Navy Yard are being delayed.

The Joint Committee would appreciate being advised as to the facts concerning any delay in the schedule of the *Tinosa* and any relationship the delay may have to facts developed during the investigation of the loss of the sister ship, U.S.S. *Thresher.*

Sincerely yours,

JOHN T. CONWAY, *Executive Director.*

DEPARTMENT OF THE NAVY,
OFFICE OF LEGISLATIVE AFFAIRS,
Washington, D.C., June 18, 1963.

Mr. JOHN T. CONWAY,
Executive Director, Joint Committee on Atomic Energy,
Congress of the United States,
Washington, D.C.

DEAR MR. CONWAY: This is to acknowledge your letter of June 14, 1963, in which you inquire regarding a reported delay in the completion of tests of the nuclear submarine *Tinosa.*

The Chief of the Bureau of Ships has been contacted for this information, which will be forwarded to you immediately upon receipt.

Sincerely yours,

H. V. BIRD,
Rear Admiral, U.S. Navy,
Chief of Legislative Affairs.

DEPARTMENT OF THE NAVY,
OFFICE OF THE SECRETARY,
Washington, D.C., July 1, 1963.

Mr. JOHN T. CONWAY,
Executive Director, Joint Committee on Atomic Energy, Congress of the United States, Washington, D.C.

MY DEAR MR. CONWAY: This is in further reply to your recent letter regarding a delay in the schedule of the nuclear submarine *Tinosa*, in which you asked if such delay was related to the submarine *Thresher.*

As has been previously reported, the completion of the *Tinosa* was delayed in order that misplaced radiographs of certain weldments could be redone to insure compliance with required quality control procedures. As you can appreciate, all safety measures must be observed in the construction of these submarines. Also, the integrity of certain piping systems in the ship is being verified by a newly developed ultrasonic testing procedure.

As a matter of interest, I am enclosing a copy of a news release concerning the submarine *Thresher* which mentions this new ultrasonic test.[1] To specifically answer your questions, there is no direct connection between the sinking of the *Thresher* and the delay in the completion of the *Tinosa.* The *Tinosa*, originally scheduled for completion on June 15, has been delayed until October 19.

Sincerely yours,

H. V. BIRD,
Rear Admiral, U.S. Navy,
Chief of Legislative Affairs.

---

[1] See app. 6, p. 149.

CONGRESS OF THE UNITED STATES,
JOINT COMMITTEE ON ATOMIC ENERGY,
July 6, 1963.

Rear Adm. H. V. BIRD,
U.S. Navy, Chief of Legislative Affairs, Office of the Secretary, Department of the Navy, Washington, D.C.

DEAR ADMIRAL BIRD : We received your July 1 letter which was sent in response to my June 14 letter requesting information on delays in the scheduled completion of the nuclear submarine *Tinosa.*

Your letter does not appear to be completely responsive. In reply to my question concerning relationships between the delay in the *Tinosa* schedule and facts developed during the investigation of *Thresher,* you responded concerning the connection between the delay in *Tinosa* and the sinking of the *Thresher.* I would appreciate a response to my original question which concerned the facts developed during the *Thresher* investigation and the *Tinosa* schedule.

Another point on which I would appreciate clarification concerns your reference to a previous report of the reason for the delay in *Tinosa.* Please identify the report you refer to which, accordng to your letter, cited the misplaced radiographs as the reason for the delay.

Sincerely yours,

JOHN T. CONWAY, *Executive Director.*

DEPARTMENT OF THE NAVY,
OFFICE OF THE SECRETARY,
Washington, D.C., July 10, 1963.

Mr. JOHN T. CONWAY.
Executive Director, Joint Committee on Atomic Energy, Congress of the United States, Washington, D.C.

DEAR MR. CONWAY : This is to acknowledge your letter of July 6 in which you refer to previous correspondence and request further information regarding the delay in the *Tinosa* schedule.

The Chief of the Bureau of Ships has been contacted for this information, and it will be furnished to you immediately upon receipt.

Sincerely yours,

H. V. BIRD,
Rear Admiral, U.S. Navy, Chief of Legislative Affairs.

DEPARTMENT OF THE NAVY,
OFFICE OF THE SECRETARY,
Washington, D.C., July 23, 1963.

Mr. JOHN T. CONWAY,
*Executive Director, Joint Committee on Atomic Energy,
Congress of the United States,
Washington, D.C.*

DEAR MR. CONWAY : This is in further reply to your recent letter in which you requested the identity of a report referred to in earlier correspondence and further questioned the connection between the delay in the scheduled completion of *Tinosa* and the *Thresher* investigation. The Chief of the Bureau of Ships has provided the following information.

The delay in the scheduled completion of *Tinosa* was reported by the Navy to the press on June 7, 1963. A copy of the release is enclosed for information.

There is no direct connection between the investigation of the *Thresher* disaster and the delay in the completion of *Tinosa.* However, as indicated in Rear Adm. H. V. Bird's letter of July 1, 1963, to you, the need for application of newly developed ultrasonic inspection techniques to submarine high pressure piping systems was emphasized as a result of the investigation. Application of these newly developed techniques may take longer than the taking and examining of the additional radiographs. Both types of work are being conducted concurrently.

Sincerely yours.

R. Y. MCELROY, Jr.,
Rear Admiral, U.S. Navy, Chief of Legislative Affairs.

"TINOSA" INFORMATION

The Navy today announced that the *Tinosa* (SSN–606) now under construction at the Naval Shipyard, Portsmouth, N.H., has been ordered drydocked for the purpose of taking additional radiographs of certain hull sections.

These additional radiographs are necessary because a block of radiographs has been misplaced. Such documentation is required not only before the shipyard commander may certify the ship as ready for sea but also as a matter of permanent record.

The commissioning of *Tinosa* previously scheduled for June 15 will be delayed for several weeks. The delay has no relationship to the loss of U.S.S. *Thresher*.

JOINT COMMITTEE ON ATOMIC ENERGY,
CONGRESS OF THE UNITED STATES,
July 31, 1963.

Hon. FRED KORTH,
The Secretary of the Navy,
Washington, D.C.

DEAR MR. SECRETARY: During our recent hearings on the loss of the nuclear submarine *Thresher*, testimony was received concerning the loss or misplacement of radiographs of welds on both the *Tinosa* and the *Thresher*.

We would appreciate receiving additional information concerning the circumstances of the loss of these radiographs.

We would like to know the following:

1. Has the reason for the missing radiographs of *Tinosa* hull welds been investigated? If so, what were the results of this investigation? Has it been definitely established that radiographs that are missing were actually taken?

2. What were the results of the recent re-radiography of the *Tinosa*'s hull welds? Did all welds meet Navy specifications?

3. Have the circumstances concerning the missing *Thresher* hull radiographs been investigated? If so, what were the results of the investigation?

4. Do results of re-radiography of the *Tinosa* hull welds shed any light on what may have been the condition of the *Thresher*'s hull welds at the time of her loss?

5. The court of inquiry fact No. 40 states:

"That *Thresher* was commissioned and delivered on August 3, 1961; the condition of the ship was defined by the certificates of condition furnished by the commander, Portsmouth Naval Shipyard, and the report of the Board of Inspection and Survey. In general, the ship was built in accordance with specifications and was in generally good material condition."

Was this finding of fact by the court based on its own determination whether the *Thresher* hull radiographs—

   (a) Were all actually made;
   (b) Were available; and
   (c) Showed that her hull welding met Navy specifications?

6. Are all the hull radiographs available for ships other than the *Tinosa* currently being built at Portsmouth? Have they been re-examined in light of the *Thresher* loss? What were the results of this re-examination? Do the hull welds meet Navy specifications?

7. What investigations have been made to determine whether the situation at Portsmouth with respect to hull welding is or is not typical of conditions at other naval and private shipyards building nuclear submarines? What are the results of these investigations?

We would appreciate a prompt response to this request since the committee would like to have this specific information during its present review of the loss of the *Thresher*.

Thank you for your assistance in this matter.

   Sincerely yours,

JOHN T. CONWAY, *Executive Director.*

DEPARTMENT OF THE NAVY,
OFFICE OF THE SECRETARY,
Washington, D.C., August 13, 1963.

Mr. JOHN T. CONWAY,
Executive Director, Joint Committee on Atomic Energy, Congress of the United States, Washington, D.C.

MY DEAR MR. CONWAY: Your letter of July 31, 1963, requested answers to various questions concerning the loss or misplacement of radiographs on *Tinosa* and *Thresher.* You indicated that the committee desires this information to use during its review of the loss of the *Thresher.*

The Chief, Bureau of Ships, has provided the desired information, which is set forth in the enclosure to this letter. I trust that this information will be helpful to you and the committee. If you should have additional questions, please do not hesitate to communicate with me.

Sincerely yours,

PAUL B. FAY, Jr.,
Acting Secretary of the Navy.

___

ANSWERS TO QUESTIONS PRESENTED IN JULY 31, 1963, LETTER FROM EXECUTIVE DIRECTOR, JOINT COMMITTEE ON ATOMIC ENERGY

1. Q. "Has the reason for the missing radiographs of *Tinosa* hull welds been investigated? If so, what were the results of this investigation? Has it been definitely established that radiographs that are missing were actually taken?"

A. The reason for the missing *Tinosa* radiographs has been informally investigated, both by Bureau of Ships and by Portsmouth Naval Shipyard personnel. The results of the investigations indicate the breakdown of an outdated accountability system. Over the past 15 to 20 years radiography has grown from infancy to a widely used method of nondestructive testing. The number of radiographs per submarine has increased from a few hundred to tens of thousands. The development of an accountability system has not kept pace with the increased employment of radiography as a nondestructive tool. Best evidence, according to the Bureau of Ships investigators, indicates that the majority of missing radiographs were not taken because the accountability system did not trigger a radiographic request. The accounting system has been altered to require a positive checkoff as assurance that all hull weld radiographs are requested, **checked** for acceptability, accounted for, and available for review in submarines being built at Portsmouth at this time.

2. Q. "What were the results of the recent re-radiography of the *Tinosa*'s hull welds? Did all welds meet Navy specifications?"

A. The results of the recent re-radiography of *Tinosa* hull welds revealed numerous small defects over a low percentage of the weld length in those areas where radiographs, according to the record, had not been previously taken. Where radiographs were made of areas which the records indicated had been radiographed but no radiographs could be accounted for, the defect rate was found to be significantly less (by a factor of approximately 10) than the areas that had been previously radiographed.

Some of the hull welds did not meet Navy specifications. Those areas revealed to be substandard are being repaired.

3. Q. "Have the circumstances concerning the missing *Thresher* hull radiographs been investigated? If so, what were the results of the investigation?"

A. The circumstances surrounding the missing *Thresher* hull weld radiographs have not been directly investigated. It is the Bureau of Ships opinion that the situation for the *Thresher* radiographs will be similar to the radiographs of *Tinosa* and other ships being built at Portsmouth Naval Shipyard at that time as outlined in paragraphs (1) and (2) above.

4. Q. "Do results of re-radiography of the *Tinosa* hull welds shed any light on what may have been the condition of the *Thresher*'s hull welds at the time of her loss?"

A. No audit has been conducted to determine exactly which hull weld radiographs are missing for *Thresher.* This audit has not been conducted because this area of investigation does not seem fruitful since all evidence appears to point away from the hull as the source of the original casualty which led to *Thresher*'s loss. The radiographs of *Tinosa* add one more piece of evidence in that the defects found during re-radiography were small and of the type which might affect fatigue characteristics but would not contribute to a catastrophic failure. The review of radiographs taken during *Thresher's* post-shakedown availability led to the same conclusion.

5. Q. "The court of inquiry fact No. 40 states: 'That *Thresher* was commissioned and delivered on August 3, 1961; the condition of the ship was defined by the certificates of condition furnished by the commander, Portsmouth Naval Shipyard, and the report of the Board of Inspection and Survey. In general the ship was built in accordance with specifications and was in generally good material condition.' Was this finding of fact by the court based on its own determination whether the *Thresher* hull radiographs: (a) were all actually made, (b) were available, (c) showed that her hull welding met Navy specifications?"

A. There is no readily available information as to the specific reasons which led the court to their finding of fact No. 40. It is noted that finding of fact No. 40 refers to certificates of condition furnished by commander, Portsmouth Naval Shipyard, and the report of the Board of Inspection and Survey. It is, therefore, inferred that these documents in all probability led the court to this finding of fact.

6. Q. "Are all the hull radiographs available for ships other than the *Tinosa* currently being built at Portsmouth? Have they been re-examined in light of the *Thresher* loss? What were the results of this re-examination? Do the hull welds meet Navy specifications?"

A. All of the hull radiographs are not available for ships under construction at Portsmouth as in the case of *Tinosa*.

A local audit of all radiographs was underway at Portsmouth prior to loss of *Thresher*. This audit was a part of a normal shipyard quality assurance check. As a result of loss of *Thresher* this audit has been expanded and extended and is not yet completed.

Results of the audit reveal missing radiographs in all ships under construction in Portsmouth as in case of *Tinosa*. These missing radiographs are being retaken.

The hull welds did not in all cases meet Navy specifications. Substandard welds are being ground out and repaired.

7. Q. "What investigations have been made to determine whether the situation at Portsmouth with respect to hull welding is or is not typical of conditions at other naval and private shipyards building nuclear submarines? What are the results of these investigations?

A. Prior to the *Thresher* loss, radiographic problems appeared in the area of pipe welding. The resulting investigation and action improved radiographic techniques, radiographic interpretation, and started some reforms in the area of radiographic recordkeeping. The process of radiography for both pipe and hull welding involves the same personnel, equipment, and record filing. These investigations revealed that the general conditions existing at all private and naval shipbuilding yards were approximately the same insofar as the field of radiography is concerned. After *Thresher* loss the Bureau of Ships instituted the submarine shipbuilder audit which is to be executed prior to the first sea trial of every new construction submarine. The first of these audits was conducted prior to *Barb* (SSN-596) sea trials in Ingalls Shipbuilding Corp., Pascagoula, Miss., in June 1963. Only minor discrepancies were noted during this audit and suitable corrective action is being taken at Ingalls. It is planned to continue this audit program at all submarine construction yards until such time as the Bureau is satisfied that the radiography of hull welding has reached a satisfactory level of quality and accountability.

APPENDIX 8

CORRESPONDENCE CONCERNING CLASSIFICATION OF INFORMATION RELATING TO THE LOSS OF U.S.S. "THRESHER"

DEPARTMENT OF THE NAVY, OFFICE OF THE SECRETARY,
Washington, D.C., August 13, 1963.

Mr. JOHN T. CONWAY,
Executive Director, Joint Committee on Atomic Energy, Congress of the United States, Washington, D.C.

DEAR MR. CONWAY: I am returning one copy of the transcript of the executive session hearing before the Joint Committee on Atomic Energy on July 23, 1963.

This copy indicates those editorial changes which are considered desirable by the witnesses concerned.

In addition to a review of the July 23 transcript for editorial changes, you requested that the transcripts for June 26 and 27, and July 23 be reviewed for classification and marked to indicate the specific information which is classified for security reasons. After a thorough review and most careful consideration of the situation, I do not believe it is in the best interests of the Navy to undertake any declassification action at this time. I consider the entire subject classified, and until the Court of Inquiry records have been reviewed, and the hearing completed. I would be loath to release portions of the hearings. Such patchwork release allows testimony to be taken out of context and, as you are well aware, could be damaging to public confidence in the Navy. At a later date, I believe that declassification of portions of the testimony could be undertaken, and I would be most pleased to work with your staff.

Accordingly, I ask your understanding and assistance in this matter.

Sincerely yours,

FRED KORTH.

Enclosure: (1) Transcript of the executive session hearing, Joint Committee on Atomic Energy, July 23, 1963, re: loss of the U.S.S. *Thresher* (Joint Committee on Atomic Energy Classified Document No. 7675 copy 2 of 10 A).

JOINT COMMITTEE ON ATOMIC ENERGY,
CONGRESS OF THE UNITED STATES,
August 19, 1963.

Hon. FRED KORTH,
Secretary of the Navy,
Washington, D.C.

DEAR MR. KORTH: I have read your letter of August 13 to Mr. Conway, executive director, Joint Committee on Atomic Energy, and I must say I am astonished by the idea that the entire subject of the loss of the *Thresher* is classified.

I am particularly amazed in view of the detailed article by Hanson W. Baldwin, appearing in the July 31, 1963, issue of the New York Times, which goes into a great deal of discussion on the technical aspects of our present nuclear submarines and characteristic planned for our future submarines in connection with the *Thresher* loss. I can only assume that Mr. Baldwin obtained his detailed information from knowledgeable individuals in the Navy. Also, on July 26, when you first testified before the Joint Committee, the Joint Committee was furnished a 17-page unclassified summary of the testimony.

I believe thoroughly and completely in protecting defense information and restricted data but I do not believe that you would wish to use security classification to protect the people from the truth, nor to keep embarrassing information from the public. Accordingly, I request that you reconsider your decision and specifically designate what information in the hearing records is properly classified for security reasons.

Sincerely yours,

CLINTON P. ANDERSON,
Chairman, Subcommittee on Security.

[From the New York Times, July 31, 1963]

NAVY STUDIES FLAWS IN ATOM SUBMARINES

(By Hanson W. Baldwin)

A thorough restudy of the design and construction of the Navy's nuclear submarines has started as a result of the loss of the *Thresher* and a number of pipe failures in other submarines.

The loss of the *Thresher* with 129 persons, in 8,400 feet of water 220 miles east of Cape Cod, April 10, is believed to have been caused by flooding in the engine room. The wreckage has not yet been found, although oceanographic research ships are continuing the search. The Navy's bathyscaphe *Trieste*—a deep-diving research craft with limited mobility—may resume diving operations within a few weeks.

The Navy court of inquiry that investigated the *Thresher* case believed that a piping failure subjected the interior of the *Thresher* to "a violent spray of water and progressive flooding" that "in all probability" flooded electrical circuits and caused a loss of power.

The court's findings and the current restudy were influenced by the fact that piping failures and part floodings have occurred in a number of U.S. submarines in recent years. None of them, except the *Thresher*, have involved loss of the submarine or of life.

None of them involved nuclear reactors and none of them resulted in the release of any radioactivity. All of these materiel failures were checked or compensated for before major damage was done.

The intensive reexamination of nuclear submarines—built, building and planned—is just starting. It has found nothing so far, Secretary of the Navy Fred Korth noted, "to cast doubt on the basic soundness of the program" or on the nuclear reactors, or on the general shape of the now standard, tear-dropped shape, or shark-shaped, hull form. Rather, it is taking the form of a scientific and engineering "who-done-it" to discover why such failures occur and how they can be minimized.

RESEARCH IS STIMULATED

The studies have been greatly stimulated by the *Thresher's* loss. However, the Navy Bureau of Ships, research departments of various industries, oceanographic institutes and Government and private laboratories already had been engaged for some years in wide-ranging studies directed toward submarines capable of cruising silently at greater and greater speeds and greater and greater depths with greater and greater safety.

These studies have involved new concepts. The experimental submarine *Albacore*, for instance, was fitted with dive brakes and a drag parachute, which was released from the top of the sail, or superstructure, to test the effects upon underwater maneuvering and rate of descent.

The highest priority is now being given to checking all submarines for structural integrity, particularly high-pressure piping and safety features. Until these checkouts are completed, arbitrary depth limits have been established that are considerably less than the test depths for which operating submarines have been designed.

The complex nature of this inspection task is brought about by the changes in submarine design that nuclear power has caused. Conventional submarines utilize electric batteries that supply power to electric motors for submerged cruising.

The fission of nuclear materials simply provides heat that must be transformed into energy that can be harnessed to the submarine's propeller shafts. This is done by utilizing the heat generated by fission to change fresh water into steam in a heat exchanger, or boiler. The steam is then used to drive conventional turbines geared to the propeller shafts.

FRESH WATER IS REUSED

Any such steamplant utilizes the fresh water in its system over and over. After the steam expands through the turbine blades, it is piped back to a condenser, where it is cooled and, in the form of water, passes into the heat exchanger or boiler once again in a closed-cycle system. The cooling in the condenser is done by passing the steam over pipes filled with cool seawater.

Thus, the development of nuclear power meant that a maze of piping—much more than in an electric-powered submarine and all of it open to sea pressure—had to penetrate the strong pressure hull of the submarine and be routed through her interior.

In addition to the sea water for the condenser, other high-pressure piping is used for the evaporators, which make fresh water from salt water; for the ship's toilet system; for air lines to ballast tanks; and for some other purposes.

Thus, to a far greater degree than the old electric battery submarines the nuclear submarine not only has the tremendous pressure of the sea outside the hull, but also inside in high-pressure piping, bending and curving through the ship.

FASTER CRUISING SPEEDS

Moreover, the submarine has been built to cruise much faster and far deeper than its World War II predecessors. The greater the depth, the more difficult the problems. Packing boxes around the propeller shafts, piping joints and piping and the hull itself are subjected to tremendous pressures—more than 44 pounds a square inch for each 100 feet of depth.

For these reasons the complexity of the task of insuring safety has greatly increased. The maze of piping presents the major problem to date. There are more than 3,000 pipe joints in the nuclear submarine. During construction each of these joints and the pipe itself is carefully inspected and tested by several methods. The pipe joints are formed by welding, wherever space, which is precious in the constricted interior of a submarine, permits, or by a process called silver brazing, where space is limited.

Welding provides a built-up seam with new metal joining the two ends together; silver brazing, utilizing a silver alloy, is a physical bonding of the two ends of the pipe with the application of heat, somewhat similar to soldering.

There are various types of pipe joints, some inherently stronger than others. No one type, because of space and other reasons, can be used for all purposes. Welding normally is a somewhat stronger process than silver brazing, but both have been used successfully for some years for joining high-pressure piping. Silver brazing, however, is not used for joining high-pressure steam lines. The developed inspection techniques for welded joints offer a much higher guarantee of a good joint than do those for a brazed joint.

JOINTS ARE INSPECTED

In construction, physical inspection of the joint is the first step. A trained inspector can tell a good deal by looking at a welded or brazed joint. X-ray or gamma ray photography is then used on all welded joints to take a picture of the cellular condition of the metal. Trained operators are required to read the photographs.

X-rays cannot be used for brazed joints, but ultrasonic inspection—the utilization of sound energy passing through the joint and the measurement on an oscilloscope of the reflected sound waves—can give a trained operator a picture of a sound or faulty joint.

After these inspections, there are various blowdown and hydrostatic tests. It has been found that even fine dust left in a piping system may jam or slow the closing of a high-pressure valve, ground to fine tolerances. High-pressure air blows out the system. The piping and the joints are then subjected to hydrostatic pressure tests—that is, water is pumped in under a pressure equivalent to that to which the submarine and her high-pressure sea water piping would be subjected at the deepest depth at which she will normally operate, and then at her crushing depth.

In addition to this inspection procedure during construction, the pipe metals themselves and some sample joints are tested again and again to the breaking point under extreme hydrostatic pressure to determine the effect of metal fatigue.

It is this kind of testing that is now being done on all U.S. nuclear submarines. The testing will extend ship overhaul periods, but it will not materially interfere with the *Polaris* submarines now on patrol and with the operating schedules of attack submarines. The inspection will be done as each returns to the yard for overhaul. Lagging is stripped off all pipes and any suspected weak joints will be replaced.

HULL SECTIONS X-RAYED

At the same time, hull sections will be X-rayed to discover any deterioration. Any modifications in design—such as the relocation, or protection, of electrical switchboards from exposure to flooding by broken piping than can be made will be made.

More major design changes will be incorporated in submarines not yet built. But just what they will entail no one can now say. So much has to be packed into a small hull in a submarine, and a submarine is subjected to so many stresses—the exact nature of some of them unknown—that any design must represent a compromise between optimum combat effectiveness and optimum safety. Diving deep into the sea at great depths is inherently hazardous, as every submarine sailor knows; the problem is what level of risk should the designer accept.

But it is already rather clear that future submarine designs will reduce materially the number of piping joints. The chances of failure, some designers believe, are multiplied by the number of joints. The quality control of workmanship needed is so high that the possibility of human failure by inadequately trained or careless inspection personnel increases.

Bending, rather than joining, of pipes wherever possible; rerouting them so that welds rather than brazing would be possible; and eventually, perhaps, the development of some sort of propulsion system that would eliminate, or at least reduce, the piping subject to sea pressure within the hull are all part of the planned changes.

So, too, is a system called Frisco (fast reaction integrated submarine control), an automatic reaction type of submarine control and safety system. By means of computers and electronic and hydrostatic monitors and controls, this system will provide the quick reactions that human reflexes cannot for the high-speed, deep-diving submarines of tomorrow.

The size of the sail planes—the ventral fins that stick out from either side of the submarine superstructure called the sail—is another issue in debate. Some submarine sailors believe that they should be somewhat larger so that the planes themselves—like the wings of an airplane—would provide a certain amount of buoyancy, or "lift" and could compensate for some negative buoyancy in case of unexpected flooding.

Changes in design will be influenced by the experimental submarines now operating or under construction. The *Albacore*, with its tear-drop-shaped hull for high speed underwater and its sensitive airplane type of controls, pioneered the deep high-speed trend. Its hull form, sometimes slightly modified, is now standard for attack submarines.

The *Albacore* is being used for many experiments, with different combinations of propellers and rudders and varying types of controls. She has recently been reequipped with what are believed to be the world's most powerful electric batteries, which give her an underwater speed of about 33 knots for short periods.

Another experimental submarine, the *Dolphin*, is being built for the Navy. It is designed for far deeper dives than any submarine afloat. Its test depth has not been disclosed, but it is believed that it will be at least three to four times the limits of the *Thresher* class. The *Thresher*'s top speed and depth limits were secret, but speculative published reports indicated that she had a test depth of perhaps 1,000 feet, and a top underwater speed of more than 25 knots.

The *Dolphin* will have only a seven-man crew, but she will be highly instrumented and automated. She will have a computer-recorder to tape and assimilate the immense amount of data she is expected to record. She will be used to assist in the solution of such seemingly simple but actually complex engineering problems as how best to seal a propeller shaft bearing against the tremendous pressure of hundreds and thousands of feet of water.

The *Aluminaut*, to be built of high-strength aluminum forgings bolted together, is under construction by Reynolds International and the Electric Boat Division of General Dynamics Corp. She is designed as a research submarine for use down to depths of 15,000 feet by the Woods Hole Oceanographic Institution. She will carry a crew of three and will have a horizontal radius of about 80 miles.

In addition to these submarines, an extensive oceanographic program includes a projected construction program of six to eight small research submarines for exploratory operations down to 15,000 to 18,000 feet. Another and improved bathyscaphe, capable of reaching the deepest parts of the ocean—estimated at more than 36,000 feet—is also planned.

New materials, of greater strength than any now available, are being developed. The United States Steel Corp. has recently received a contract to develop a new type of tough steel alloy for hull plates of deep submergence submarines. Welding techniques of greater strength are also to be developed.

DEPTHS ARE ESTIMATED

The Navy believes that these, and many other developments, may make possible test depths for operating submarines (as distinct from research and development submarines) of a maximum of about 4,000 feet in the period of 1970–80. Many officers see no combat or military requirement for any greater depth capability, but some disagree.

In any event, the present and future designs and capabilities of the Navy's submarines are now being put under the microscope. A board of experts and submarine "elder statesmen"—including naval officers and civilian scientists—has been established under the Assistant Secretary of the Navy for Research and Development. It is called the Deep Submergence Systems Review Group and is headed by Rear Adm. E. C. Stephan, a former Navy oceanographer.

DEPARTMENT OF THE NAVY,
OFFICE OF THE SECRETARY,
Washington, D.C., August 29, 1963.

Hon. CLINTON P. ANDERSON,
Chairman, Subcommittee on Security, Joint Committee on Atomic Energy, Congress of the United States, Washington, D.C.

DEAR SENATOR ANDERSON: I am in receipt of your letter of August 19, 1963, requesting a reconsideration of my decision to maintain the *Thresher* hearing records classified. As you can well appreciate, I carefully considered the matter prior to making this decision, and in reviewing the situation, I believe the rationale to be completely sound. The hearings transcript should at this time maintain its classified status.

I am informed that the hearings have not been completed, and of course the records of the court of inquiry have not been reviewed. In my opinion, it would be a poor time indeed to release piecemeal the facts and assumptions documented by your hearings. Such action could materially downgrade our offensive-defensive submarine weapons systems, both in the public mind and the minds of our officers and men that man them. This would certainly lead to many comments and speculations. Such public knowledge would undoubtedly aid our enemies in their intelligence assessments and possibly in their own undersea program. Other important factors to be weighed are the concern which could be generated in the minds of our allies and in the world in general. Also such release could have an extremely detrimental effect on the Navy's current endeavors to integrate qualified volunteer line officers into the nuclear submarine program.

I am informed that Mr. Baldwin visited the Bureau of Ships on July 17, 1963, and discussed unclassified aspects of the *Thresher* disaster, chiefly with regard to technical matters of piping system joints which are of common shipbuilding knowledge, with Rear Adm. Charles A Curtze, U.S. Navy Deputy Chief and Capt. D. H. Kern, U.S. Navy head of the Submarine Branch, Bureau of Ships. Although Mr. Baldwin's article, because of his broad experience and background in Navy matters, was more informative than would have been expected of the average newspaperman, the Navy considers that its security interests were properly safeguarded.

I trust, Senator Anderson, that this letter details my concern regarding declassification of portions of the hearings transcripts at this time. As you know, we are deeply involved with our comprehensive review of records, procedures, and conditions relating to the nuclear submarine program, and as a result, I am certain that many changes will be forthcoming.

Sincerely yours,

FRED KORTH.

CONGRESS OF THE UNITED STATES,
JOINT COMMITTEE ON ATOMIC ENERGY,
March 16, 1964.

Hon. PAUL H. NITZE,
The Secretary of the Navy.

DEAR MR. SECRETARY: On June 26, 27, and July 23, 1963, the Joint Committee held executive hearings on the loss of the nuclear submarine, *Thresher.*

In correspondence with Secretary Korth, subsequent to the hearings, the committee on July 3 and 31, and August 19, 1963, requested that the Navy review the hearing record and mark those items of a classified nature, so that such items could be deleted preparatory to the publication of an unclassified record.

In response, former Secretary Korth, on August 13, and again on August 29, 1963, stated in letters to the Joint Committee that the entire transcript should be maintained in a classified status.

I would like to reiterate my request that the Navy review the record of the hearing and specifically designate that information in the hearing record which is classified. In addition, please indicate why the specific item is classified.

As you may know, I have always encouraged the agencies of Government to maintain the security of defense information and restricted data. However, it is equally my conviction that security classification should not be used to protect the people from the truth or to keep embarrassing information from the public.

In my view, the Navy's refusal to identify specific areas of the *Thresher* transcript which are classified is based, in part, on a desire to withhold information which rightly belongs in the public domain. There can be no satisfactory justification for this attitude.

Accordingly, should the Navy persist in its refusal to identify those areas of the *Thresher* transcript which are classified, I plan to initiate action leading to the preparation of a report on the *Thresher* hearings, pursuant to the duty and authority vested in the Joint Committee on Atomic Energy by sections 202 and 206 of the Atomic Energy Act of 1954.

Your prompt attention to this matter will be appreciated.

Sincerely yours,

CLINTON P. ANDERSON,
Chairman, Subcommittee on Security.

DEPARTMENT OF THE NAVY,
OFFICE OF THE SECRETARY,
Washington, D.C., March 25, 1964.

Hon. CLINTON P. ANDERSON,
Chairman, Subcommittee on Security,
Joint Committee on Atomic Energy,
Congress of the United States,
Washington, D.C.

DEAR CLINT: I appreciate your interest in the Navy, and your desire to make public an unclassified report on the *Thresher* hearings. Pursuant to the request contained in your letter of March 16, I have taken action to review the transcript with view to designating those areas which are classified. In addition, it is believed that there are matters, while not of a classified nature, that may not be in the best interests of the Government to release. To the extent such is contained in the record, in the judgment of the Navy, these will be separately designated and the reasons set forth. As you can well appreciate, this endeavor must be handled by my most knowledgeable people, considering well the impact of such release both within this country and to our potential enemies. We are proceeding with sanitization. When sanitization is completed and the transcripts submitted, as stated earlier by my predecessors Mr. Korth, we will be pleased to cooperate with your staff and assist in any way possible.

Since the *Thresher* and our nuclear submarine program are of such vital importance to the defense posture, it is suggested that a review of your report prior to publication might prove beneficial to both the Joint Committee on Atomic Energy and to the Navy.

Sincerely yours,

PAUL NITZE.

DEPARTMENT OF THE NAVY,
OFFICE OF THE SECRETARY,
Washington, D.C., May 26, 1964.

Hon. CLINTON P. ANDERSON,
Chairman, Subcommittee on Security.
Joint Committee on Atomic Energy,
Congress of the United States, Washington, D.C.

DEAR CLINT: Enclosed is the transcript of the *Thresher* hearings, as I promised in my letter of March 25.

As I am sure you will understand, it was a most difficult task to isolate just those parts of the transcript which must properly bear a security classification. Mr. Conway and his staff worked closely with the Navy team engaged in this long endeavor, and were most helpful.

I understand that further updating hearings on *Thresher* and subsequent corrective actions are scheduled to be held next month. The consolidation of the two phases of the hearings into a single report will place the matter in proper perspective and should serve a constructive purpose. In this regard, I would appreciate the opportunity to review the galley proofs prior to report printing. You may be assured that I will be pleased to cooperate in any way possible.

Sincerely,

PAUL [NITZE].

DEPARTMENT OF THE NAVY,
OFFICE OF THE SECRETARY,
Washington, D.C., July 22, 1964.

Mr. JOHN T. CONWAY,
Executive Director, Joint Committee on Atomic Energy,
Congress of the United States, Washington, D.C.

DEAR MR. CONWAY: In response to your letter of July 9, one edited and sanitized copy of the transcript of executive session hearings on *Thresher*, July 1, 1964, is enclosed. This transcript has been edited for accuracy by the cognizant witnesses, and their correction noted in green pencil markings. The areas considered classified have been bracketed by red pencil markings.

In addition, two pieces of Navy correspondence are enclosed which have been sanitized, with the classified areas bracketed by red pencil markings. These include my February 5, 1964, letter to you summarizing developments since the loss of *Thresher*, requested by your July 9 letter; and, Chief, Bureau of Ships letter of August 28, 1962, to commander, Portsmouth Naval Shipyard, concerning silver-brazed piping on *Thresher*, requested by your July 15, 1964, letter.

I believe this completes any outstanding Navy responsibilities in this area. This material should assist in the generation of a factual and informative report. As previously agreed, it is requested that the Navy be allowed to review the galley proofs prior to printing of the report.

If I can be of any further assistance, please do not hesitate to call upon me.

I have designated Captain Robbins, Director of Congressional Investigations as my representative in these matters.

Sincerely,

PAUL H. NITZE.

Enclosures:
   (1) Transcript of executive session *Thresher* hearings, July 1, 1964.
   (2) Secretary of Navy letter of February 5 to Mr. Conway.
   (3) Chief, Bureau of Ships, letter of August 28, 1962, to commander, Portsmouth Naval Shipyard.

APPENDIX 9

CORRESPONDENCE CONCERNING ADDITIONAL INFORMATION REQUESTED BY JOINT COMMITTEE

DEPARTMENT OF THE NAVY,
OFFICE OF THE SECRETARY,
February 5, 1964.

Mr. JOHN T. CONWAY,
Executive Director,
Joint Committee on Atomic Energy,
Congress of the United States,
Washington, D.C.

DEAR MR. CONWAY: Recently several members of your staff enumerated various areas of interest concerning the *Thresher* hearings about which the Joint Committee on Atomic Energy was desirous of obtaining additional information. Accordingly, I have had material assembled on those specific items mentioned and am enclosing it herewith for your information. In addition to this material, it was requested that your staff be given a personal briefing by Rear Admiral Stephan pertaining to his work in hull tests, search, and rescue vessels. As the admiral has not conducted investigations in the area of hull tests, this portion of your request is not entirely clear. Hull tests currently specified for submarines are contained in shipbuilding specifications and the Bureau of Ships' technical manual. If this is the type of information which is desired by the Joint Committee, it can be provided on your request.

It is hoped that the enclosed information meets the requirements of your committee on this matter. You may be assured that the Navy is most pleased to cooperate with you in this manner, and you will be informed with regard to future changes that are considered significant.

Sincerely yours,

PAUL H. NITZE,
Secretary of the Navy.

"THRESHER" HEARINGS, ADDITIONAL INFORMATION REQUESTED BY THE JOINT
COMMITTEE ON ATOMIC ENERGY

(a) Design study group

The *Thresher* Design Appraisal Board (Design Study Group) appointed by
the Chief, Bureau of Ships, completed deliberations and submitted its report
of July 15, 1963. This group made various recommendations concerning improvements of design, fabrication, and testing directed toward improvement in
submarine safety. These recommendations have been incorporated into the
Bureau of Ships submarine safety program for evaluation and are being implemented as appropriate in new construction and operating submarines.

(b) Blow rate, capacity

Computer studies conducted prior to and following loss of *Thresher* have been
utilized to evaluate the adequacy of stored compressed air and the rate at which
main ballast can be blown from submarines at deep depths. As a result of these
studies changes are being or will be made in submarines under construction to
improve their flooding recovery capability. Present intent of the Bureau of
Ships is to provide a higher main ballast tank air blow rate in all submarines
having a design test depth of [classified matter deleted] feet or greater. Indications to date concerning the need for increased air storage are that little if any
increase in capacity is required or will be required for most classes of submarines. However, some increase is anticipated for some classes and redistribution of existing air banks may be required for others. This increase in blow
rate and redistribution or increase in high-pressure air storage where applicable
is currently underway in new construction and is planned for operating submarines during first overhaul. Studies conducted to date on new construction
and operating submarines showing recovery capability as a function of various
system parameters and flooding holes sizes will be provided the Joint Committee
staff if desired.

(c) Personnel policy

(1) It has been and will continue to be the policy of the Chief of Naval
Personnel that both the commanding officer and executive officer not be relieved
during construction, postshakedown availability, or regular overhaul of nuclear
submarines. The exception to policy in the case of *Thresher* was authorized
because of urgent requirements for commanding officers of Polaris submarines—
the Nation's highest priority program. The Chief of Naval Personnel is embarked on a determined effort to obtain additional qualified officer personnel
for nuclear power training which should increase his flexibility for officer
rotation.

(2) At Portsmouth Naval Shipyard, officers in the ship supervisor category
have been extended as necessary in order to complete the entire yard period of
the submarine to which assigned. Additional officers in excess of allowance
have been ordered into the design, construction, and repair areas to assist in a
rapid return to a satisfactory production level.

(d) Fabrication changes, including specifications

The most significant changes in fabrication requirements for submarines as a
result of *Thresher* loss have been in the area of critical piping system joints. The
basic instructions covering sil-braze for submarine piping have been combined
and reissued and have been modified to incorporate new techniques in inspections
(ultrasonics), more stringent training of production and inspection personnel,
closer inspection, and more thorough accountability. Design changes have also
been implemented to decrease the amount of piping and the number of joints
subject to submergence pressure. Increased radiography of castings in critical
piping systems has been called for in new construction and improved nonferrous
radiography standards have been issued. The requirement for improved assurance in sil-braze piping system joints and increased requirements for radiography
of castings will be applied to operating submarines and will require considerable
additional effort over normal overhaul work.

(e) Rework or modification of boats in operation

The Bureau of Ships has developed a work package consisting of items required
for the improvement in submarine safety dictated by the above and other improvements in systems and components. This package will be accomplished in all new

construction submarines and in all operating submarines having a design test depth of [classified matter deleted] feet or greater.

The following items constitute the Bureau of Ships safety certification package directed toward an order of magnitude increase in the safety of submarine operations and the removal of current restrictions on submarine operating depth. Accomplishment of the complete package on a particular submarine will provide maximum reasonable assurance within existing state of the art that failure of vital systems or components will not occur under the most severe operating conditions during peace or war. Accomplishment of portions of this package will significantly reduce the hazards inherent in submarine operations at any depth. Completion of the mandatory portion of the certification package will minimize the risk of catastrophic failure sufficiently to permit BuShips to certify the material condition for unrestricted operations to design test depth.

Certification package.—(1) Certification of critical piping systems: Sea water, hydraulics, high-pressure air and oxygen.

   (*a*) Weld and inspect radiographically or silbraze to the new standards and inspect ultrasonically certain critical piping system joints as specifically identified for each submarine or class of submarines.

   (*b*) Radiograph vital castings in sea-water systems to insure integrity.

   (*c*) Remove all unsatisfactory forms of aluminum bronze where in contact with sea water.

   (*d*) Provide more reliable flexible piping in sea-water systems.

   (*e*) Remove unsatisfactory K–Monel.

(2) Certification of the hull boundary: Review the design, construction, and testing performed for new design (*Thresher* depth) submarines to insure adequacy in all respects. Such items forming the hull boundary as sea-water systems, trash ejector, torpedo tubes must be evaluated from a safety standpoint.

(3) Improvement in flooding control and recovery capability:

   (*a*) Insure remote operated air bank valves fail in such a way to provide air to MBT blow system (in event of an electrical failure).

   (*b*) Insure MBT blow filters are of proper type and properly located.

   (*c*) Insure adequate high-pressure air stowage is provided.

   (*d*) Provide a separate emergency blow system for increased ballast ejection.

   (*e*) Provide remote, central control of sea water valves.

   (*f*) Insure there is adequate access to vital equipment for operation or repair in an emergency.

(4) Insure the stern plane control system is in peak mechanical condition.

Complete details of the extent to which Bureau of Ships intends to accomplish the certification package on individual ships and the intended time of accomplishment (overhaul/delivery schedules) for operating and new construction submarines respectively will be provided to the Joint Committee staff if desired.

(*f*) Operating limitations

(1) All deep diving submarines have been restricted to a maximum operating depth of [classified matter deleted] feet. On July 23, 1963, authority was granted by the Chief of Naval Operations to conduct a single deliberate carefully controlled dive to [classified matter deleted] feet in a specified area of limited depth for each new construction submarine during builder's trials. Such a dive will provide assurance that, in an emergency, an overshoot to [classified matter deleted] feet would be safe. This dive is authorized only upon certification by the Bureau of Ships that the workmanship, construction techniques, inspections, and test programs, used in construction of the submarine are adequate and in all respects meet established standards and requirements. The Bureau of Ships specifically determines certification for this [classified matter deleted] foot dive based upon audit and review of the shipyard's procedures and records including such vital areas as nondestructive testing of sil-brazed piping joints, radiography of welded hull and piping joints, test and inspection records, material identification and control, special pretrial tests and adequacy of damage control equipment. A single dive to [classified matter deleted] feet is considered entirely safe due to its controlled nature and increased margin of safety provided by thorough inspection and improved recovery capabilities.

(2) Reinstatement of design test depth is planned on a ship-to-ship basis when the certification package for each ship is accomplished.

(g) Discipline action re Hecker

No disciplinary action has been taken or is contemplated concerning Lieutenant Commander Hecker's involvement in the *Thresher* incident. He is still in command of the rescue vessel *Skylark*. He will be due for normal rotation from his present command in June 1964.

(h) Search summary

(1) On September 5, 1963, the associated operational aspects of the search for the nuclear submarine *Thresher* were terminated. This decision was made due to need for a thorough overhaul of *Trieste* and the rapidly deteriorating weather conditions during the fall in the *Thresher* search area.

(2) During this search effort, which lasted nearly 5 months and involved more than three dozen ships and thousands of men, the *Trieste* made a total of 10 dives. The most significant dive was made on August 28, 1963, when the bathyscaph took a number of extremely valuable photographs and made a unique recovery from the ocean floor 8,400 feet from the surface. The item recovered was a piece of brass piping and a fitting with markings which definitely established that it came from *Thresher*. The piping was picked up by a mechanical arm operated from inside *Trieste*'s gondola in the first successful test of this device.

(3) Much of the burden of the 5 months' search fell largely to four research ships; the Military Sea Transportation Service ships *Gilliss* and *Gibbs*, the Lamont Geological Observatory ship *Conrad* and the Woods Hole Oceanographic Institution vessel *Atlantis II*. Using deep-towed still and television cameras, magnetometers, and sonars, the ships made exhaustive electronic probes of the bottom and took thousands of photographs. As a result, the area of the search is now better known to oceanographers than any area of similar depth in the world.

(4) Although no part of *Thresher's* pressure hull was sighted or photographed, the amount of evidence collected in the form of debris sighted, photographed, and recovered leaves no doubt as to the general location of the sunken submarine. From analyses of many water and bottom samples taken in the search area, there is no indication of any radiological hazard, even to marine life. Periodic surveys will continue to be made in *Thresher* area using oceanographic research ships. Further exploratory work in the field of deep submergence vehicles and underwater reconnaissance is being planned under the direction of the Chief of Naval Research.

APPENDIX 10

THE NEED FOR A HIGH IQ (INTEGRITY-QUALITY)

Remarks by Rear Adm. Charles A. Curtze, U.S. Navy Deputy Chief of the Bureau of Ships at the Ninth Annual Gas Turbine Conference and Products Show sponsored by the Gas Turbine Power Division of the American Society of Mechanical Engineers, Houston, Tex., March 4, 1964

Mr. Chairman, distinguished guests, gentlemen, ordinarily you might expect me to talk about gas turbines or some new, intricate, and interesting device and how it does its job for the Navy. I am not—I am going to tell you what you are going to have to do for me if I am going to be successful in my job.

I need primarily a high IQ—I need ship and component integrity and quality and you, gentlemen, representing the scope of industrial disciplines that you do, are going to provide it for me.

Today, I propose to tell you how the Navy is going to extract it from you because, in recent years, as I will point out later, IQ has not necessarily been automatically discharged without a lot of pump priming. We simply cannot tolerate or afford deficiencies in Navy ships and equipment. Too much is at stake. Frankly, our ships are not all we would like them to be, and further, are not all we know how to make them be and lastly, intend to make them be.

We are faced with critical operating and maintenance problems due to the introduction of ultracomplex systems into the fleet. Many of these new systems are not performing to promise because they are not reliable and are difficult to maintain. There are a number of remedial actions we can take to bring these problems under control. The purpose of my remarks here today is to plead for intelligent help from you through generating an understanding of Navy problems that you, as engineers, can do something about solving.

I find it not only convenient but good antifrustration medicine occasionally to review how things used to be and why, and how things are now and why; how we ran the gamut from simplicity, dependability, maintainability, and excellent cost effectiveness to complexity, questionable reliability, diminishing maintainability and high-cost hardware in our quest for major increases in combat effectiveness.

Our lives as engineers, measured against the problems of our times, have never been simple. That's why we like what we do. Under the old guild system, the master was responsible for conceptual design and execution. The materials available to him were basic. Long association of his forebears with these materials gave him knowledge of their limitations. The consumer public trusted him implicitly as evidenced by the German quip: "What the master does is well done, but the apprentice needs to be beat about a bit."

During the industrial revolution in England, product complexity increased. It became impossible to embody in one man all of the required skills and disciplines within the fast-changing time and cost frames. Even then, if Dickens is any authority, a mechanic and engineer with ambition became the owner-manager-mechanic who hired others to help him share the load. The measure of a man was reflected in Dickens' comment that wherever such a man goes, "they'll know that there is a man as knows his tools, and, as his tools knows, knows how to use them. If that ain't a man, where is a man?" It's still true although new tools are added to our kits.

It was possible, because of the length of time it took to produce anything, for the manager-artificer to keep a continuing check on quality and progress; only an ultimate operational checkout, test run was required before delivery and acceptance.

Further down the pike, the end of that era, perhaps 25 years ago, I went through Browne & Sharpe in Providence and saw some automatic screw machines on test. The foreman was rough-checking machine output for true circularity by revolving test spindles between his fingers. He modestly admitted that he could never really depend on this if one required an accuracy of anything better than a thousandth or two.

At the beginning of World War II our designs were conservative. The required skills and materials were available and completely familiar to all hands; specifications had been refined by years of fire and hammering. Equipment was standardized, at least in design, so almost anyone who had machinery to operate was able to maintain it. In short, dependability, maintainability, and reliability, under the conditions of loading usually encountered, was no problem.

We fought World War II largely with designs already firm at the beginning of the war. Our crews were stable and could maintain the ships. They had to, could, and did.

The period immediately after the war gave us time to look at a whole line of new things—and away we went. We did not sufficiently appreciate that the skills had been diluted and a whole new set of rules applied. Things changed—but fast.

We can't afford to let ourselves become hypnotized by our own cleverness. The nonengineering public has been conditioned by the press and national pride to think only in terms of bearded scientists, beetle-browed mathematicians, recluse physicists, harried engineers, and table-thumping executives. In the public eye, to this team, all is possible. They simply pour data into tireless computers of their own making. These regurgitate everything from the formula for Revlon's intimate perfume to nuclear powerplants—on demand.

If we had had an early enough awareness of the shape of things to come, we could have progressively kept ahead of the tide on many of the quality, reliability, and maintainability problems we are facing today. Unfortunately, although developments shot up exponentially, we kept running on a straight-line function.

For a look at the present: Included in our equipment troubles was a recent rash in our submarines. We selected one group of ships to look at, as alike as ships in 1 year's flight can be with diversified builders and component suppliers. The nuclear propulsion system was already adequately covered and reported.

During a 1-year period over 9,000 items were found deficient. These 9,000 were supplied by some 270 manufacturers. This also made it clear that something was wrong with us, too. At least specification precision was lacking; inspection less rigorous than necessary. The sweat needed to do things right just is not being generated.

Checks in building yards disclosed material errors indicating poor control in manufacturers' plants, and our own. We seemed to have lost the control we needed to guarantee the kind of product we required. It was painfully apparent that we could no longer depend on the methods of the past. I feel we got a bit sloppy as an industrial nation—a tendency to engineer price or profit and not value?

Admiral Rickover, who has addressed himself with force and effect on many occasions to this area, summed this up as clearly as I have seen it anywhere as follows:

"In many instances it is impossible to 'inspect' for the desired quality in complex equipment, especially after the equipment has been fabricated. The desired quality must be built into the equipment during all stages of design and manufacture. No amount of inspection can fully assure the desired quality; further, it is impracticable for the purchaser to duplicate all inspections and checks that have to be made by the manufacturer. Therefore, in the procurement of high-quality complex equipment it is most important that the purchaser assure himself that the manufacturer he selects is not only capable of providing equipment having the desired quality, but, whenever possible, is actually delivering similar high-quality equipment."

So much for how we got where we are and what's wrong. What's the fix?

The guiding thesis in our solution of these difficulties is first to establish an orderly and systematic description of them. We think we can cope with these difficulties once we have measured them and have established a solid quantitative basis on which to build. We want to do away with vague will-o'-the-wisp opinion surveys and reports and come up with good, solid figures and facts. We are now making real progress along this road and have started in the education of our own people and industry in what we are trying to do. Unfortunately, our problem is not a simple one, for we have had to apply the most advanced technology to provide modern ships in support of our national position as a seapower. We are certain that we must have these systems to have the seagoing fighting force the Nation needs.

Now every young engineer is dedicated to the thought that technology is a wonderful thing but pragmatically it is not always an unmixed blessing. At any time, the new nuclear-powered, missile-equipped, jet-age Navy is in danger of bogging down in technological quicksand if we don't manage properly—this concerns me to motivate you.

It is no national secret that the necessary increases in combat capability of our ships and equipment have been won thus far with concurrent skyrocketing costs and almost overwhelming complexity. We have invested heavily in the technical promises for improved systems and in the process we traded off some older and in most cases more reliable systems to get them. Those were the tradeoffs. What happened to the payoffs? Unfortunately, some are still in the state of promise and not yet performance.

I have already given you some illustrations of essentially engineering inadequacies in a number of areas. I will also describe some of the systematic approaches we have recently given renewed credence to help us eliminate our troubles.

I mentioned earlier that the roles have changed—technology is advancing so rapidly, particularly in the missiles systems areas that we have been hard pressed to develop parameters for material support or eqipment maintenance. Our standard maintenance management program is designed to fill this need.

We think the Bureau of Ships design work-study program gives us the start we need to insure a ship system that can in fact be controlled from design through delivery to operational dependability. It helps point out the areas of large, quick, cheap, and easy return—we can initially attack where the payoffs are greatest; it sets the relatively bloodless stones in good perspective—we don't waste time squeezing them.

The increase in space and complement required by the new systems to meet the new threats caused ships growth to the extent that a present-day escort ship is bigger than most World War II destroyers. The new systems have improved the eyes, ears, and kill capabilities of the new ships but the price in greater cost in men and money was high. The complex new systems brought with them difficult problems in maintenance, reliability, and communications.

Design work study is basically a logical, systematic, factfinding method of determining the requirements for effectively operating and maintaining a ship—how it can best be done, by whom and how fast. Just how complex a ship do we need? Can we go conservative to maintain the basic ship and machinery with lower levels of skills and fewer men? What are the optimum machinery arrangements for easy maintainability? Do we need complicated feed systems and high pressure lube oil systems when a return to lower pressures, lower bearing loadings permit us to get along with familiar, tried and true hardware, carbon moly pipe, horizontal blowers? Is the price in tonnage too much to pay? Size, per se, really is the cheapest thing we build into a ship. It's what occupies the larger volume that costs money.

The first ship design using the work study approach was the escort ship in the Navy's 1964 program. The new approach resulted in an initial weight saving of about 300 tons. This paid off in room for equipment and systems that significantly increased the operational capability while permitting a substantial reduction of personnel.

Because of the excellent results obtained with this ship, design work study is now being applied to the design of a tank landing ship (LST) and a submarine tender (AS) in our 1965 program. We envision design work study as a way of life in ship design by 1970.

Considerations of maintenance and logistic support of our work studied ship caused us to dust off the reports of World War II "automatic flow of spare parts," from which we never really recovered but merely walked away from, and progressive maintenance. We found we had no "use data" for the new equipment in our ships.

The standard maintenance management system gave us the tool. This really is not a new idea to the Navy or to industry. What started in 1947 as a punch card operation, for systems sake, has come into its own—been given the support to make it fly.

The new program set up by the Fleet Maintenance Division of the Chief of Naval Operations was established specifically to define what maintenance had to be done and when—and to provide a system which would allow complete control—yet be clutched rather than geared to possible changes in the operating schedules. Although only about a year old, this program is paying off in more than 200 ships. We are now able to get the shipwork done with existing personnel in less time. Breakdowns are on the decline, weak links in the components defined and corrective action possible.

This gives us a formal line management and technical feedback system that will provide the fleet, Chief of Naval Operations, technical bureaus and you with the data each of us needs to improve and control our singular efforts. As you would guess—the most difficult part of this development is not so much defining what we need to know as learning how to get this data factually from our sailors. They are still disposed to fix and forget.

One of the facts of our lives is competitive procurement. It's always mentioned in the same breath with low costs. It does give everyone a chance but it complicates logistic support. There is always conflict between "inital buy" and "cradle to grave" thinking.

The maintenance management program is expected to reduce casualties by at least 50 percent through the accomplishment of engineered preventive maintenance. This in turn will reduce spare parts burnup and costs; the feedback will provide us with data to assist in making more sensible buys and reduce initial buys for new ships. A spinoff of the hoped for reduction in complexity of basic plant hits at the heart of spare parts requirements.

To attack the problem of increased numbers and caliber of men on our ships, both programs are involved. Work study integrates men with equipment, systems, and spaces and already has reduced the numbers of men required to operate our ships. On the other hand, the maintenance management program has materially reduced the maintenance time required of our sailors—lowered the level of skill to accomplish the preventive maintenance tasks. A fringe benefit is the reduction in training requirements and costs.

We intend to assure ourselves of "cradle to the grave" control. You control your contributions for us. It would be quite impossible and in fact, from our respective points of view, not only undesirable but unnecessary to have it otherwise. Our quality assurance program is a planned and systematic pattern of actions necessary to provide confidence that the product will perform satisfactorily. This definition envisions progress that will insure quality at each stage the product goes through we will require the control systems by spec and conduct audits for adequacy and conformity. This is a touchy point but the facts support the requirement.

As the most important outgrowth of these things, we will have the information on which to base and support our specification requirements. Our specifications never were goals, they were and are requirements. There will be no waivers of them as such. If a change is supported by sound engineering logic, we will change the specification. We are thinking about extending the use of nondeviation plans in areas where the payoff is worth it.

We are going increasingly into full-scale space mockups to insure engineering maintainability and planned easy replacement of components when necessary. From these we are extending the use of dimensioned drawings—less and less will be left to pipefitters' choice or chance.

You may ask—how can you talk of cost effectiveness and engineered value in the face of all this? We are buying maintainability, reliability and long life. We thought we were still getting it—we weren't. Our yardstick for cost is ship life cost as opposed to initial buy. One of the least used tools of value engineering is conservative engineering, at least let's use it where we can.

In summary, there is no single magic system that will assure this high IQ. No matter how sharp the tools, they can only be used effectively if all personnel involved are diligent. Top management must be attentive and relentless in nit picking the details involved.

Effectiveness is in this case—as in all worthwhile things—largely proportional to the sweat expended.

We are underway—I ask you to join, we need your help.

APPENDIX 11

April 10, 1964.

FLOOR STATEMENT BY CONGRESSMAN CHET HOLIFIELD: IN HONOR OF THOSE WHO WERE LOST IN "THRESHER"

On the morning of April 10, 1963, the nuclear submarine, *Thresher*, was lost at sea, 200 miles off Cape Cod, while undergoing a series of test dives.

Exactly 1 year has passed since the tragic loss of the *Thresher* and the 129 brave men who were lost with her. In this past year, the 129 men of the *Thresher* have become part of the history of American heroes who have given their lives in the defense of freedom.

Yet, it is not enough to merely pay tribute to these men, for tributes—no matter how heartfelt—are only words. We must learn something from this tragedy so that similar tragedies will not occur.

The Joint Committee on Atomic Energy, of which I am vice chairman, held extensive hearings last year on the events surrounding the loss of the *Thresher*. Our main objective was to assure that all measures were being taken to prevent a similar tragedy. The record of the hearings was classified for security reasons, but the Joint Committee has made every attempt to have the unclassified information made public. Recently, the Secretary of the Navy agreed to assist the committee in his endeavor. We now believe that a useful unclassified document may be released in the near future.

Our investigation was undertaken not with the purpose of ascribing blame, but rather with the objective of developing all the lessons that could be learned from the loss of the *Thresher*, so that it could be truly said that these 129 men did not die in vain.

No words can soften the grief of the widows, the orphans, the mothers, the fathers, the loved ones left behind by the men of the *Thresher*. We share their grief, but we cannot erase it. We can only take comfort in the knowledge that these men gave their lives in the defense of their country on the great, silent battlefield of the cold war.

APPENDIX 12

MEMORANDUM CONCERNING SUBMARINE SAFETY STEERING TASK GROUP

DEPARTMENT OF THE NAVY,
OFFICE OF THE SECRETARY,
OFFICE OF LEGISLATIVE AFFAIRS,
Washington, D.C., July 17, 1964.

Memorandum for Mr. Conway.

Subject: Names and titles of the submarine safety steering task group.

1. The subject information was requested by the JCAE during testimony by Rear Admiral Curtze, Deputy Chief, Bureau of Ships, on July 1, 1964. This information has been provided by the admiral, as follows:

Deputy Chief of Bureau (code 101), chairman, Rear Adm. C. A. Curtze, U.S. Navy.

Director, Ship Design Division (code 410), vice chairman, Capt. N. Sonenshein, U.S. Navy.

Head, Submarine Branch (code 525), Capt. D. H. Kern, U.S. Navy.

Director, Applied Research Division (code 340), Capt. M. L. Pittman, Jr., U.S. Navy.

Head, Machinery Design Branch (code 430), Capt. W. R. Riblett, U.S. Navy, relieving Capt. W. E. Weisert, U.S. Navy, detached, July 7, 1964.

Director, Hull Division (code 630), Capt. D. L. Creed, U.S. Navy, relieving Capt. R. Riley, U.S. Navy, retired, July 1, 1964.

Director, Machinery Division (code 640), Capt. D. G. Phillips, U.S. Navy.

Director, Assurance Systems Engineering Division (code 705), Cmdr. R. J. Leuschner, U.S. Navy, relieving Capt. T. V. Hennessey, U.S. Navy, retiring September 1, 1964.

Submarine safety project officer (code 525), recorder, Cmdr. J. E. Rasmussen, U.S. Navy.

    Very respectfully,

SPENCER E. ROBBINS,
Captain, U.S. Navy,
Director, Congressional Investigations.

APPENDIX 13

Status of shipbuilding program for nuclear-powered ships authorized by Congress

SUBMARINES

Hull number and name	Ship-building program fiscal year	Builder	Sea trials completed
Attack type:			
SSN 571 *Nautilus*	1952	Electric Boat	1955
SSN 575 *Seawolf* [1]	1953	___do___	1960
SSN 586 *Triton*	1956	___do___	1959
Small attack type:			
SSN 578 *Skate*	1955	___do___	1957
SSN 579 *Swordfish*	1955	Portsmouth	1958
SSN 583 *Sargo*	1956	Mare Island	1958
SSN 584 *Seadragon*	1956	Portsmouth	1959
Guided-missile-type Regulus: SSGN 587 *Halibut*	1956	Mare Island	1959
Hunter-killer attack type: SSN 597 *Tullibee*	1956	Electric Boat	1960
Fast attack type:			
SSN 585 *Skipjack*	1956	___do___	1959
SSN 588 *Scamp*	1957	Mare Island	1961
SSN 589 *Scorpion*	1957	Electric Boat	1960
SSN 590 *Sculpin*	1957	Ingalls	1961
SSN 591 *Shark*	1957	Newport News	1961
SSN 592 *Snook*	1957	Ingalls	1961
SSN 594 *Permit*	1958	Mare Island	1962
SSN 595 *Plunger*	1958	___do___	1962
SSN 596 *Barb*	1958	Ingalls	1963
SSN 603 *Pollack*	1959	New York Ship	1964
SSN 604 *Haddo*	1959	___do___	1964
SSN 605 *Jack*	1959	Portsmouth	___
SSN 606 *Tinosa*	1959	___do___	1964
SSN 607 *Dace*	1959	Ingalls	1964
SSN 612 *Guardfish*	1960	New York Ship	___
SSN 613 *Flasher*	1960	Electric Boat	___
SSN 614 *Greenling*	1960	___do___	___
SSN 615 *Gato*	1960	___do___	___
SSN 621 *Haddock*	1961	Ingalls	___
SSN 637 *Sturgeon*	1962	Electric Boat	___
SSN 638 *Whale*	1962	Bethelem	___
SSN 639 *Tautog*	1962	Ingalls	___
SSN 646 *Grayling*	1963	Portsmouth	___
SSN 647 *Pogy*	1963	New York Ship	___
SSN 648 *Aspro*	1963	Ingalls	___
SSN 649 *Sunfish*	1963	Bethelem	___
SSN 650 *Pargo*	1963	Electric Boat	___
SSN 651 *Queenfish*	1963	Newport News	___
SSN 652	1963	___do___	___
SSN 653 *Ray*	1963	___do___	___
SSN 660	1964	Portsmouth	___
SSN 661	1964	Unassigned	___
SSN 662	1964	Mare Island	___
SSN 663	1964	Unassigned	___
SSN 664	1964	___do___	___
SSN 665	1964	___do___	___
SSN 666	1965	___do___	___
SSN 667	1965	___do___	___
SSN 668	1965	___do___	___
SSN 669	1965	___do___	___
SSN 670	1965	___do___	___
SSN 671	1965	___do___	___

Total attack submarines authorized 51; completed 22.

See footnote at end of table.

Status of shipbuilding program for nuclear-powered ships authorized by Congress—Continued

SUBMARINES—Continued

Hull number and name	Ship-building program fiscal year	Builder	Sea trials completed
Fleet ballistic missile-type (Polaris):			
SSB(N)598 *George Washington*	1958	Electric Boat	1959
SSB(N)599 *Patrick Henry*	1958	....do	1960
SSB(N)600 *Theodore Roosevelt*	1958	Mare Island	1960
SSB(N)601 *Robert E. Lee*	1959	Newport News	1960
SSB(N)602 *Abraham Lincoln*	1959	Portsmouth	1961
SSB(N)608 *Ethan Allen*	1959	Electric Boat	1961
SSB(N)609 *Sam Houston*	1959	Newport News	1962
SSB(N)610 *Thomas A. Edison*	1959	Electric Boat	1961
SSB(N)611 *John Marshall*	1959	Newport News	1962
SSB(N)616 *Lafayette*	1961	Electric Boat	1963
SSB(N)617 *Alexander Hamilton*	1961	....do	1963
SSB(N)618 *Thomas Jefferson*	1961	Newport News	1962
SSB(N)619 *Andrew Jackson*	1961	Mare Island	1963
SSB(N)620 *John Adams*	1961	Portsmouth	1964
SSB(N)622 *James Monroe*	1961	Newport News	1963
SSB(N)623 *Nathan Hale*	1961	Electric Boat	1963
SSB(N)624 *Woodrow Wilson*	1961	Mare Island	1963
SSB(N)625 *Henry Clay*	1961	Newport News	1964
SSB(N)626 *Daniel Webster*	1961	Electric Boat	1964
SSB(N)627 *James Madison*	1962	Newport News	1964
SSB(N)628 *Tecumseh*	1962	Electric Boat	1964
SSB(N)629 *Daniel Boone*	1962	Mare Island	1964
SSB(N)630 *John C. Calhoun*	1962	Newport News	1964
SSB(N)631 *Ulysses S. Grant*	1962	Electric Boat	1964
SSB(N)632 *Von Steuben*	1962	Newport News	1964
SSB(N)633 *Casimer Pulaski*	1962	Electric Boat	1964
SSB(N)634 *Stonewall Jackson*	1962	Mare Island	1964
SSB(N)635 *Sam Rayburn*	1962	Newport News	1964
SSB(N)636 *Nathanael Greene*	1962	Portsmouth	1964
SSB(N)640 *Benjamin Franklin*	1963	Electric Boat	
SSB(N)641 *Simon Bolivar*	1963	Newport News	
SSB(N)642 *Kamehameha*	1963	Mare Island	
SSB(N)643 *George Bancroft*	1963	Electric Boat	
SSB(N)644 *Lewis and Clark*	1963	Newport News	
SSB(N)645 *James K. Polk*	1963	Electric Boat	
SSB(N)654 *George C. Marshall*	1964	Newport News	
SSB(N)655 *Henry L. Stimson*	1964	Electric Boat	
SSB(N)656 *George Washington Carver*	1964	Newport News	
SSB(N)657 *Francis Scott Key*	1964	Electric Boat	
SSB(N)658 *Mariano G. Vallejo*	1964	Mare Island	
SSB(N)659	1964	Electric Boat	
Total fleet ballistic missile submarines authorized, 41; completed, 29.			

SURFACE SHIPS

Guided missile cruiser: CG(N)9 *Long Beach*	1957	Bethlehem	1961
Aircraft carrier: CVA(N)65 *Enterprise*	1958	Newport News	1961
Guided missile frigate (destroyer leader):			
DLG(N)25 *Bainbridge*	1959	Bethlehem	1962
DLG(N)35 *Truxtun*	1962	New York Ship	
Total surface ships authorized, ; completed, 3.			
Grand total of all nuclear ships:			
Authorized, 96.			
Completed, 54.			

[1] USS *Seawolf*, originally commissioned in 1957, was recommissioned in 1960.

APPENDIX 14

EULOGIES PLACED IN THE CONGRESSIONAL RECORD, APRIL 22, 1963, BY SENATOR
JOHN O. PASTORE

[New York Times, Apr. 13, 1963]

"THRESHER"

She was the finest product of the shipwright's art and one of the maritime marvels of this technological age.

Like the great fish for which she was named, her kingdom was the ocean and its black depths. She was the lead ship of a class designed to run silent, run deep, and run fast—deeper and faster than any submarine of the past. She was shaped like a teardrop and powered with the fissioned energy of the atom. Her cylindrical pressure hull of heavy steel was designed to withstand the crushing weight of deep water.

When the klaxon sounded and the command "Dive! Dive!" echoed through the boat last Wednesday morning there were no intimations of disaster. *Thresher* had already established her preeminence and power. Today, with Lieutenant Commander Harvey and his crew, she lies many fathoms deep off the Continental Shelf. The Navy that built her and manned her may never know what destroyed her; the silent forces of the deep are implacable enemies to detailed investigation.

Yet no investigation is needed to reiterate certain verities. Death—of a ship or a man—is not an end but a beginning; man builds upon the past. Throughout the history of the sea men have died and ships have sunk. In the endless history of conflict between man and nature men have lost but man has triumphed. The earth's mountains have been conquered; the blue sky and the realm of space are sealed and now the forbidding depths—so long beyond the reach of man—are in process of conquest.

Man's indomitable spirit has never in history faltered in such extensions of man's kingdom. The *Thresher* is gone but *Thresher* lives.

————

PRAYER BY FRANCIS CARDINAL SPELLMAN

Let us pray. O God, the Creator, Redeemer of all the faithful, hear our supplications and through Thy infinite love and mercy graciously grant the souls of Thy servants departed remission of all their sins by which they may have deserved the severity of Thy divine justice and punishments in the world to come. Vouchsafe to them grace and mercy before the divine tribunal and let them attain to everlasting rest and happiness through the infinite merits of Jesus Christ. O God, great and omnipotent Judge of the living and the dead, before whom we are all to appear after this short life to render an account of our works, let our hearts, we pray Thee, be deeply moved at this sight of death. Let us be mindful of our own frailty and mortality, that walking always in Thy fear and in the ways of Thy commandments, we may after our departure from the world, experience a merciful judgment and rejoice in everlasting happiness through the same Christ our Lord.

Grant, O Lord, we beseech Thee, that while we lament the departure of Thy servants, our brothers, out of this life, we may bear in mind that we are most certainly to follow them. Give us grace to make ready for that last hour by a divine and holy life. Teach us how to watch and pray that when Thy summons comes, we may go forth to meet the bridegroom and enter with him into life everlasting through the same Christ our Lord. Almighty and most merciful Father, who knowest the weakness of our nature, bow down Thine ear and pity unto Thy servants upon whom Thou hast laid the heavy burden of sorrow. Take away out of their hearts the spirit of rebellion and teach them to see Thy good and gracious purpose in all the trials that shall descend upon them. Grant that they should not languish on unabandoned grief nor sorrow as those who have no hope, but through their tears look meekly up to Thee, the God of all consolation through Jesus Christ our Lord. Amen.

I feel sure that all of us have been consoled by the eulogy by Bishop Feeney and in sympathy and sorrow we offer our prayers to Almighty God that God will grant eternal rest to our heroes. Certainly very few tragedies in recent years can so touch the heart of all Americans with sympathy and sorrow— abiding sorrow and a desire to be helpful in their prayers. As Bishop Feeney was speaking I thought of a few stanzas of a verse I learned long ago. "The bravest battle that ever was fought shall I tell you where and when. On the map of the world you find it not—it's in the hearts of the mothers and wives of men," and I am sure that all of us feel and grieve deeply with you in the loss of your dear ones. They, however, have reached the goal of eternal life. In the prayers we are reminded that after this short life, and even the longest life is short, but we can be happy in the thought that these men who did their duty to their God and their country have received the award and the reward of eternal life. I like to think that when that last cry echoed through the *Thresher*, "Dive," that shortly afterward the men of the crew heard the response—the response that came from Almighty God—their Creator, their Redeemer, and their Saviour—"Well done," and now you faithful servants enter thou in the procession of the kingdom prepared for you from the beginning of the world.

THE MEMORIAL MESSAGE BY BISHOP HENRY KNOX SHERRILL

We are met together this afternoon for meditation, for worship, in order to pray for strength and courage and in order to thank God for lives which have been given in the service of the Nation and the free world. It is not a time, therefore, for long and intricate speech, as Mr. Lincoln said at Gettysburg so long ago. "It is not what we say here that matters," but certainly the whole Nation, indeed the entire world, has been saddened and shocked by this event. This does not change the hard reality of loss; the tragedy still remains, and it must not or cannot be underestimated, but the fact that in countless churches on Easter Day throughout this Nation prayers were offered for the families of these men, the fact that everywhere people are praying for God's blessing upon them must be a sustaining and a strengthening force in the realization of the great company who share this experience to some degree with you.

These men were, of course, unusual in their gifts. They were chosen because they had special aptitudes of training, of native ability, and, above else, of character, in order to serve in a pioneer enterprise, in a new type of service for the protection of the Nation and of the free world. So there are many memories of what they were and what they did and a very deep sense of thanksgiving for their service. We live in a strange world; it's a world in which there is peace, and yet there is no peace. A world in which, unfortunately it seems, to the moment impossible, to have international understanding and a genuine concord among the nations of the world. This kind of service in days of so-called peace is never as dramatic as wartime service. Someone said to me this morning that perhaps this tragedy will make the ordinary casual citizen realize more deeply all that the armed services are doing for us today, many times so undramatically. It has been my lot at various times to be in similar situations. I recall conducting a service in Honolulu Harbor over those who were lost in the attack at Pearl Harbor. I remember conducting service during two World Wars where there was again this tremendous loss. But what I would say now is from the point of view of the Nation, these men have given their lives for home and country just as much as if they had been at Pearl Harbor or in the Coral Sea or in the events of actual war.

I am confident that they did not wish war. I am confident that there was no hate of others in their minds or hearts. I have always found in a long experience there is more hatred expressed by those who are at home far away from action, than by those who are actually engaged in the struggle itself. No, they were performing a very important service in keeping the peace of the world.

in making it impossible for aggressors to destroy our liberties, our heritage, and all that is meant by freedom, in many nations of the world. So we owe them a tremendous debt for they gave their lives very truly, not only that the rest of us may be safe but that liberty and justice and freedom may pass on from our generation to those yet unborn. Again, what I'm saying does not break the impact of the hard loss but I say that here is a cause of humble pride. We are not our own because we have been bought with so great a price. What can be said in the way of comfort and strength? I must be honest, there are no easy answers to many of the things which happen in this world. Again and again, as a parish minister, I have been in difficult circumstances and you just do not know what to say. People say, "Why must this have been?" "Why?" and I have to answer, "I do not know." There is a mystery in life and there is a mystery in death, and no one, I think, clearly can see the way. But I have faith in the Easter hope that someday, freed from the limitations of time and of space when we do not see any more through a glass darkly but face to face, somehow, sometime, in the goodness of God, these strands will be brought together and in God's Eternity we will find the will of God and know this answer. The problem is as old as suffering, sin, and death. St. Paul asked the question that I am suggesting now. St. Paul said, "What can we say to these things? What can we say to these things?" Then after discussing some of the tribulations which come to the children of man, he closes with that magnificent statement, which is part of the Christian experience of the ages, and of us all, "For I am persuaded that neither death nor life, nor things present, nor things to come, shall be able to separate us from the love of God, in Christ Jesus, our Lord." I had an only friend in Boston, a wonderful old man who lost a brilliant son at an early age. His son was a remarkable physician. Before him were all sorts of opportunities for overcoming illness and disease and suddenly he was stricken just at the beginning of the manifestation of his powers. And I met his old father on Beacon Street in Boston and I said, "We have all been thinking of you and have been helped by the courage and faith which you and your family have shown during this difficult time." The old man said, "Yes, thank you. 'I had a letter yesterday. The letter read, you have been conquerors, you and your family, through this experience.'" The old gentleman smiled and then he said, "I wrote back. 'You entirely misunderstand. We have been more than conquerors through Him that loved us.'" So we do not meet these changes and circumstances of life by ourselves, there are great invisible spiritual forces, the love of God, the presence of the living Christ who rose from the dead himself, the promise of strength and courage and peace even of deep abiding joy that is the Easter message that is true for all times. So we pray to those who are immediately and specially bereaved that they may feel underneath God's everlasting arms, that they may feel something of this Easter joy. Death is swallowed up in victory. And we pray that we may entrust to God's loving care all those who are dear to us for this life and the life to come. May God give you strength and courage and the everlasting hope.

EULOGY BY BISHOP DANIEL FEENEY

Blessed are the dead who die in the Lord. Your Eminence, Your Excellency. good friends all in Christ, it is with the deepest conviction that I believe in the immortality of the soul of man. It is not because great thinkers and philosophers of all shades and culture over the ages have accepted this truth—no. I have a stronger and a sounder basis for the conviction that is mine. We are still within the period of the commemoration of the event that raises the ceremony of this kind above the level of soft sentiment to the very lofty heights of reality. How futile it would be, however permeated almost with mockery. Yes, more, how degrading to the proud who still lives the ceremony of this kind meant only that death was a completion of man's existence. The event that we commemorate this last Friday taught us that death is no more a mystery, but rather that it does not indicate the extension of man but is only an incident in the path of man's existence from this life to the realization, the yearnings, the longings that the human soul has ever experienced that can be satisfied only in the bosom of the Infinite, the Inexhaustible and the Eternal God. This thought alone gives dignity to a ceremony of this nature. The soul of man is immortal. The dominant thought in our minds this noon is union, union of the temporal living with those eternally living. In this spirit of union we cherish the love that has united us over the years. We esteem the memory of friendship and the appreciation of the character and the virtues of the loved ones. We know that the character of a good man does not die, but continues to exercise its beneficent influences just so long as those are those who are to carry on his memory. In this spirit of loving union, we gather here this morning to express also our deep gratitude to those whose services have been offered in behalf of our great country. Many of them had already exposed their lives before for us, others in the first great challenge had already indicated the will to place themselves in peril for us. Heroism is not always in the act, but frequently is it found in the determination and the will and the acceptance of what life may have for them. They have been sacrificed on the alter of freedom. We are not deceived today that our freedom is secure, for our freedom is still in danger and it is those who are willing to accept the risks that we took as its guardians. On this sad and yet solemn occasion I think it is not consolation or even sympathy that those who commemorate their loved ones are seeking from us, but rather I think we all should be actuated by the spirit of mutual suffering and distress in union with those who are suffering and in distress. With the wives, children, fathers, mothers, and all the close kin of those today we commemorate, we do unite in spirit, suffering, sadness, and distress and we all pray together the Almighty Father of us all may look with pitying eye upon them and grant them the release from their suffering. There was a noble President of the United States who had the gift of sympathy and of mutual suffering with those who sought his help and on one occasion in the dark days of the Civil War, Abraham Lincoln penned a letter to a mother who suffered. With a bit of paraphrasing, you will permit me to read it. The great Lincoln said, "I feel how weak and fruitless must be any word of mine which should attempt to beguile you from the grief of a loss so overwhelming, but I cannot refrain from tendering to you the consolation that may be found in the thanks of the Republic for which they died. I pray that our Heavenly Father may assuage the anguish of your bereavement and leave you only the cherished memory of the loved and lost and a solemn pride that must be yours to have laid so costly a sacrifice upon the altar of freedom. May God bless us all, protect us all, and make us worthy of those whose memory this morning we cherish."

MEMORIAL ADDRESS DELIVERED BY J. FLOYD DREITH, CHC, U.S. NAVY, DIRECTOR OF THE CHAPLAINS' DIVISION, GIVEN AT MEMORIAL SERVICES FOR U.S.S. "THRESHER" AT THE PORTSMOUTH NAVAL SHIPYARD, APRIL 15, 1963

Distinguished guests, ladies and gentlemen, but particularly you, the bereaved members of the families of the departed officers and men of the *Thresher*. The entire Nation went into a state of shock last week when the word was flashed on the news wires that the U.S.S. *Thresher*—with 129, both civilian and naval personnel aboard—was lost at sea. Prayer groups were started among those, one by Mrs. Korth, the wife of the Secretary of the Navy, beseeching Almighty God, that He might find it in His wisdom and mercy to bring that ship and those men safely back. In His wisdom and mercy He decreed otherwise. The fact that the Nation went into shock is a high compliment to the U.S. Navy. Seldom a week goes by that we don't read about an airplane crash. Daily, hundreds of lives are taken upon our highways. We take all this more or less for granted. But when a ship of the U.S. Navy is lost in peacetime, the entire Nation is astounded, because it so seldom happens, and because the Navy has demonstrated such high regard for the safety and welfare of its personnel. Those men that went down on that ship were God's men, and I say this without having had the privilege of knowing any one of them personally. A Russian cosmonaut may encircle the globe and find no evidence of the existence of God. An American sailor when he goes to sea is very much aware of the fact that he is God's child and in God's hands.

It is given unto all men once to die. We seldom know when and the time is never propitious whenever it does come for any of us, it seems, and we seldom know how. But if we had the choice, the free choice given unto us by Almighty God today, I'm sure that we could ask for no higher honor or glory than that accorded to those men to give their lives in the service of their country upon the altar not only of that country, but the altar of human dignity and freedom throughout the world. And were they here now to speak to us I'm sure that they would ask us not to grieve for them, because they could have selected no higher honor or glory than that which was accorded unto them. The young son of Dr. Keuster, a Navy scientist, who was aboard that ship, said to his mother, "Since God holds the ocean in the hollow of His hands, our daddy is safe." And so in that sense particularly you bereaved members, loved ones of the departed, may I commend unto you that God holds them in the hollow of His hand and as we commend them to the depths of the sea which they loved and their souls to His tender mercy, may we here and now commit ourselves to a nobler service of God in the service of our fellow men. To that may our Heavenly Father strengthen us and bless us.

REMARKS BY COMDR. KARL G. PETERSON, U.S. NAVY PROTESTANT CHAPLAIN, AT MEMORIAL SERVICES FOR U.S.S. "THRESHER," AT THE PORTSMOUTH NAVAL SHIPYARD, APRIL 15, 1963

Wives, parents, children, relatives, and friends of those lost in *Thresher*, we are gathered here to honor and to show our esteem for your loved ones, and to express our sincere sympathy to you in your sorrow and to assure you of the deep appreciation of our Nation for the gallant services of those lost in *Thresher*. There are present representatives of our Government, the Department of Defense, the Navy Department, and other agencies dedicated to the protection of our Nation, local and national. Time permits the mention of only the following:

The Honorable Kenneth E. BeLieu, Assistant Secretary of the Navy (Installations and Logistics); Vice Adm. W. R. Smedberg, Chief of Naval Personnel; Vice Adm. E. W. Grenfel, Commander, Submarine Force, U.S. Atlantic Fleet; the Honorable John W. King, Governor, New Hampshire.

The loyalty, dedication, and selfless sacrifice of those lost in *Thresher* demands recognition of our common debt of gratitude. They have written a page in naval history that will not be forgotten.

Almighty God, Heavenly Father, to Thee be honor and glory forever. By Thy divine guidance Thou hast led us; by Thy providence Thou hast blessed us, Thou hast lifted us up to be a favored people. These manifestations of Thy power and goodness give substance to our faith in Thee, as we turn to Thee in this memorial service.

O Thou who are the strength of the weak and the consolation of the sorrowful be attentive to the prayers of Thy grief stricken children who turn to Thee now in these solemn moments laden with their sense of tragedy. As Thou hast known the anguish of suffering and sorrow in the death of Thy beloved Son, we beseech Thee in Thy compassion to bring balm and healing to those whose hearts are wounded and burdened with grief. Through Thy gift of faith may the assurance of our Saviour's victory over death proclaimed in the Easter message bring them strength and comfort and provide them with that peace which passes understanding. May the bright rays of the resurrection light shine into every dark place in life. Now we commit to Thy love and mercy, the souls of the shipmates and those builders and engineers who made their last voyage in *Thresher*. Vouchsafe to them light and rest, peace and refreshment, joy and consolation, and the companionship of Thy saints, and in Thine own presence, O Thou gracious, risen Saviour. Amen.

REMARKS BY RABBI ABRAHAM I. JACOBSON, D.D., AT THE MEMORIAL SERVICES FOR U.S.S. "THRESHER" AT THE PORTSMOUTH NAVAL SHIPYARD, APRIL 15, 1963

Psalm 121: "I will lift up mine eyes unto the mountains; from whence shall my help come? My help cometh from the Lord, who made heaven and earth. He will not suffer thy foot to be moved; He that keepeth thee will not slumber. Behold, he that keepeth Israel doth neither slumber nor sleep. The Lord is thy keeper; the Lord is thy shade upon thy right hand. The sun shall not smite thee by day nor the moon by night. The Lord shall keep thee from all evil; He shall keep thy soul. The Lord shall guard thy going out and thy coming in, from this time forth and forever."

Prayer

Out of the depths we call unto Thee, O God, our heavenly Father. In Thy hands are the souls of all the living and the spirits of all flesh. Thy loving kindness is never withdrawn from us, but abides with us, in death as in life. In Thy wisdom, Thou hast laid upon us this heavy burden. Mayest Thou in Thy mercy, give us the strength to bear it.

Guide us and sustain us. Give us the strength of faith that shall keep us from murmuring against the justice of Thy dispensation, even when Thou dost afflict us. Grant us we pray Thee the understanding which shall enable us to recognize that the hand that woundeth is the hand that bindeth up again. Enable us always to be supported by the knowledge that these dear ones whom Thou in Thy wisdom hast seen fit to take from us have reflected their deep love for our country, their loyalty to their oath, and their courage in the face of their supreme trial. What greater glory than to die for our beloved country. Thou art the life of all life.

Kaddish memorial recited in Hebrew

Go your way for the Lord hath called you
Go your way and may the Lord be with you.
May your righteousness go before you and the glory of the Lord receive you.
     Amen.

REMARKS BY THE HONORABLE KENNETH BE LIEU, ASSISTANT SECRETARY OF THE NAVY AT MEMORIAL SERVICES FOR U.S.S. "THRESHER" AT THE PORTSMOUTH NAVAL SHIPYARD, APRIL 15, 1963

While we gather in solemn reverence in memory of our gallant comrades both civilian and military, it's appropriate to remember the President's words, for he said the courage and dedication of these men of the sea, pushing ahead into depths to advance our knowledge and capabilities is no less than that of their forefathers who led the advance on the frontiers of our civilization. These brave men have joined their comrades 1,500 of whom were lost in submarines in the fight for freedom in World War II. The future of our country will always be sure when there are men such as these to give their lives to preserve it. Secretary McNamara desired that I convey to you these words today. Today the entire Nation and people of the free world as well mourn the brave men of the *Thresher*. The sorrow in our hearts is symbolized by this memorial service. Only those whose loved ones gave their lives can feel the deep sense of personal loss. But that does not preclude us in the Defense Department from our own feeling of grief. The bereaved families may take some measure of comfort from knowing that their men died serving their country. The world will continue to live in freedom as long as men like these devote their lives to the highest service on the land, in the air, and on and under the sea, and as you and I are in memory of these gallant men let us not leave this ceremony alone as the only symbol of our honor. Rather let us resolve here today of this instant that you and I will somehow, someday, each day, in some way, perform some continuing act of patriotism, so in the future when and if we are to give an account to them, they shall know they did not die in vain and we carry the torch with them.

APPENDIX 15

REVIEW OF INSPECTION PROCEDURES FOR HY–80 SUBMARINE HULL WELDS

3960
Ser 634B–284
13 June 1960

Report on travel
Person making visit: H. S. Sayre, GS–13, Code 634B.

Date	Place visited	Persons consulted
Apr. 12–13, 1960	Portsmouth Naval Shipyard	Capt. B. A. Strauss, planning officer. Comdr. H. A. Jackson, design superintendent. Ens. R. G. Davis, assistant production officer. F. Dunham, code 250. M. Watts, code 250A. T. L. Sheehan, code 375. H. E. Dickerman, code 375A. B. I. Roberts, welding engineer. C. E. Cole, foreman welder. R. McConnell, chief quartermaster welder.
Apr. 14–15, 1960	Electric Boat Division, Groton, Conn.	Supervisor of shipbuilding, U.S. Navy. Capt. W. E. Hushing, supervisor. Comdr. R. Aroner, inspection officer. L. T. Korn, assistant, quality control. R. Dugsley, head inspector. C. Claus, head hull inspector. R. Taylor, hull inspector, Electric Boat Division. E. Franks, welding engineer. J. Hall, head, radiographic department. A. Bort, assistant radiographer. H. Chapman, assistant chief inspector. A. E. Dohna, head, quality control division. R. McCormick, quality control division.

1. *Purpose.*—This visit was to review the procedures used for nondestructive inspection of the HY–80 submarine hull welds and to review production radiographs to determine quality level of the hull weld radiographs.

2. *Background.*—As the basis of the findings during recent review of the radiographic inspection procedures and production radiographs at the Mare Island Naval Shipyard it was considered desirable to visit other submarine building activities to review the nondestructive inspection procedures used for inspection of the HY–80 hull welds. The information obtained will be of value in development of the inspection requirements by the HY–80 welding task group.

3. *Brief.*—The radiographic facilities, procedures, production radiographs, and methods of control of inspection and the magnetic particle inspection methods were reviewed in each activity visited. The following is a summary of findings.

Portsmouth Naval Shipyard: Radiographic inspection is done by the shipyard laboratory when requested by shop 26. The production radiographs taken prior to obtaining the present iridium 192 sources were of very poor technical quality. The radiographs taken with iridium 192 sources although better, showed lack of control of techniques and processing and do not represent 100 percent coverage of the hull butts and seams. The review of the radiographs for defects appeared good although many areas could not be interpreted because of poor quality. Until recently no adequate identification method was used and most radiographs taken on the SS(N)593 and 602 cannot now be identified with location on the submarine hull. Shipyard personnel advised that 100 percent coverage of hull butts and seams cannot be obtained due to obstructions inherent to construction and removal would delay production. It was recommended that steps be taken to insure closer control of the radiographic taking and processing techniques to provide better quality radiographs and to insure complete radiographic inspection of the hull welds as required by specifications. Since the shipyard radiographic procedures have not been qualified, it was requested that steps be taken to qualify in accordance with MIL–STD–271 and NAVSHIPS 250–1500–1.

Electric Boat Division: The radiographic inspection of the submarine hull welds was at high quality. The production radiographs aside from occasional minor items were excellent and represented almost complete coverage of the head welds. The radiographs are reviewed for defects by qualified personnel in the Electric Boat radiographic laboratory, the shipyard inspection office and the supervisor's office. The identification method is good and all radiographs can be identified within close limits as to location. An accurate cross check is maintained at all production inspection, both radiographic and magnetic particle. The Electric Boat Division radiographic procedures have been qualified in accordance with the MIL–STD–271 requirements.

4. *Action required.*—Following completion of the review in each activity a meeting with yard personnel was held and the findings were discussed. No further Bureau action is required at this time. On receipt of Portsmouth Naval Shipyard radiographic qualification tests necessary action will be taken to expedite review and report of tests.

5. *Detailed discussion.*—Portsmouth Naval Shipyard: All radiographic inspection including taking the radiographs, processing, and review is under cognizance of the shipyard laboratory. When a welded joint is ready for inspection, shop 26 notifies the laboratory and the radiograph is taken as time permits. In order not to delay production the radiograph is taken as quickly as possible and, in general, time is not taken to remove obstructions such as scaffolding, braces, etc. The completed films are processed and reviewed in the X-ray laboratory. In the case of welds requiring repair, the films are sent to shop 26 where they are taken to the job for location of the defect. The repaired weld is radiographed. If there is disagreement on interpretation between the laboratory and shop 26, the radiograph may be referred to the shipyard welding engineer. It is stated, however, that this situation does not occur very often. Shop 26 may request reradiograph of a weld if they do not consider a radiograph of good quality.

Radiographic procedure: The radiographs initially taken on the SS(N)593, 605, and 606 hull welds were made with X-ray using calcium tungstate screens and coarse grain medical-type film. About October 1959, iridium 192 sources were obtained and DuPont 506 fine grain film was adopted as a standard with no screens. Cobalt 60 is used for radiography of thicknesses of plating 2¼ inches or over. In general butts were not flock-shot but on the SSB(N)602 some flock shots were taken with cobalt 60 sources.

Quality of radiographs: The radiographs taken using X-ray and medical film were of very poor quality. The films were grainy and the exposure varied across the film. The radiographs in general showed penetrometers of the old type. Many films were water streaked and showed pressure marks and the calcium tungstate screens had been patched with Scotch tape so that the image of the tape was superimposed in many cases across the weld area. In a number of instances the films were taken with cables, wire baskets, or other obstructions superimposed across the weld area. Shipyard personnel advised that the production schedule did not permit removal of many obstructions.

Identification: Logs are kept of radiographs taken on each hull. Each component such as butt weld, seam weld, pipe joint, etc., is assigned an item number in sequence as radiographed and each radiograph taken of the item is numbered or lettered sequentially. Individual radiographs are identified only with the hull number, item and sequence number. Logs are kept to identify the item with the component radiographed and to record the radiographic procedure used. Until recently, identification of the radiograph to a particular hull location was maintained only until the radiographs had been reviewed and necessary repairs made. Correlation of radiographs to hull location can no longer be made for subsequent inspection purposes. Last fall. on the 593, 605, and 606 hull welds, a more uniform system was established by starting butt inspection at the 12 o'clock position looking forward, numbering the films sequentially counterclockwise, and seams starting at one end. Shipyard personnel did not consider that accurate identification within a couple of feet of a location is possible after the initial inspection is completed and ink location marks on the hull have been obscured. A set of sketches of hull structure have been prepared by shop 26 for use in connection with future inspection records. The radiographs are filed as completed in boxes, roughly by date, and it was difficult to locate particular radiographs for review.

Review of radiographs: All radiographs are reviewed for compliance with acceptance standards by one of three experienced men in the radiographic laboratory. Survey of random production radiographs indicated the shipyard review to be good with regard to detection of defects. However. in a number of instances technically poor radiographs had been accepted for final weld inspection. Radiographic personnel advised that production schedules precluded retaking of radiographs in most instances. The viewing facilities were, in general. poor and not conducive to accurate reading of films.

Repair of defects: The rejected areas found are marked and the films are sent to the shop for identification on the hull and repair. The defective areas are arc air gouged and repair welds are made. The weld areas are preheated with 24-inch strip heaters and after repair the heater is left until the heat evens out, then allowed to cool in air or under asbestos protection depending upon surrounding atmospheric conditions. It was reported that the indident rate of cracks in butts and seams is approximately 15 per hull and about 1 to 2 percent repair due to slag-type defects. Repair welds are radiographed.

Radiographic sources available: Iridium 192 sources, two 100 curie, one 50 curie, one 30 curie; cobalt 60 sources, one 10-curie source; X-ray, one 250-kilovolt Triplett Barton machine and two CE kilovolt machines.

Magnetic-particle inspection: Magnetic-particle inspection is made by welders in shop 26 trained for inspection by an instructor qualified by the shipyard laboratory. All butts and seams are magnetic-particle inspected on inside and outside surfaces, using alternating-current yoke inspection units. Code 303 spot checks the inspection on butt and seam welds and on high-pressure tanks.

Electric Boat Division.—Electric Boat Division radiographic inspection is made in accordance with Shipyard Standard Procedure 3.20 Rev. A., Inspection Instruction No. 20. The responsibility for exposing, identifying, location marking, developing, and evaluating radiographs is assigned to the radiographic section of the welding department. They are also responsible for originating and maintaining radiography records and custody of all radiographs. The inspection department requests radiographic inspection of final production welds in duplicate one copy of which is kept by the inspection department as a check. The completed films are processed and reviewed by either the head of the laboratory or his assistant. The films are never taken to the job in order to avoid damage to the films. In the case of weld repairs a tracing paper overlay is made of the film and this is used in locating the defect on the job. A four-copy record sheet is kept of all radiographic inspection. This sheet includes a complete description of the welded joint covering all details of the welding procedure which is of invaluable assistance in review of the films. The details on inspection of each film is made by the radiographic department on this record sheet and reason for each rejection are given in detail. When the radiographic department has reviewed the films, repaired joints and retaken as necessary, the radiographs are submitted to the Electric Boat Division inspection with the record sheet. The inspection department evaluates all final production films to assure compliance with all requirements for identification, technical requirements, quality of radiograph, and acceptability of evaluation. Following review by the inspection department all final production films are submitted to the supervisor of shipbuilding for review. The films are all reviewed and the supervisor's office is currently keeping an accurate record of the quality of all radiographs with view to future use of a sampling inspection by the supervisor rather than 100-percent inspection. The copies of the record sheet are kept as a permanent record in the folder with the film, and in radiographic department, inspection department, and supervisors' files.

Radiographic procedure: The radiographs are made on type AA film using iridium 192 sources with lead screens for material thickness less than $2\frac{1}{4}$ inches and cobalt 60 for thicker materials. All radiographs were single exposure and no flock type inspection is done.

Quality of radiographs: Films viewed were of excellent quality. Approved penetrometers were visible on all films. In all except a few films where there was interference from framing, the exposure and sensitivity was consistent across the film. The films were free from developing defects such as streaks or water spots and through handling techniques the films were free of scratches.

Identification: Films were marked with the boat number, section, seam or butt number, film number (such as S16A, where S-starboard, 16-film number, A-first repair). All films were correlated by measurement as to location on the hull. Electric Boat Division personnel reported that the radiographs could be later identified with the hull location to within a few inches. All films of individual butts or seams are filed together and through the copies of the radiography report in the files and with the film, particular radiographs can be readily located for later review.

Review of radiographs: The viewing facilities for review of radiographs was good. Survey of production radiographs showed the review to be good and in all instances where radiographs were of defective quality the shots had been retaken.

Radiographic sources available: Iridium 192 sources, 10 sources ranging from approximately 3 curies to 450 millicuries; cobalt 60 sources, 7 sources ranging from 4 curies to 500 millicuries; X-ray, one 250-kilovolt Triplett and Barton machine.

Magnetic particle inspection: Magnetic particle inspection is done by the Electric Boat Division inspection department. All magnetic particle inspection supervisors have completed commercial courses in magnetic particle inspection. All men doing the inspection work are given shipyard courses in magnetic particle inspection and must pass a comprehensive written examination. Inspection is done using alternating current yoke inspection units except where accessibility requires use of direct current prods. All yokes are checked daily using drilled test blocks.

Records: A complete record is kept by the inspection department of the radiographs and magnetic particle inspection of all welds including date inspection, and result of inspection. At any time the status of any weld inspection can be immediately given from card records. Prior to launching the design department makes a complete list of all hull penetrations below the waterline which is double checked to insure complete inspection and acceptance.

HARRISON S. SAYRE.

APPENDIX 16

PHOTOGRAPHS OF "THRESHER" DEBRIS

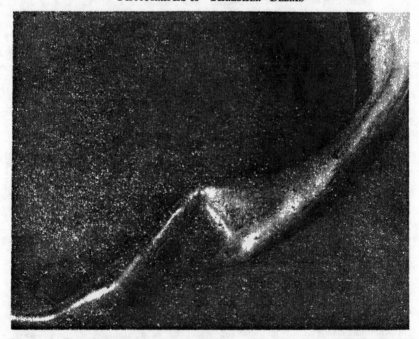

FIGURE 1. Brass pipe with the inscription: "JO 10 * * * 3–0–5091–05; DM 263B–109–61; PL–1862791 pe. 75; 1.050 x .065.593 boat" recovered in second series of dives in the search for the U.S.S. *Thresher*.

FIGURE 2. Starboard side of the U.S.S. *Thresher* sail with portions of the hull number "593" visible.

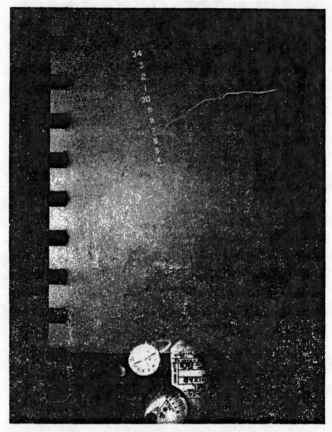

FIGURE 3. Draft markings on the top-side rudder of *Thresher*. Part of the port stern plane of the sunken sub can be seen in the foreground.

FIGURE 4. Overhead view of the top-side rudder of U.S.S. *Thresher.*

APPENDIX 17

"THRESHER" (SS(N)593) CHRONOLOGY

July 2, 1956—Authorized by the Congress.

October 1957—Construction and working plan preparation assigned to the Portsmouth (N.H.) Naval Shipyard.

March 1958—Ship's detailed specifications issued.

May 28, 1958—Keel laid.

July 9, 1960—Launched.

March 10, 1961—Reactor brought to critical.

April 30, 1961—Commenced sea trials.

August 3, 1961—Commissioned and assigned to Submarine Force Atlantic Fleet.

September 24 to October 16, 1961—At Portsmouth (N.H.) Naval Shipyard for minor modifications, maintenance, and repairs.

October 17 to November 28, 1961—Underway operations.

November 29 to February 8, 1962—At Portsmouth (N.H.) Naval Shipyard for minor modifications, maintenance, and repairs.

February 9 to April 15, 1962—Underway operations.

April 16 to May 19, 1962—At Electric Boat Division, Groton, Conn., for modifications in preparation for high shock testing.

May 20 to June 16, 1962—Underway operations.

June 17 to June 29, 1962—Tested for ability to withstand controlled underwater high shock off Key West, Fla.

June 30 to July 15, 1962—Underway operations.

July 16 to April 9, 1963—At Portsmouth (N.H.) Naval Shipyard for major overhaul.

April 9, 1963—Underway from Portsmouth for sea trials following overhaul.

April 10, 1963—Lost at sea.

INDEX

CPSIA information can be obtained at www.ICGtesting.com
Printed in the USA
LVOW06s0927130913

352198LV00029B/122/A